JESUS AND THE CHRISTIAN

Published by James Clarke & Co. Ltd.
31 Queen Anne's Gate, London, S.W.1

Printed in Great Britain by
Latimer Trend & Co Ltd, Plymouth

Contents

Introduction

When William Manson died on Good Friday, 1958, many of us were suddenly deprived not only of one whom we regarded as a profound Teacher but of one whom we loved as a man of God. He influenced me more intimately than any other of my teachers and over the years he had become to me more and more a spiritual father. But he was taken away from us just when he was about to produce his main works on the theology of the New Testament Scriptures after a life-time of historico-critical and source-critical research on them. What this would have been like some of us can gather from his unforgettable lectures on the first eight chapters of the Epistle to the Romans when with only the Greek text and no notes in front of him he spoke out of the fulness of his understanding of the New Testament. Sketches of what he had intended were found among his papers, while the St. Giles addresses delivered in the previous year and published after he died under the title *The Way of the Cross*, offered in a popular form an indication of part of what was planned to come. But in the last five years his thought had been changing and developing so remarkably as he re-examined everything in a distinctively theological way that the final result would certainly have been very fresh and rather different from what most would have expected.

In an introductory note to one of William Manson's earlier works *Christ's View of the Kingdom of God*, 1918, H. R. Mackintosh wrote, "He is a master of the scholarly debate and this is much. But also he has a persistent spiritual judgment which is not intimidated by random appeals to the modern mind." That was characteristic of all Manson's work. He never shirked the critical problems or looked for an easy way round the difficulties raised by other scholars, and his positive contributions were always the stronger for it. The more I study *Jesus the Messiah*, published in 1943, the more I am convinced that it is one of the really great books in New Testament studies in our generation. In it he faced squarely the full challenge of Form-criticism

to let the texts bear witness to themselves, in order to develop their significance as far as possible out of themselves and their own inherent dynamic, that is to say, to let them impress upon us the appropriate frame of reference for our understanding of them. This applies to a text not only in its character as a literary creation which once took shape in a writer's mind, in its style, diction, form and emotional quality, bears witness to the distinctiveness of his spirit, and not only to it as a work of historical significance in the sense that it springs from and reflects a contemporary situation in some quarter of the Early Christian Church, but as a confessional and theological document in which it bears witness to the religion of the New Testament Church. This was the approach he adopted, for example, in his exceedingly fresh examination of the Epistle to the Hebrews, but no less in his life-long work on the Synoptic Gospels where he found 'the primitive stuff already dyed in the grain with revelational meaning and indeed to a far greater extent than the redactors sometimes get credit'. In other words, as he put it, 'the revelational significance of Christian history is not a mere epiphenomenon, an interpretation which has settled on the events ab extra, but adheres to the very nature of the events'. It was characteristic of Manson's approach that historico-critical penetration into the interaction of spirits and events lying behind their own intention and spiritual discernment into the divine purpose at work in them, should go hand in hand, each aiding the other in the work of interpreting the message of the Gospels.

(iv) A primary question that Manson insisted had to be asked if adequate interpretation of the New Testament is to be undertaken, relates to the very existence of the Christian Church. How are we to account for it? It is at this point that the theory of the Form-critics that the Gospel springs not so much from a fund of reliable historical reminiscence as from a myth which the Church evolved out of a few uncertain traditions round the life of its Founder, breaks down completely, for it not only leaves us with no adequate explanation of the Church's own existence, but creates acute and serious conflict with the features of the tradition which can only be regarded as objectively given. When we examine the primitive Christian witness itself, however, we find a narrative of events affirmed to have happened on the plane of human and historical existence, and a claim of absolute significance made for these events. The New Testament writers report that Jesus came with the [illegible] in existence in the present of the Kingdom of God with power, and that to render it to let the texts bear witness to themselves in order to develop their significance as far as possible out of themselves and their own inherent demands, that is to say, to let them impress upon us the appropriate frame of reference for our understanding of them. This applies to a text not only in its character as a literary creation which once took shape in a writer's mind and by its style, matter, moral and emotional quality, bears witness to the distinctiveness of his spirit, and not only to it as a work of historical significance in the sense that it sprang from and reflects a contemporary situation in some quarter of the Early Christian Church, but as a confessional and theological document in which it bears witness to the religion of the New Testament Church. This was the approach he adopted, for example, in his excitingly fresh examination of the Epistle to the Hebrews, but no less in his life-long work on the Synoptic Gospels where he found "the primitive stuff already dyed in the grain with revelational meaning and indeed to a far greater extent than the redactors sometimes grasped". In other words, as he put it, "the revelational significance of Christian history is not a mere epiphenomenon, an interpretation which has settled on the events *ab extra*, but inheres in the very nature of the events". It was characteristic of Manson's approach that historico-critical penetration into the interaction of agents and events laying bare their own intention, and spiritual discernment into the divine purpose at work in them, should go hand in hand, each aiding the other in the work of interpreting the message of the Gospels.

(iv) A primary question that Manson insisted had to be asked if adequate interpretation of the New Testament is to be undertaken, relates to the very existence of the Christian Church. How are we to account for it? It is at this point that the theory of the Form-critics that the Gospel springs not so much from a fount of reliable historical reminiscence as from a myth which the Church wove out of a few uncertain traditions round the life of its Founder, breaks down completely, for it not only leaves us with no adequate explanation of the Church's own existence, but comes into serious conflict with many features of the tradition which can only be regarded as objectively given. When we examine the New Testament witness itself, however, we find a recitative of events affirmed to have happened on the plane of human and terrestrial existence, and a claim of absolute significance made for these events. The New Testament writers report that face to face with Jesus they found an irruption into their existence in the present of the Kingdom of God with power, and that in order to know this power of God men must break with the existing order of the world and with its interests and values. That is to say, they were forced to interpret the Kingdom of God and therefore the person of Jesus Himself from an objective ground beyond themselves, against the grain of their natural existence and in sharp conflict with their own forms of thought. What they apprehended was forced on them against their will and desire, for it arrested them and constituted them witnesses in a way they could not resist. It is only such an incursion of supernatural and divine power into human life, setting it on a wholly new basis, Manson claims, that is capable of explaining the existence of the Christian Church. But it also makes complete sense of those basic elements in the tradition in which we can discern profound conflict between the witnesses and that to which they bear witness, giving unmistakable evidence of the character and source of that to which they bear witness as objectively thrust upon them. It is in this connection that Manson sees the profound link between the preaching of the Kingdom of God and the crucifixion of Jesus in which there becomes revealed the conflict of God with the demonic forces that have entrenched themselves in human existence and clothed themselves with its forms of being and life. Thus the Kingdom of God as proclaimed by Jesus is not to be interpreted, as Bultmann would have it, through an assimilation to our own relation to life but through a renunciation of ourselves with our preconceptions in a movement of crucifixion with Christ.

(v) There is another important aspect of Manson's thought which must be noted, for it played an increasingly important part in his thought and exegesis of the New Testament, the conviction that we cannot think of faith except as faith in the God of the Resurrection, and that we cannot think of Jesus except as the Priest of the Resurrection. So far as the growth and development of the evangelical tradition is concerned this means that its "forms" must be interpreted not so much from the creative spirituality of the Early Christians but from the creative impress of the divine Spirit upon them, as the Kingdom of God intersected their mundane existence in the life and work of Jesus Christ, and related it directly to God's redeeming and renewing power. This is the real eschatological situation constituted by the coming of the Son of God and inaugurated through the death and resurrection of Christ, in which there was injected into the world an entirely new ethical tension with transforming results, and an entirely new perspective of history in which the Church is caught up in the know this power of God each must break with the existing order of the world and with its interests and values. That is to say, they were forced to interpret the Kingdom of God and therefore the person of Jesus Himself from an objective ground beyond themselves, against the grain of their natural existence and in sharp conflict with their own forms of thought. What they apprehended was forced on them against their will and desires, for it arrested them and constituted them witnesses in a way they could not resist. It is only such an insertion of supernatural and divine power into human life, setting it on a wholly new basis, Manson claims, that is capable of explaining the existence of the Christian Church, but it also makes complete sense of those basic elements in the tradition in which we can discern profound conflict between the witnesses and that to which they bear witness, giving unmistakable evidence of the character and source of that to which they bear witness as objectively thrust upon them. It is in this connection that Manson sees the profound link between the preaching of the Kingdom of God and the crucifixion of Jesus in which there became revealed the conflict of God with the demonic forces that have entrenched themselves in human existence and clothed themselves with its forms of being and life. Thus the Kingdom of God as proclaimed by Jesus is not to be interpreted, as Bultmann would have it, through an assimilation to our own relation to life nor through a reconciliation of ourselves with our preconceptions in a movement of crucifixion with Christ.

(5) There is another important aspect of Manson's thought which must be noted, for it played an increasingly important part in his thought and exegesis of the New Testament: the conviction that we cannot think of him except as faith in the God of the Resurrection, and that we cannot think of Jesus except as the Christ of the Resurrection. So far as the growth and development of the evangelical tradition is concerned this means that its 'forms' must be interpreted not so much from the creative spirituality of the Early Christians but from the creative impress of the divine Source upon them, as the Kingdom of God intersected their mundane existence in the life and work of Jesus and [illegible] directly to God's redeeming and renewing grace. [illegible] the Kingdom of God [illegible] was first put into the world [illegible] with life-renewing power [illegible] as a perspective of history [illegible] the Church was caught up in the

CHAPTER I

New Testament Criticism in Relation to the Christian Religion[1]

I

The first task of the New Testament student is, of course, to understand the New Testament itself, and to give its text a chance. So simple and obvious as this principle may appear, it is by no means superfluous in a day when generalizations based on comparative religion, or theories of religion based on modern psychology, conspire to run away with the student, and to relegate philology and exact linguistic science to a secondary place in his mind. Over and over again we need to remind ourselves that only the tested and measurable fact has moral value, whereas the untested hypothesis may be the most immoral and debilitating thing in the world. In the development of a philological conscience, therefore, and in the calling to his side of whatever aids the linguistic and textual calculus of the present day affords, the student has his primary task, one which he may not depute, and which is morally prior to the speculative ventures of his mind. Whatever value comparative religion and psychology may possess, the New Testament religion is still more important. It is more important than any analogies which may be discovered to it elsewhere, and it is more important than any theory of the way in which religion is developed and nourished within the brain. Psychology may determine the mode of religious as of other experiences, it cannot decide as to their validity. If pursued to the point at which all forms of consciousness are given the same value, or at which they are all given no value at all, psychology is not a science of reality, but sheer nihilism.

Again, the student whose primary task is thus with the scientific exegesis of the New Testament, will always, as part of the reality with which he is dealing, remember the peculiar sanctity which belongs historically to these writings in the confessional life of humanity. Whatever theory we may or may not hold of Holy Scripture, these are the writings to which in every age since the first the Christian soul has

[1] Inaugural Lecture, New College, Edinburgh, 8 October 1925.

gone, and in which it has found anew the redeeming love of God. Such a fact cannot be abstracted from upon any true perception of the reality of these documents. At an early time the Christian Church drew a circle round a certain group of books. It proclaimed them as the fair and just norm of Christian truth, and since that time the New Testament documents, *plus* or *minus*, have possessed, in addition to their text, another claim to be objectively considered, a claim which, only secondarily to their text, is part of their historical reality.

And now a further consideration falls to be mentioned, which is perhaps not quite so obvious. From the linguistic and textual study of the New Testament books, the student will proceed to the literary question proper, the question of sources and of authorship. Now here it needs to be noted that into whatsoever sources we may analyse the Gospels, or the Acts of the Apostles, or the Apocalypse, it was not these *sources* that received or retained the official sanction of the Church, but the later books into which the sources were worked. This is a principle, the clearness and value of which are better perhaps appreciated within the Old Testament than within the New, if only because the Old Testament documents come to us from over a longer span of time. From whatever sources the Pentateuch may have been derived, it was not these original documents which were received by the Church in Israel, but the completed Pentateuch. Hence it follows that the religious value which belongs historically to any particular episode is not to be assessed finally by consideration of its context in the archaic source from which it was drawn, but only by the spiritual significance with which it was invested by the time when these books became Bible. Jacob's dream at Bethel, for example, or his wrestling at Peniel, may be interesting enough in the light of the original sense which attached to them in J or in some other archaic document, but their claim to be in the Bible rests not on that but on the spiritual truths which they suggested at a later time in Israel, and these, we may conjecture, were not very different from the truths which they suggest to us today.

Perhaps, in the New Testament the same principle has not an equally direct truth of application. Jesus stands at the close of the Old Testament, and therefore each later formation in the religion of Israel may, relatively to the earlier, be regarded as marking a higher stage of advance to the final truth of things. Jesus stands at the beginning of the New Testament, and therefore later formations within the New Testament may conceivably be connected with a decline from the highest point attained. But this criterion must not be pressed too far in either direction. Without entering here into a discussion of later and earlier in the New Testament, it is surely obvious that apocalyptic ideas, for example, and other vestigial remains of Judaism incorporated in the Christian writings have to be evaluated not from the Jewish, but solely from the Christian standpoint. The Christian mind, in other words, has the sole proper access to the New Testament. And even as regards the original sources of books, the dropping in so many cases of an early document, and the adoption instead of the later gospel or other book in which the source was integrated, has surely some directive significance. If we insist on valuing the New Testament solely for the primitive facts or formations which it contains, the pure age of a document will be the sufficient index of its worth. But if our standards of measurement are widened to include consideration of the growing religious experience in which the primitive facts were developed and enforced, the mere criterion of age ceases to satisfy. Early formations are not necessarily to be preferred to later formations in every case. The Q-elements in Matthew and Luke, for instance, are not necessarily more valuable than the other constituents of these composite works. This is a point on which, as it seems to me, not a few modern exegetes have gone astray through theory, so that a word of caution will not be out of place.

From linguistic and literary criticism, we pass next to historical criticism proper, i.e. to the question of the relation in which the New Testament records and the New Testament religion stand to the original facts of Christian history, and here it is necessary to speak at somewhat greater length. Historical criticism is a necessary part of a New Testament student's work, first of all, because the Christian Church is anchored in the experience of an historical revelation. It was this conviction which in the second century, when Gnostic speculation threatened to dissolve the Christian religion in an atmosphere of myth, kept that religion true to its own character, and perpetuated its form. Yet time, which is thus a necessary coefficient in the working out of the Christian experience, always threatens by its by-productiveness to obscure the continuity of that experience and to silt up the foundations. Here, therefore, the historian whose spiritual perception of the meaning of Christianity keeps pace with his scientific engagements, is the true fundamentalist. Much of the silt by which each earlier phase of Christian theology is overlaid by a later is due to pure tear and wear, to the natural detrition of language, through which the expression of an earlier day ceases properly to convey the underlying reality to the mind of the next successive age. Hence, like the archaeologist, we have to uncover the upper strata of the time-deposit in order to get at the lower, and thus ultimately to work back to foundations. In the excavation of the Roman Forum the silt of ages had to be removed before the men of today could walk on the platform on which Cicero and Caesar walked, and before they could see with their own eyes the foundations on which the great of Rome had looked. So is it in Christian theology, if we would walk with St. Paul and with the apostles. Here, indeed, the New Testament has kept its foundations from ever being wholly obscured, yet even in the New Testament we see the process taking place. We find in the later writings of the New Testament the conception of a "faith once delivered to the saints". This implies a consciousness that thought has travelled somewhat from its starting-point, and that the time process has already to be resisted. Going still farther back, we find ourselves confronted by the questions, What was the true historical relation of St. Paul to the primitive Church, and what was the true relation of that Church to Jesus?

But there is a second reason why historical criticism must take a prominent place in the work of the student, and that is because in the study of a developing religion, as opposed to that of a mere series of facts, to get back to the beginning is really rather a moving to the centre. There is an illusion latent in our sense of time which leads to the mistaken idea that because one thing is temporally prior to another, it is therefore actually at a farther remove from us. This is not true of the world of ideas, unless Plato is farther from us than the Academy, or Jesus farther from us than St. Paul. Here let St. Paul himself be spokesman. Jesus is to Paul, not the beginning only of the Church's life, but its eternal centre. The words "I live" is not considered by Paul an adequate expression of his own experience. He withdraws it in favour of the other expression: "No, not I, but Christ liveth in me." And so it is in all Christian experience. We cannot think of Jesus merely as one who lived nineteen hundred years ago, and then ceased. He is one who is eternally present and eternally central through the Spirit. Here the Pauline formula ἐν Χριστῷ becomes specially filled with light. Jesus while on earth had said: "If any man will come after Me, let him deny himself, and take up his cross, and follow Me." There you have the old thought of the religious life as a *Halakhah* or "walk". Paul does not use this metaphor to express the characteristic relation of the Christian to his Saviour. He says, not "If any man is after Christ, it is a new creation," but "if any man is *in Christ*, it is a new creation". This points to a very different relation from the mere time-sequence.[1]

Yet historical criticism, which is thus so necessary and so valuable a part of the New Testament discipline, getting as it does to the heart of things, is perhaps today at a discount. Partly, it is assailed by psychology, which is today the fashionable science. Professor Burkitt, in his latest book *Christian Beginnings*, foresees ruefully that the valuable work done in recent years by the New Testament historian may cease to interest the modern mind if only because the stock of facts with which the historical investigator works is meagre compared with that which is open to the psychologist, while the latitude assigned to his hypothesis is relatively small. What would the result be, supposing that this took place, and that psychology triumphed? Simply that all religious reality within the New Testament sphere would, so far as its scientific character is concerned, be resolved into a never-ceasing, ever-fading stream of impressions. The Pauline theology would be a subjective freak, an abnormality only to be explained by Paul's abnormal mentality. The Christ of the Church's devotion would be replaced by this or that man's conception of Christ. The Jesus who lived on earth would be but an inorganic link in an irrational chain of impressions. Time and change would be the only realities. Eternity would be nowhere. Psychology would thus be the destruction of any intelligible conception of history. But we need not pursue the thought, for psychology sooner or later will discover its own limits.

A more serious obstacle to the student's confidence in the historical method is constituted, not by the meagreness of the facts at his disposal, but by the bewildering variety of the reconstructions to which the facts have given rise. The student of today, while feeling and approving the rightness and necessity of the critical method, finds himself face to face with what seems a hopeless jungle of conflicting interpretations, through which, for a long time at least, he sees no paths leading to assured results. Hence he is tempted, if not to lose faith in criticism, at least to lose interest, and to turn down some pleasant byway where his fancy is more free to assert itself. In particu-

[1] Thus by history we transcend history. And should the idealist, not content with this, say that truth has no relation of any kind to history, we may answer that that may hold very well of the ideal world in which he lives, but hardly applies to the actual conditions of existence, to the empirical world in which we creatures of time dwell, and in which we have to work out an empirical salvation.

lar, he finds himself in confusion upon the two main issues emerging in the New Testament field, viz. (1) of the historical validity of Paulinism with reference to primitive Christianity, (2) of the historical validity of primitive Christianity with reference to Jesus. With regard to the first of these issues, he finds it asserted—and the assertion is perhaps only too congenial to the modern mind—that Paul did not continue the right line of early Christianity, but switched it on to a false course, partly through his subjection to Judaistic conceptions of God, and partly through a leaning to Hellenistic-Oriental mysticism. Thus, instead of continuing the ethical tradition of Jesus' teaching, he transformed Christianity into a "mystery" having two centres, atonement and mystical union with Christ. With regard to the second issue, the relation of early Christianity to Jesus, the student finds it asserted, on the one side, that the Messianic element in early Christianity was a pure importation lacking any historical support in Jesus' own declarations regarding Himself; on the other side, that this Messianic element, Jewish and visionary and time-conditioned as it was, was only too authentic a part of Jesus' pronouncement, was indeed the whole ground and substance of His work, to which everything in His teaching is relative, and by which everything in His teaching is bounded.

But while historical criticism thus presents a tangle of conflicting interpretations oscillating between the extremes which I have stated, and sufficiently alarming to the student at first sight, I venture to think that its total trend is somewhat more reassuring. Paths of a definite and central direction, and leading to reasonably solid results, are being blazed through the wilderness, and we may, I think, on the main things expect a still larger measure of agreement in the future. As regards the textual and literary criticism of the New Testament this is obvious. One needs only to refer to Canon Streeter's recent work on *The Four Gospels* to indicate what notable advances towards the clearing up of textual and literary problems have been made in our generation by one brilliant investigator. But not to speak of these results here, there are signs that on the central questions of St. Paul's relation to the early Church and of the early Church's relation to Jesus, the area of more or less assured results is steadily widening. Both of these relations are being stated today in much more positive terms than they were fifty or even twenty-five years ago. It is no longer customary for an historical critic to draw an absolute line either between St. Paul and the primitive Church, or between the primitive

Church and Jesus. The issues here are so important that I may without special apology devote what remains of this lecture to their discussion.

II

As regards St. Paul, it will readily be admitted that, in the peculiar working out of his system of theology, auxiliary ideas both of Jewish and of Hellenistic-Oriental provenance played an important part. The Jewish conception of the Divine righteousness gave Paul a language by which to think out the Christian principle that "Christ died for our sins according to the scriptures". The language of Hellenistic-Oriental mysticism gave him a form in which to present the relation of the redeemed soul to the Redeemer-Lord. Yet these elaborations affect only the superstructure which Paul built on the Christian foundations: neither Jewish legalism nor pagan mysticism created the Christian experience itself. Let us, if you will, regard the equations which can be made out between Paul and Judaism or between Paul and the mysteries as a time-element, the silt which a developing process has brought with it. We can, I think, clear away this silt, and show what solid foundations exist underneath. Not to speak of the extent to which St. Paul's "Judaistic" presuppositions can claim the support of universal and ever-renewable experiences in the domain of the soul's relation to God, or of the extent to which the language of mysticism is unavoidable in any inward statement of the Christian relation to Christ, St. Paul's own statements, carrying back the initial truths of his theology to the apostles or to the Lord, are convincing and sufficient evidence of the real sources of his inspiration. On his own showing, the faith which he preached from his conversion onwards was the same faith which once he destroyed: the principle, so central to his system, that "Christ died for our sins according to the scriptures" was one which he had "received": the doctrine that Christian men are made right with God not by legal works, but by faith, is appealed to as common-ground between him and Peter, as Christian matter of fact which needs only to be mentioned in order to be conceded. In the light of these personal pronouncements of Paul, and with all due respect to the individuality and thoroughness of mind with which he wrought the principles out, it is surely unreasonable to speak of Paul's singularity within the early Church, and not rather of his solidarity with the rest of his brethren. St. Paul—it comes to this—even in the most characteristic working out of his ideas represents not a breakaway from the early Christian direction, but the central, summit wave of the movement, the wave which rose highest and has washed farthest on to future shores. His contemporaries were behind him in realizing the far-reaching logic of their position, but their position was not therefore essentially different from his.

It is not possible within the limits of this lecture to go into the whole question of St. Paul's relation to Christianity and to Christ. What can and, I think, ought to be said is that while not all of Paul can be included in the Christianity which was before him, nevertheless his system is built perpendicularly upon the historic Christian foundations. His reasonings regarding the Atonement are only the further working out of what was already given in the primitive Christian postulate, that Christ died for our sins according to the Scriptures. In other words, Paul starts with the Cross of Christ, and in all that he says about sin, and law, and the conditions of Divine forgiveness he is really arguing backwards from that Cross as a *datum* of Christian history. In the same manner the Pauline conception of life ἐν Χριστῷ, while it may possibly owe something to the prevailing tendency to mysticism, is on Paul's own showing synonymous with the life which springs from faith in the Crucified. These are important recognitions. Having determined the Christian character of the basic presuppositions of Paulinism, we are in a position to deal with the Pauline superstructures, and to give them the value which belongs to them. This means just the value which they possess in the eternal nature of the Christian experience of God. Hence the merely "Jewish" and merely pagan elements, if such exist, need not trouble us.

Perhaps this solidarity of St. Paul with original Christianity is most clearly seen in his identification of the Spirit, by which Christians live, with the personal Christ. I need not enter here into the causes which obliged Paul to circumscribe so carefully the nature of the supernatural principle to which Christians looked for guidance and help. Suffice to say that Paul found his converts threatened by false analogies from the ethnic religions by which they were surrounded, and which also recognized the principle of pneumatic inspiration, and that he had therefore to safeguard the special character of the Christian πνεῦμα. This Paul does partly by proclaiming that the Spirit is a moral, as opposed to an anarchic, principle, partly by setting the Spirit in its proper antithesis to the flesh. But most of all Paul does it by always and everywhere associating the Spirit with Christ, and by definitely orienting the spiritual life to the Cross as to a moral centre. St. Paul would have agreed with the teaching of the Fourth Gospel that the Spirit of God in Christian experience does not create a new or special consciousness of its own, but always and everywhere a consciousness of Christ. Now this position is interesting not only as revealing the historical foundations of St. Paul's peculiar mysticism, but as suggesting that his knowledge of Christ was circumstantial, far more so than is ordinarily supposed.

It comes, as it seems to me, to this. It is incredible that St. Paul, working in so free a field and with so naturally mystical a bent, should have transferred the emphasis in his teaching from the Spirit to the Lord, if in the Lord he did not recognize the concrete lineaments of the Jesus who had lived and taught upon earth. His exchange of terms is obviously from the abstract to the concrete, from the purely mystical to the definitely historical. It is not apparent why he should have substituted the Lord for the Spirit, if his Christ were the theological abstraction which He is commonly represented to have been, for in that case his choice would have had little latitude. It is true that St. Paul draws a certain distinction between the "Christ according to Spirit" and the "Christ according to flesh". His Christ κατὰ πνεῦμα transcends and completes the Christ κατὰ σάρκα, but while He thus transcends and completes Him, He does not therefore unmake or remove Him. Therefore, without going so far as one of my Canadian friends who holds that St. Paul may have been the actual source of a great part of the special matter of St. Luke's Gospel, I would regard it as practically certain that he was well acquainted with the Church's traditions regarding Jesus, and that he subsumed these in his thought of the spiritual Christ.

The question regarding St. Paul's relation to primitive Christianity is thus on a fair way to being settled. There remains the question of primitive Christianity's relation to Jesus, and to this subject our attention must now be transferred.

III

People are saying today, Why trouble with St. Paul at all? Why not drop him altogether, and go back to Jesus Himself, by which they generally mean, go back to the teaching in Galilee, back to the ethics of the Sermon on the Mount? Now if this means, go back from a Christ who is a theological abstraction to one who was clothed with flesh and blood, and who lived an historical life, the principle, as we have seen, is already conceded by Paul. Paul identifies the Spirit with the Lord, and therefore the teaching of Jesus, as well as His death for sins, is a norm of the spiritual life. But if the modern cry "Back to Galilee!" means, Back to a Christianity which consisted of purely ethical teaching, without any reference to Him who was its centre, the sufficient answer is that no such Christianity ever existed, or at least that none such is on record. The Christian religion, in the form in which we know it from the beginning, started not from Galilee, or from the Sermon on the Mount, but from Jerusalem, from the Upper Room and the Cross. Its Jesus—the real historic Jesus—was one who had not only taught and laboured, but who had died on Calvary, and dying had drawn the faith of His followers from temple and from sacrifices, and from law to Himself. Unless we rule out all developments taking place in Jesus' life subsequently to the Galilean mission, we have no warrant for making Christianity originate in the Galilean ethics. Indeed, to do so is to leave Christianity suspended in the air. We may, I think, go further and say that primitive Christianity not only did not, but could not have lived purely by Jesus' teachings, if only for the reason that the traditions of these teachings which were available did not contain any sufficiently visible principle of unity within themselves. Even today scholars are baffled when it comes to comprehending the Synoptic data within the limits of any single formula, whether of an apocalyptic or of any other kind. Plainly the force behind early Christianity was not a programme but a Person. The Jesus, who had died, but who had returned to His followers in visions, prophecies, and revelations of Himself, alone gave unity to Christianity. In this scheme of life the teachings of Jesus, the Sermon on the Mount, and the Galilean history have, of course, their place. They are an expression of the living Jesus, an instrument and organ of His Spirit. They are not *per se* the source of the Christian life, as our advocates of the "Back to Galilee" cry are apt to assume, but simply a determining mode of the whole consciousness which is associated with the Christian Lord.

The great question in this field is, of course, whether the Messianic faith of the early Church goes back to the consciousness of Jesus, a point about which there is some dispute. Personally, it seems to me that the controversy is largely one about words, rather than about real things. Even if Jesus Himself never employed Messianic language or allowed its use by others, even if He never drew to Himself any of the prophetic passages or imaginative symbolisms of the Old Testament, some kind of language was necessary by which His followers could explain to themselves the nature of the religious experience which had come to them in Him, and which was inseparable from Him. But even if they, not He, first uttered the word "Messiah", they were still only registering an existing religious reality, not adding to or creating it. We cannot too often remind ourselves how very indeterminate and inconstant a quantity the Jewish belief in the Messiah was. We deceive ourselves if we think that in Jesus' time the name of the Messiah was trembling on every lip. If Jesus by the sheer force of His spirit had not created the substance of His followers' religion and pushed them beyond the confines of all ordinary language, it is hard to imagine that these followers would have thought of the nomenclature on which they finally united. Something very concrete and extraordinary, like the passion and the blood of Jesus, was necessary to recall so shadowy and unsubstantial a revenant as the Messianic idea. But the scepticism which denies to Jesus what it concedes as possible for His followers is surely overwrought. It does not appear why Jesus in the course of that wondrous life with God should not have come to the point where only the Old Testament language about the One who was to bring the Kingdom of God could explain His own mysterious fortunes at the Father's hands, and, above all, His extraordinary engagement to bring His nation to God. That this engagement, springing from Jesus' unique sense of the love of God, was the *prius* of the Messianic vision, and not the Messianic vision the *prius* of the redemptive passion, seems to me certain. At any rate, such a view, which carries the Messianic vision back to the later stages, at least, of Jesus' own consciousness, consorts better with the later creed of His followers, and would seem to be required upon any reasonably objective view of the evangelical tradition.

The thing we have to grasp is that Jesus set up in the souls of His followers a religious movement of infinite consequence, which required climatic language. This is a point on which most modern books dealing with the early Christian development seem to me inadequate. Early Christianity has been treated from the standpoint of its Christological concepts, which were mostly borrowed and inadequate. It has been treated from the standpoint of its public activities, which were worthy but not fully indicative of its essence. What has not been adequately treated is the history of the Christian soul, the spiritual experience which finds expression in words like: "He loved me, and gave himself for me"—"He died for our sins according to the Scriptures"

—"He sitteth at the right hand of God in the glory everlasting." If we can fathom and explain these convictions, all that follows of faith in Christ—His Messiahship, His Lordship, His eternal Sonship, His identification with the Logos—becomes intelligible. The gulf between Christianity and Jesus will have been bridged.

And, indeed, a thorough sifting of the early Christian materials would seem to involve the carrying back of these convictions to the direct impact of Jesus upon the souls of men. When we come to Jesus certain facts emerge which, upon any just evaluation, must be regarded as constituting an irreducible minimum of historical certainties.

(1) Jesus brought to men a new experience of the living God, uttering itself in the cry, "Abba, Father." This is what the Christian tradition means when it says that Jesus at baptism received the Spirit of God, and heard the voice: "Thou art my Son, the beloved, the object of my desire." Jesus Himself, baptized with the Spirit, touched by the power, kissed by the love of God, is the beginning of Christianity. Accordingly, when Jesus preaches, men are amazed at His authority, His power over the spirit of man, for He speaks not like the scribes from book, but straight from the heart of the truth itself. There arises in human hearts a new God-consciousness of which Jesus is the fount. With this there comes an orientation of the religious life, no longer to tradition, but to God as revealed to experience. Jesus found on the statute-book old principles like "Eye for eye, and tooth for tooth", which went back to the desert, and which but for the codification of Israel's laws in a holy book would have gone the way of all obsolete things, but whose retention in the holy book was fatally retarding the soul of Israel. Jesus struck away these obsolete things. He broke through the sacrosanct book, and opened a way for the Spirit. He removed the fatal arrest which legalism had imposed on men's spirits. He put forward the hands of the clock until the ideal of human duty chimed again with the holy love of God. All this is history, and creative history, and I cannot but feel that Dr. McGiffert is wrong when, in his recent work *The God of the Early Christians*, he seems to deny it. If Jesus laid any foundation at all, it was through and in a new realization of the Divine Fatherhood. St. Paul confesses as much when he says: "God has sent the Spirit of his Son into your hearts, crying, Abba, Father." Here you have the natal cry, the primordial recognition of Christianity. And with the Lord's Prayer daily upon Christian lips, I do not see how it could have been otherwise.

(2) The task to which Jesus gave Himself, and in which He realized

His calling, was the reconciliation of His nation to God. It was to save "many", i.e. as many as He could, that He preached and taught, laboured, hungered, and suffered, and it was on the same mission of reconciliation that He sent the Twelve. Jewish scholars, while contending that the ethics of Jesus may be paralleled from Rabbinical sources, admit that to this fundamental redemptive passion of Jesus there is no Jewish parallel. Here, then, we strike a second historic foundation of the Christian religion. The history of the Christian Church has been written from the standpoint of its apocalyptic visions and of its Messianic cryptograms, but I believe that the mission to humanity was more central, more constitutive, and more original than any of these.

(3) The Christian society could never from the start dissociate the new experience of God and the new passion for humanity from the personality of Him through whom they came. They called Jesus the Messiah, the Anointed of God, because no other language was adequate to His transcendence. But it is important to grasp on what experiential basis this historic language was moulded and riveted. In the soul of Jesus the Messianic prophecies of the Old Testament came into position through His determining and inalienable consciousness of being sent to save His nation. In the faith of His followers the Messianic language signified the confession that this salvation was real. Nor could these followers, in virtue of that consciousness, ever think of Jesus' functions being alienated, or of His place ever being taken by another. Jesus was and remained the final messenger of God. Such a conviction, welded and annealed on Jesus' word and spirit, was, it is clear, primordial, coeval with Christianity.

(4) "Christ died for our sins according to the scriptures." It is quite certain that this conviction which came to constitute the finally determining aspect of Jesus' Messiahship, was also present in the natal consciousness of the Church. We have seen that there is no New Testament Christianity in which it is not the central, indeed the characteristic, element. The death of Jesus, which was at first the darkest of all mysteries, became very soon the focal point of light. From saying, "Though He was the Messiah, He was crucified," they came to say, "He is the Messiah, just because He was crucified." What was the specific experience which enabled this transition of thought to be accomplished, and made the Cross for ever the fascinating centre of all interest? I need not speak here of the objective significance of the death of Jesus as an event standing between the

followers of Jesus and the world, nor of its ethical significance as marking the contrast between the Messiah's Kingdom and the kingdoms of the world, or as annulling earthly dreams of glory. Another direction of mind was implicitly present from the start, a pathway starlit by flashes of Jesus' own thought, in the conception that His death was part and parcel, nay, was the final and all-determining element, in that reconciliation of the "many" to God, which Jesus came to effect. His death a ransom? His blood the sign or seal of a new covenant? These spear-pointed flashings of spiritual prediction on Jesus' own part were too consistent with the tenor of His whole life not to draw the eyes of His followers to them, and not to fill the foreground of their thought. So as they stood face to face with the fact of the Cross, some glimmering of what that whole reconciling life had meant gave guidance to their spiritual instincts. Gone to God for us? Giving Himself for the sins of Israel? Faith felt that it might indeed embrace that thought. As they pondered the mystery, the followers of Jesus realized that something had happened. The veil of the temple had been rent in twain. Faith and hope had transferred themselves from temple and sacrifices and law, and rested on the head of the Crucified.

(5) Jesus brought to men, and founded His Church upon, the assurance of immortality. The specific form of His message was the Jewish idea of the world-displacing, world-renewing Kingdom of God, for which apocalyptists looked. There was much in this Jewish idea which was natively and naïvely contingent and time-conditioned. The Jewish conception was largely a protest against the culture and institutions of the civilized world. But at the heart of the dream of the imperial glory of God there was something more. There was the dream of resurrection, the passion for what we call immortality. I believe that in the century and a half preceding Christ, and in the century and a half that followed Him, this quest of immortality was the predominant passion, and that the Jewish belief in the Kingdom of God was but the characteristic national form of it, a form in which the pure spiritual element was still involved in much crude matter. And what Jesus did, while carrying forward the form of the Jewish idea, was to liberate the spiritual substance, and to give it wings. The emphasis in Jesus' teaching is not on the material nature of the Kingdom, but on the quality of that life with God which is its condition and its inner essence. So that what Jesus gave to His followers, along with the conception of the life with God, was the assurance of immortality,

as founded on Himself, and above all on His passion and death. I would stress this point at the close of our survey of the Christian foundations. I cannot but think that much of the emphasis which modern scholars have placed on the outward form of Jesus' eschatology is largely mistaken and unwarranted. Jewish scholars are not greatly troubled by the apocalyptic element in the literature of Israel. It is only when Western minds, accustomed to the external and prosaic valuation of ideas, get to work on the symbolism of the primitive faith that we lose touch with Jesus.

And so, beside the principle, "He died for our sins according to the scriptures," rises the other and complementary principle, "He sitteth at the right hand of God in the glory of the Father." On these foundations everything else is built.

CHAPTER 2

The Early Ministry of Jesus According to St. Mark: A Theological Approach

I

As starting-point we shall take the triple aspect under which the synoptic gospels, including St. Mark, come before us.

(1) The books are *literary* creations which, however much they may have drawn on oral and written sources, came to their present form under the shaping and ordering powers of individual minds. There was a time when the *books* were not, and when they did come to be, they did not produce themselves. While, therefore, our attention must continue to be given to questions concerning the source and the literary interdependence of the documents, there must be no overlooking of the selective and constructive insights—and freedoms—which go with individual authorship.

(2) They are *historical* documents which, as incorporating the most ancient traditions of the Church concerning Jesus, raise questions as to the character and order of the underlying events. There was a time when the facts were not. What now is the relation of the books to the facts? How, for example, do the parables as recorded compare with the terms and the intention of the original pronouncements of Jesus. How does the eschatology of Mark xiii and its parallels answer to His authentic vision of the things to come? How, finally, do the Passion-narratives of the gospels stand with reference to the course of events at the trial and death of Jesus?

(3) They are memorials of *Christian faith and doctrine* which are grounded on the belief in Divine events operative in the Person and work of Jesus. There was a time when this *faith* was not. As it is, the books take us into a dimension of reality lying beyond the ordinary range of historical perspective. They come to us on the level not of secular but of sacred history [*Heilsgeschichte* as the Germans call it], and even there the books make for themselves a singular and incomparable claim.

An immense amount of labour has been expended on the study of the Gospels but, in modern times at least, the work has been for the most part in two dimensions only. We have projected the text of the Gospels on to a plane surface, and have sought to take its measure by reference to grammar and ideas. First, we have, with every instrument of philological precision, placed the language of the books against the background of the historical development of the Greek tongue. We have called in the aid of the papyri, of the LXX translation of the Old Testament, and of the vocabulary of contemporary Hellenistic religious literature, while not neglecting Aramaic studies. We have in this way surveyed the material along its axis of *length*, that is, by reference to the evolution of language. Secondly, for the illustration and appraisal of its ideas we have adduced analogies from the field of Comparative Religion. We have amassed parallels from Jewish apocalyptic eschatology, Greek and Oriental gnosis, Hermetic mysticism, and what not, and now there has been opened to us the very fertile new source of knowledge which has come with the Dead Sea Scrolls from Qumran. We have here been computing the *breadth* of the New Testament material. There remains now, thirdly, the theological substance, or depth dimension of the Gospels. This has not had anything like the same attention directed to it. Exegetics have indeed been warned not to intrude into this area. Even Dr. Vincent Taylor shakes a warning finger at us. In his great commentary on St. Mark, *à propos* of the turning of the tide of Synoptic studies in the direction of theology, he reminds us that neglect of literary and historical criticism of linguistic and textual studies in the supposed interest of theology "can only result in a new Gnosticism". We agree. Yet Dr. Taylor acknowledges that theology has a place—and now that the great guns of his fortress-commentary are in position, less danger is to be apprehended from occasional raids into the area of the evangelist's third dimension. *Depth-soundings*, depth-exegesis are clearly wanted, and in case of accidents, accidents occurring over the frontier, there is always the stronghold built by Dr. Taylor to flee to.

The present essay is a venturesome effort to act out some of the things in the opening chapters of Mark which invite beyond literary and historical criticism to *depth exegesis*.

II

The Gospel of Mark opens with the words: "Beginning of the gospel (i.e. the glad news, or apostolic message) about Jesus Christ."

I brush aside the temptation to ask in passing whether these words may not be a rubric subsequently prefaced to the book, and meaning: "This was the first book to be written about Jesus Christ." In the absence, however, of any evidence that the literary priority of Mark among the Gospels was recognized in the patristic period, it is safer to resign oneself to the ordinary, less exciting interpretation.

We know that Mark's was the first Gospel to be written, but it may well be that the comparative simplicity and indeed *naiveté* of the Markan narrative have disguised from us the tremendous part which this little book may have played in determining the whole cast of our thought regarding the life-story of Jesus. Yet what are the facts? Matthew and Luke are more comprehensive and informative Gospels than Mark, yet they depend upon Mark almost entirely for their scheme and construction of the evangelical history, the writer of Matthew at Antioch finding nothing better to do than to take over and supplement Mark, and the writer of Luke using Mark to fill and cement together his looser collections of traditional material. This being so, we may have to allow in Mark, more than in the other Synoptists, for original elements of inspiration and freedom expressing themselves in the narrative. He first put the facts together and interpreted them. In respect of originality he has no rival but John.

Whether now it is to the architectonic genius of Mark that we owe the impressive general picture of events in the life of Jesus we shall probably never know. It can be made out from a notable passage in Acts that in the ordinary kerygma of the Church the sacred history began, after the baptism of John, with the anointing of Jesus with the Holy Spirit and power, and ended with the events of His passion and resurrection. Between these two points the kerygma made reference to the beneficent works of Jesus and His healing of all oppressed by the devil; because "God was with Him" (Acts x. 36–42). But the structure of the events in Mark is a far more elaborate affair than this. The Gospel falls into two main sections: the one, running from Mark i. 1 to viii. 30, describes how Jesus was revealed to His disciples as the Messiah; the other running from viii. 31 to xvi. 8, tells how He made known to them the further mystery, the Christian mystery proper, of His rejection, death, and resurrection. Both sections near their beginnings have a colourful picture for frontispiece; in the one case it is the Baptism of Jesus, where Jesus as Son of God is anointed with the Holy Spirit (i. 9–11); in the other case it is the Transfiguration where the Divine Sonship is unveiled to the inner circle of His followers (ix. 2–8).

In the first section, Jesus is known only to Himself, His Christhood being supra-historical, a secret hidden from men. In the second section, the Christhood comes out into the open, but solely in relation to the historical events of His rejection, suffering, and death (viii. 31, ix. 31, x. 32 f., x. 45). [He is the Messiah, not after the mind and will of man, but after the mind and will of God (viii. 32–3). He calls Himself the "Son of Man".] Whereas, therefore, in the first section Jesus speaks of His mystery only indirectly and enigmatically (ἐν παρα βολαῖς, iv. 11), He now declares it openly and unambiguously (παρρησίᾳ viii. 32). And, interestingly enough, in this second section we are at points taken over the same ground as in the first, but on a higher level of perceptive insight. Thus there are the references after the Transfiguration to John the Baptist who is now seen as the predicted Elias (ix. 11–13, xi. 28–33), to the Baptism of Jesus Himself which is now seen as a baptism for death (x. 38–40), and to Satanic temptation which He endured, this time at the hands of a confessing disciple (viii. 32–3). It is difficult to think of all this structure and arrangement without assigning some part in it to the evangelist's inspired height of Christological insight.

III

St. Mark's account of *John the Baptist* is brief but theologically loaded. Nothing in the narrative suggests that he is introduced for his own human interest. He is important only for his place in sacred history. After two scripture citations bringing out his function in that history, the evangelist records John's appearance at the Jordan and his dramatic calling of Israel to baptism. This is described as "baptism of repentance" (βάπτισμα μετανοίας) which probably means "baptism *for* repentance". John's baptism was to inaugurate the great repentance of Israel in view of approaching judgement. Mark gives no details of John's message other than that "What he preached was, 'After me there comes the Mightier than I (ὁ ἰσχυρότερός μου)' ". Who this Mightier [this eschatological agent of God] is and what he is to be mightier for, John does not say. He only knows that He will baptize, not like himself in water, but in a higher medium: "with the Holy Spirit", as Mark says. A reference, however, to Matthew and Luke, where the Q source has come under contribution, makes it reasonably certain that, while John may have said "with Holy Spirit", he also said "with fire", doubtless the *refiner's fire spoken of by the prophet Malachi*, iii. 1–3, iv. 1 (cf. Luke xii. 49–50).

We have learned enough of contemporary religious movements to know that John's demand of baptism was not an altogether isolated phenomenon. Proselyte-baptism was practised as part of the admission of Gentile converts as "new creatures" into Judaism and we now know from the Qumran scrolls that ritual ablutions were a condition of initiation into and continuance within the "New Covenant" society of the Essenes. John's baptism differed from these, however, in not being self-administered, in not being demanded of proselytes or of a sect but of all Israel, in not being administered more than once, and in not being oriented towards spiritual perfectionism but towards the immediate approach of the Eschaton. What stands out is the uniqueness of John as the Way-maker for God. Jesus was to say of him that "Among those born of women there has not arisen a greater than John the Baptist" (Matt. x. 11, Luke vii. 28) and He was to identify him with the "Elias to come" (Matt. xi. 14, Mark ix. 12–13). Mark knows this and in his description he invests John with the marks of Elias. But, following Jesus also in this, he goes further back, and in the first of his scriptural quotations introducing John, Mark links him with the Exodus of Israel from Egypt: "Behold, I send my messenger before thy face, who shall prepare thy way" (Exod. xxiii. 20; cf. Matt. xi. 10, Luke vii. 28). In the second quotation he links him with the later exodus of the same people from Babylon (Isa. xl. 3). So John's significance in salvation-history is clinched.

The *Exodus* is indeed the beginning of all salvation-history in the Biblical sense, and it retains significance for the whole of that history. When we today think of *history*, we think of it as a series or stream of events, in which the earlier are always dropping behind the horizon as the new events come on. But in the Bible *time* is not a stream but a structure. It is a structure of Divine acts in which all the parts are held together. First there is the Exodus from Egypt, then to this is added the prophetic interpretation of Israel's calling based on that event, then to this in turn is linked the later eschatology of Israel having part of its roots in the same event. So Israel's religious history becomes a coherent unity. Its elements are like the linked components of a moving train with the Exodus travelling forward like the rest and bringing up the rear. In the shaft of light within which the Bible presents the history of salvation the beginning and end of the process are interconnected. So John appears in Mark as the fulfilment of an Exodus promise, and when Jesus at His baptism passes through the waters of Jordan He is inaugurating the completion of what was begun at the Red Sea.

IV

"It came about in those days", Mark writes "that *Jesus* came from Nazareth" (i. 9). Not a word is said as to who Jesus is, nor is that necessary for a Church which already knows Jesus as Lord and Christ, the Son of God. Here, as elsewhere, the depth-exegesis of the Gospel requires that wherever the names Jesus, Son of God, and Son of Man occur, we shall read into them all the weight of christological meaning which they had acquired in the apostolic Church for which Mark was written. But it may also be noted as an additional reason for Mark's silence that at the time when Jesus comes to be baptized, He is His own mystery, He is known only to Himself. Mark, therefore, offers no explanation why Jesus takes His place with the sinners at the Jordan. A later question put by Jesus however (xi. 28–30), "The baptism of John, whence was it?" makes it plain that, for Mark, John's mission was the supreme sign from God to the age preceding Jesus, while the word of Jesus in Matt. iii. 15 about fulfilling "all righteousness' in coming to John reveals His acceptance of *baptism* as an act of obedience to God, an act cohering in the closest possible manner with His whole identification of Himself with Israel in His mission to bring that nation to God.

In the narrative of Mark what happened at the Jordan is presented as an inward experience imparted to Jesus alone. The *Spirit* descends on Him. The *Voice* from heaven speaks to Him. The Divine enlightening and ordering Spirit which had brooded over the waters at creation, which had come at moments on kings and prophets and men of genius in Israel's sacred history, and which had been promised against the last times, now hovers over the water of Jesus' baptism. It is the sign of His eschatological calling and of the coming of the Age of Grace. The heavenly gift does not yet descend upon others; that awaits a later date (cf. John vii. 39). The Voice "*Thou art My Son*", which has its ultimate theological background in Adam's creation in the image of God, connects specifically with the calling of Israel at the Exodus: "Israel is my Son, my firstborn; let my Son go that He may serve Me" (Exod. iv. 22–3). Even more specifically the voice echoes the Divine decree pronounced at the enthronement of the King of Israel: "The Lord hath said to me, Thou art my Son" (Psalm ii. 7). The further words: "My beloved, on thee have I set my choice" recall the function of Israel as God's servant (Isa. xlii. 1) and suggest a vicarious destiny for Jesus. So through the transparent of the Voice at Jordan there shines the vast representativeness of the Divine nomination of Jesus. He is the second Adam or Son of Man, He is Israel, He is the King of Israel. He is the righteous servant who is to raise up the tribes of Israel. Such at any rate Jesus has come to be for the apostolic church for which and out of which Mark was written. And what is it that constitutes the reality behind every aspect of this function? *It is the Son's obedience.* It was to obedience that original man was called and that Israel and her kings were called, though unsuccessfully. It is to obedience now that Jesus as the "Son of God" is consecrated, that "being found in fashion as a man" He may, for the first time, truly resist the devil, and obey God "even to death" (ὑπήκοος μέχρι θανάτου, Phil. ii. 8).

Mark does not dwell much on the obedience of Jesus Christ. But certain utterances spoken at great moments in the life of Christ, for example His repeated announcements of the necessity (δεῖ) of His Passion (viii. 31, ix. 31, x. 32), His rebuke to Peter, "Thou hast no sense of the things of God" when Peter tried to divert Him from that destiny (viii. 33), and the cry in Gethsemane, "Not what I will, but what Thou wilt" (xiv. 36) reveal the deep sub-structure of the Divine Sonship of Jesus in its ethical manifestation. This is more fully stated in the Q teaching embedded in Matthew and Luke, and comes to pointed expression in their narratives of the wilderness temptation. Mark knows of Jesus after His baptism being "tempted by Satan" (i. 13), and leaves it to be understood that Jesus, alone with the beasts, but ministered to by the angels, is the blessed one of the 91st Psalm who, being under the shadow of the Almighty, passes unhurt through deadly perils. But Mark gives no hint what the temptation was, nor how it was answered: he only knows that Jesus is carried into conflict with the demonic power of darkness before which Adam fell in the garden, and Israel in the day of temptation in the wilderness. Matthew and Luke explain that the temptation turned explicitly on the nature and implications of the Divine Sonship. What did it mean to the Son of God? The answer was, not selfwill, not vainglory, not an empire of this world, but obedience, reverence, the sovereign claim of God.

So the Baptism at the Jordan stands as the frontispiece to the ministry of Jesus in Mark. It represents the first step towards the retrieval through Christ of that integrity with God from which man lapsed through disobedience. And we can agree with Paul Tillich that for us the *absoluteness of the manifestation of God in Christ* is constituted by the completeness and finality of His will to self-divestment in the matter of every claim but that of doing the Father's will. That obedience, by which everything purely individual to His person falls away, and His identification with man for God's sake is carried to the point of self-extinction, makes Jesus Christ the perfect transparent of God (cf. John xiv. 8–10).

V

According to St. Mark's arrangement of the history Jesus commenced His ministry in Galilee after John's commitment to prison. His message is summarized in the form: "The time has fully come, and the reign of God has drawn near; repent, and believe the good news" (Mark i. 14–15). Every word here is loaded with significance.

(1) The *time* (καιρός) that has fully come (πεπλήρωται) is the last time, the age of the End, which is to witness the salvation of God. The advent of this consummation, to which prophets and kings had looked forward, is given in the fact that God has now *named* His messiah and anointed Him for His task. The messiah, the fulness of the times, and the advent of the Reign of God belong together.

The beginnings of *Eschatology* in the age of the prophets constitute one of the most remarkable phenomena in the history of religion. Apparently the increasing pressure of the awareness of God on the minds of the prophets had thrown an ever-deepening shadow of guilt over Israel's moral life and had affixed an interrogation-mark to all its institutions. The sovereignty of the Divine righteousness, the reality of the Divine salvation, seemed withdrawn from present life. But as the faithfulness of the covenant-God could not be questioned by the prophets, the realization of what was wanting under the present order was projected into the future, and there is built up the vision of a Coming Age in which redemption will be complete. Into this future age is thrown forward the hope of a Righteous Nation, Righteous Ruler, Knowledge of God, Spirit of God, New Covenant with God, and so forth.

This rise of eschatology in Israel admits of being clearly traced in the mind of an individual prophet like Jeremiah. Jeremiah's earlier utterances are an almost unrelieved outpouring of woes and predictions of doom on princes, prophets, and priests alike for unfaithfulness and transgression. Then comes the Exile; and with the Exile a new note enters into Jeremiah's message. It is as when, after a night of storm and gloom, the star of morning appears and the first song of birds is heard. Thus (Jer. xxix. 11), "I know the thoughts that I think towards you, saith the Lord, thoughts of peace and not of evil, *to give you a latter end and hope.*" So the R.V. margin. The R.V. text has "to give you hope for your latter end". The R.S.V. renders: "to give you a future and a hope" (cf. also xxxi. 17).

Again (xxiii. 5–6), "Behold, the days come, saith the Lord, that I will raise unto David a righteous Branch, and he shall reign as King . . . and this is the name whereby he shall be called, the Lord is our Righteousness." It is added that the salvation to be effected will be an Exodus of Israel exceeding in glory the deliverance from Egypt (xxiii. 7–8). Once again (xxxi. 31 f.), "Behold, the days come, saith the Lord, that I will make a new covenant with the house of Israel . . . not according to the covenant that I made with their fathers . . . which covenant of Mine they broke."

So the sense of an eschatological *kairos*, of a coming *malkuth Jahweh*, and of a New Covenant order of life is built up.

It must be remembered, indeed, that in the age of Jesus the Jewish eschatology had advanced altogether beyond the limits marked by the prophetic teaching. An *apocalyptic* literature, beginning with the Book of Daniel, had arisen which had fitted the future hope of Israel into a grandiose cosmic framework of world-history, in which two world ages had come to be distinguished, a present age under the power of Satan and subject to sin, death, and dissolution, and a coming supernatural age, lying beyond history and marking the end of the secular world-process. The formal element in this eschatology owed much to the influence of Iranian ideas. [From the latter were derived not only the two ages but the conceptions of the Satanic character of the present age, the world-catastrophe, the resurrection, and the last judgement, and these have been taken over by the New Testament religion.] But while the eschatology of Jesus derives certain elements of colour and form from contemporary ideas, its roots penetrate beneath that soil into the subsoil of the prophetic religion of the Old Testament. And it is from the latter, as interpreted by Jesus, that its spiritual life-substance is drawn.

(2) The *Reign of God*. In the Old Testament, and in the apocalyptic

literature of Judaism, the sovereignty of the Divine righteousness involves the thought of hostile powers at war with God. The proclamation of God's Kingdom is a challenge to these affronting powers. The same is true in the Gospel, only whereas in the Old Testament the enemies are the heathen nations (cf. Psalms ii, cx, etc.), in the Gospel, as in the post-canonical Jewish writings, they are the invisible powers of the demonic world. Therefore Jesus, after His baptism, comes into conflict with Satan. He has been *named* the Son of God, and the utterance of this Name has been sufficient to arouse and organize the infernal world against Him. So in a later word of Jesus, preserved for us in another Gospel (Matt. xi. 12), we hear that "From the days of John the Baptist until now the kingdom of heaven is violently assaulted, and the violent try to seize it." The violent, I take it, are the powers of darkness, and their violence is their intolerance of the name and office of "the Son of God".

In the proclamation of Jesus this reign of God "*has come near* (ἤγγικεν)". But how near? So near that now, as Jesus speaks of it, it is to fill the whole horizon of His hearers! So near that it is to lay its total arrest on every life! So near that henceforth there is left to men no option but to accept the Kingdom or to cast away one's life! No man can serve two masters! In this manner the Reign of God, the Kingdom of the End, which hitherto had been only an apocalyptic hope, a dream, a myth that flitted before the mind of Israel as the rainbow flits before the traveller, comes into direct and *existential* relation with the lives of men. Jesus makes it a matter of life and death for the individual. What does it mean for a man that God's Reign should come to him now, and come in the absoluteness of its holiness? Here is the real "nearness" of the Kingdom, the confrontation of man with the last demand, the pressure of something which cannot be set aside or postponed to another day.

(3) Jesus says, "*Repent* (μετανοεῖτε)." But how can a man repent? How change his mind and revolutionize his life? Can he give himself a new mentality, or create in himself a new heart? The answer is, he cannot in himself, the less so in the searching light of the Divine holiness in which Jesus makes the issue to appear. But in St. Mark's presentation the demand is not simply "Repent", but "Repent and believe the glad tidings". Repentance is a new orientation of life constituted by faith in an Event which Jesus declares to be at hand and indeed knocking at the door. *God* wills to reign, and to make His righteousness effectual. This repentance is but a beginning, but Jesus

has stepped as Messiah into the human situation, and has altered the centre of gravity of man's existence. Man making or beginning by faith has henceforth *no future except God*, but he *has* that future. In this way the gospel of Jesus becomes the eschatological Event. [In this exposition we have gone beyond Mark's terms and drawn on the teaching of Jesus in Matthew and Luke, but this has been necessary to bring out the depth of meaning underlying Mark's summation.] It will be seen that the effect of the teaching, as interpreted, is a *transvaluation* of the concept of the Reign of God, a transference of emphasis from the outward realm to the realm of *spirit*.

VI

Jesus now forms a group of men around Himself (Mark i. 16–20), and as He enters on His public teaching (1. 21 ff.), these men are among His auditors. As we shall see, He is to make them conscious of the eschatological nature of their calling. He is to compare them to the companions of a bridegroom on a wedding-day (Mark ii. 18–22), and to require that they shall live the life of the New Age. He also makes known to them their responsibility as those to whom is imparted the "mystery" of the Kingdom of God (iv. 10–12, 21–2). As opposition gathers against Him, He draws these men more closely around Himself (iii. 13, 31–5). In i. 21–2 we hear of His teaching in the synagogue at Capernaum and of the impression which it produced. "They were amazed at His teaching, for He was teaching them as one who had *authority* (ἐξουσίαν) and not as the Scribes." [When we come to a closer examination of St. Mark's use of the term *exousia*—which now becomes the dominant note in the evangelist's representation of the work and word of Jesus (i. 21, 27; ii. 10, 24–8)—we find ourselves drawn into more than one field of inquiry.]

Primarily the term *exousia*, as Mark employs it, has Messianic significance. In the eschatological vision of Daniel vii the symbolic figure who there appears as "like a son of man" is said, in the Greek, to receive *exousia*, a term alternating with *basileia* or sovereignty. Thus Dan. vii. 14 in the Septuagint runs: "And there was given him authority (ἐξουσία) . . . and his authority (ἐξουσία) is an eternal authority (ἐξουσία) . . . and his kingdom (βασιλεία) one that shall not be destroyed:" Theodotion's version is similar. In Mark the eschatological context of the word comes clearly to the surface in ii. 10 where the forgiveness of sins on earth comes under the prerogative of the

"Son of Man", while in ii. 28, the "Son of Man" is Lord (κύριος) of the Sabbath. The authority of Jesus has thus a transcendent character [though its source is not as yet divulged but remains His own secret]. Mark presents it in two particular ways.

(1) There is its *psychical* aspect as shown in the extraordinary control exercised by Jesus over disordered minds, and indeed over the whole realm of psycho-physical existence. This power of Jesus penetrates beneath the rational level of the human consciousness to its subliminal depths. Thus the first reference to His *exousia* after i. 22, is on the occasion of the exorcism of the demon in the synagogue (i. 23–7), where the astonished spectators exclaim: "What is this? It is a new kind of teaching! With authority he commands the unclean spirits too, and they obey him" (i. 27). Reference to the ascendancy of Jesus over the "spirits" now becomes continuous in Mark (cf. i. 32, 34, 39; iii. 11–12, 15; v. 1–20), and in iii. 22–7, the charge made by the scribes from Jerusalem that Jesus owes the success of His work in this realm to some alliance with the prince of darkness (iii. 22) brings the whole question of the nature of His power into the open, while incidentally the use by Jesus of the parable of the strong man's castle invaded by the stronger lets the light in on the question who the "Mightier One" is of whom John the Baptist had spoken and what He is mightier for. At the same time the terrible condemnation by Jesus of the sin against the Holy Spirit (iii. 28–9) takes us back to the source of His authority in His baptism when the Holy Spirit came upon Him. Such passages-at-arms with opponents who ask for a sign from heaven, but can see in Jesus' work only a sign from hell, show the critical significance attached by the primitive Christian consciousness to the power of Jesus over disordered states of the human mind. At the same time broader issues are raised.

For one thing, the fact that in the case of healings other than those of demoniacs the Gospels sometimes employ language suggesting that a particular malady has its source in Satan's tyranny (e.g. Luke xiii. 10–17) seems to imply an extension of the principle of spiritualistic causality, to the whole domain of human suffering, and even to disorders in the external world of nature. In iv. 35–41, for example, the words with which Jesus stills the storm on the Galilean Lake are assimilated to those with which He quiets the evil spirits. Jesus "rebukes" the wind and enforces silence on the sea (σιώπα, πεφίμωσο). In this case it is patent that for early Christian thought the *exousia* of Jesus as the Messiah of God extends to realms beyond the human, and that His sovereignty in these realms too is conditioned by that perfect obedience as the Son of God by which He had resisted and overcome Satan, and is now able to destroy his works.

In fact in the Gospels and in the New Testament Jesus is Himself *the miracle of God.* "Who then is this that even the wind, etc." In the New Testament all miraculous powers are exercised only ἐν Χριστῷ. Thus we read that "John did no miracle, but all the things that John said of this man were true." All healing powers in the New Testament are effected either by Jesus or through the use of His Name.

(Similarly a dynamic-spiritualistic character is ascribed to the "*regnum Christi*" in 1 Cor. xv. 25–8. It brings about the subjugation of all enemies, the last to be destroyed being death.)

From this it follows that for the primitive Christian consciousness the *Incarnation* of the Son of God is not grasped in its full reality and consequences until we think of His entrance into our nature as not limited to the rational part of man's existence but as penetrating into the sub-conscious and the irrational, and secondly as establishing right relations between man and Nature.

(2) The second aspect under which St. Mark presents the *exousia* of Jesus has to do with the freedom into which He brings man's moral nature, the deliverance He effects not only from the guilt and power of sin, but from the inhibitions imposed by a legalistic and unreasoning tradition of religion. In the section ii. 1–iii. 5, we have a series of incidents (perhaps incorporated from a written source), of which the keynotes are these: first, Jesus as the authority through which the life of religion is liberated and reconstituted; secondly, the disciples of Jesus as the society or sphere within which that liberation and reconstitution are effected. Thus (1) Jesus declares the forgiveness of sins, defending His right to do so by reference to the power committed to the Son of Man (ii. 10). He also claims the right to break through the religious barriers erected by Judaism between the righteous and sinners by going as the physician to the sick and the lost (ii. 15–17). Further, in dealing with various questions turning on what is "lawful" (ἔξεστιν) on the Sabbath (ii. 24, 26; iii. 4), He answers by affirming His own *exousia* or by appeal to the lordship of the Son of Man (ii. 28). (2) The disciples are compared to the companions of the bridegroom on a wedding-day, and as such are exempt from fasting regulations (ii. 19). They belong, in effect, to the New Age, in which the Kingdom of God is announced. In their association with Himself these disciples are eschatological persons for whom the ritual law is

dissolved. Finally—for this is the natural meaning of the parables of the New Cloth and the New Wine (ii. 21–2)—these disciples are to wear the garments and to live the life of the *New Creation*, not to continue in the old clothes of Judaism.

In virtue of the *exousia* of Jesus, therefore, a new order of life has begun to shape itself on earth to which, as representing the fulfilment of prophetic expectation, belong forgiveness, freedom, and renewal of life. In the fellowship of the Son of God men are translated above the law, and we are on the way to that Righteousness which St. Paul describes as made manifest by God in Christ. "Now apart from Law (χωρὶς νόμου) a righteousness which is of God (δικαιοσύνη θεοῦ) has come to light, one which is attested by the law and the prophets, but which is righteousness from God, made operative by faith in Jesus Christ" (Rom. iii. 21–2).

VII

It remains to glance briefly at one or two remaining features of Mark's representation of the Early Ministry of Jesus. One is the interpretation under which in one passage he places Jesus' use of *parables* in His public teaching (Mark iv. 10–12). This notoriously difficult passage is preceded by the parable of the Sower, the obvious meaning of which is that the message of salvation, the gospel of the Reign of God, is to be broadcast to all men. Now, however, in reply to a question privately put to Him by "those who were around Him with the Twelve", Jesus draws a distinction between the open communication of truth to the inner circle and the use of figurative language in the instruction given to the many. "To you has been given the *mystery* (τὸ μυστήριον, the revealed secret) of the Reign of God, but to those outside all things are (i.e. the whole procedure is) in parables" (iv. 11). So far all is clear. If we have been right in holding that with Jesus' teaching about the *Kairos* and the nearness of the Kingdom there has come a transvaluation of the latter concept in the sense that the emphasis has been transported from the outward realm to the realm of the spirit, we have no difficulty in understanding the "mystery" which is communicated to the inner circle. That reign of God which in current Jewish expectation was embodied in a dream of national or apocalyptic glory has been turned *inwards* in the case of those who have stood in the counsel of Jesus. He has laid its arrest on their wills and consciences. He has made it for them an existential and transforming personal issue. For those on the other hand who have remained outside the counsel of Jesus the Reign of God continues to be wrapped in ideas of the visible and the material. So far, all is simple. But did Jesus use parables and tropes, not to mediate the truth to the imperfect intelligence of those outsiders, but in order to hide it from them, to produce a mental fixation leaving them where they were? Such might seem to be the surface-meaning of the words of Jesus which now follow in Mark. The teaching by parables is a measure by judgement taken against spiritually unreceptive hearers.

The words in Mark are:

To those who are without, all things are done in parables, *that* (ἵνα) *seeing they may see and not perceive, and hearing they may hear and not understand, lest haply* (μήποτε) *they should turn again*, and forgiveness be granted to them (iv. 11–12).

The difficulty about the literal acceptance of these words is that, if Jesus intended to leave these "outsiders" in their condition of spiritual blindness, it does not appear why He should wish to go on speaking to them, either in parables or in any other way, unless—though this is not stated—for the purpose of sifting out the elect. But is this alleged interpretation the only way of understanding the passage? The writer of Matthew did not think so. By substituting ὅτι for Mark's ἵνα he makes the parables an accommodation to the spiritual incapacity of the hearers, not a judicial measure against them. But even without any verbal change in the text of Mark a sense may be extracted from the passage which tends towards the sympathetic interpretation put on it by Matthew, but throws a wonderful light on the purpose of Jesus in using the parables.

The passage turns on an allusion made by Jesus to the commission given to Isaiah in Isa. vi. 10. Everything depends, however, on the purpose for which Jesus went back to Isaiah and on the possibility that He was giving to old words a transformingly new sense in keeping with His purpose of "fulfilling" the prophets. Now the Greek words used by Mark (which conform neither to the Hebrew text nor to the LXX version of Isaiah, but, as Dr. T. W. Manson has shown, to an Aramaic version preserved in the Targum and the Peshitta, and therefore possibly derived from Synagogue tradition) do admit of such a possibility. Allowing for the paratactic structure of Semitic language and thought, we may venture to translate as follows:

To those who are without, the entire procedure is in parables *in order that they may certainly see though they do not perceive, and may certainly hear though they do not comprehend, in case they may turn*, and forgiveness be granted to them.

On this understanding of the passage Jesus is subordinating the commission of Isaiah to His own overruling purpose of giving the gospel to all men. In this He is really "fulfilling" Isaiah. *Isaiah*, indeed, was sent to run his head against a wall. God said to him, in effect, "Go and fail!" The intention of *Jesus* is that what happened in the case of Isaiah shall never happen again. The superficially minded, who resist the spiritual truth (casual hearers, critics, and opponents) will at least, through the Parables, have something to carry away with them, a picture before their eyes, a story in their minds, through which the converting truth, to which they are blind and deaf, may yet break through to them with regenerative results. On this understanding the Parables of the Kingdom are an instrument of *grace*, a means by which the door of repentance is held open to "those without". They only minister judgement as their appeal is finally resisted, and the light is turned into darkness.

We may conclude, then, by saying that *through Jesus the Reign of God is demythologized for the inner circle, but for the rest of men the truth must continue to be clothed in pictorial and symbolic language if it is to gain entrance to their minds at all.*

One word more. If Jesus uses parables in His teaching of the many, it is to be added that they are of a certain kind. The parables of the reign of God cited by Mark are those of the sower, of the seed growing secretly, and of the Mustard Seed. This choice may well be thought to connect with the "Messianic mystery" in Mark. In Mark Jesus discourages all attempts to give publicity to His healing acts, especially His exorcisms, and silences all words and ovations infringing upon the secrecy of the office to which He was called at His baptism. (So i. 24, i. 34, iii. 11–12, v. 6–8). In cases other than exorcisms, He forbids the leper to speak of His healing (i. 44) and deprecates the spreading of reports about the raising of Jairus' daughter (v. 43). We all know the construction put upon this feature of the Markan tradition by Wrede in his book, *Das Messiasgeheimnis*, written about the beginning of the present century. To Wrede all this element of secrecy was an artifice concealing the fact that the historical Jesus, in His Galilean ministry made none of the Messianic claims ascribed to Him in the post-resurrection tradition of the Church.

It may be thought that Wrede's theory reflects the mentality less of the Apostolic Church than of a Liberal German theologian of the end of the nineteenth century. A less sceptical and destructive attitude becomes possible when we notice the context of the deprecations of Jesus. In Mark's representation the cry "Thou are the Son of God" and the like are confined to the evil spirits. In the Synoptic theology this goes with the fact that Satan and his minions have, from the time of Jesus' baptism, got hold of the sacred Name of Jesus as revealed at the Jordan, and are determined to turn it to their own purposes. This is attempted by Satan in the wilderness where "If Thou art the Son of God" is made the hinge on which His nefarious suggestions turn. They are designed to deflect Jesus from that perfect inwardness of obedience to God which for Him is the meaning of His call. So when the demons raise the cry "Thou art the Son of God" there is a danger that, if not Jesus Himself, at least the public for whose salvation He is concerned, may be lured to false courses. The demonic power of the world is set to divert the Messiah to false messianic paths.

Is it not possible to find here an explanation of the special character of the Parables of the Kingdom? Granting that Jesus has to use "myth" in popular teaching, we shall not expect Him to do so indiscriminately. It is, for example, significant that none of the parables of the Kingdom tell of stones being turned into bread, or of signs being given in heaven above, or of an earthly empire being awarded to the Messiah. Instead we hear of seed being sown in the ground, of seed growing to harvest secretly, of a mustard seed becoming a great tree. The *interiorization* of the Reign of God among men is what is taught. The "mystery" of the Kingdom is present even in the myths addressed to the simple. So if, more generally speaking, we are to have a Biblical Theology, let it be that of Jesus and the Apostolic Church, not that of the nineteenth and twentieth centuries.

VIII

Some points for further brief discussion in relation to the Galilean ministry of Jesus (Mark v.–viii. 30).

(1) Jesus, despite the opposition which has now developed, continues, though unknown, to exercise His Saviour-function, wherever faith is shown. His ἐξουσία is variously revealed in iv. 35–41 (over the wind and the sea), v. 14b–15 (the Gerasene demoniac), v. 19–20, v. 27–36 (ἡ πίστις σου σεσωκέν σε . . . μὴ φοβοῦ, μόνον πίστευε), v. 41–2 vi. 4–6

(unbelief at Nazareth). The *personal* nature of His power is indicated: cf. v. 30 (ἐπιγνοὺς ἐν ἑαυτῷ τὴν ἐξ αὐτοῦ δύναμιν ἐξελθοῦσαν) and vi. 2 and vi. 5–6 (καὶ οὐκ ἐδύνατο ἐκεῖ ποιῆσαι οὐδεμίαν δύναμιν' εἰ μή . . .).

(2) The *Mission of the Twelve* (vi. 7–13): calls towards Jesus the unfavourable attention of Herod Antipas. The reflections of the tetrarch (vi. 14, 16). [Does the episode recorded in Luke xiii. 31–3 belong to the situation here developing, and reflect a crisis?] The evidence of Mark vi. 30–4, and Jesus' action (vi. 35–43). Popular excitement? (Mark vi. 45. Cf. John vi. 14–15.)

(3) The feeding of the multitude (Mark vi. 35–43 and viii. 1–9. Cf. Mark viii. 17–20). Are the records duplicate traditions of a single event? . . . Was it *a Sacrament*? Notice the parallelism of the two Lake-cycles of events.

The Bread-motif.

The Lake journeys (Mark vi. 45–53, viii. 10–13).

Altercations with the Pharisees (Mark vii. 1 f., viii. 11 f.).

Appended discourses (Mark vii. 5–23; viii. 12). Cf. John vi. 22–65.

(4) Departure of Jesus from Galilee (Mark vii. 24–5, 31; viii. 13–22; viii. 27 ff.).

CHAPTER 3

The Imperative of Jesus: A Study of the "Sermon on the Mount" and the Gospel Ethics.[1]

It was my first intention to take up a somewhat broader theme than the one to which I now invite your attention. I had in mind the general relation of gospel and life in Primitive Christianity, and purposed to trace the processes of thought by which the conception of the Messianic salvation through Jesus was made to yield a norm and principle for Christian living, and how in particular St. Paul used it as the means to educe and build up in his Gentile converts a specifically ethical Christian consciousness. On second thoughts, it appeared to me that a prior, and more difficult, problem was awaiting a solution. How were these same two elements, *Gospel and ethic*, related the one to the other in the teaching of Jesus? There we have in juxtaposition, on the one hand, tidings of joy—"The Kingdom of God has drawn near", on the other hand, a demand of righteousness exceeding the righteousness of the scribes and Pharisees. The formal principle uniting these two things is that both of them come from Jesus. Both form part of our evangelical data. But what is the material principle which connects them? How are we to understand the imperative of Jesus?

How real this question is may be seen by the fact that it seems to have engaged the mind of Shakespeare. In the play of *King Richard II* we find that hapless monarch soliloquizing in prison on the dividedness, the contradictoriness of human ideas, the difficulty of finding peace by thought.

> For no thought is contented. The better sort,
> As thoughts of things divine, are intermix'd
> With scruples, and do set the word itself
> Against the word:
> As thus, "Come, little ones"; and then again,
> "It is as hard to come as for a camel
> To thread the postern of a needle's eye".
>
> ACT V, SC. V, lines 11–17

[1] Address to Glasgow Theological Club, 15 February 1937.

Revelation, religion itself sets "the word against the word". So at least it seems when we place the promises in the gospel side by side with its inexorable demand of ethics. The resolution of the apparent contradiction does not appear on the surface. Can we discover it by going a little deeper?

The imperative of Jesus shapes itself not only in *commands,* such as "Love your enemies", but *categorically* in assertions regarding the character of the Divine salvation, such as "Blessed are the poor in spirit, for theirs is the Kingdom of Heaven". It finds expression *legislatively* in pronouncements made regarding conduct, such as "Whoever is angry with his brother is liable to judgement": *conditionally* in statements of warning or promise, such as "Except your righteousness exceed that of the Scribes and Pharisees, you shall not enter into the Kingdom of Heaven": *potentially,* in averments of moral impossibility or the reverse, e.g. "You cannot serve God and Mammon": and *futuristically* in visions of a consummation not yet reached, e.g. "You shall be perfect as your heavenly Father is perfect". It is plain from the variety and character of these forms that the ethical demand of Jesus does not exclude or wave aside man's faculty of *reason* or judgement but consistently engages it in support of itself. What then is the nature of His demand? It has been styled repentance-ethic, but that description does not take us very far. We have to ask: Did Jesus teach, as some think, an *Interim-Ethic* applicable only to a situation in which this world and its interests were conceived to be passing away? Or did He teach *Kingdom-Ethic,* i.e. a rule or law of life which had reference only to a new order which was still to come? Or is the teaching of Jesus *both* these things at once? And, if so, what is it that links the words "You must" with the alternating statement "You shall be"?

It may not be possible to discover an answer to all these questions, but it is at least necessary to face them, and in any case the way must lead by consideration of that compendium of our Lord's teaching which we know as the *Sermon on the Mount.* This, I need hardly say, is a compilation put together by the Evangelist Matthew from the Logia and other documents but on the basis of a rudimentary discourse which, as we know from Luke vi. 20–49, the Logia-source contained. The compiler of Matthew, finding in Mark a reference to teaching of Jesus which amazed men by its "authority" (Mark i. 22), determined to give us a great representative instance of that teaching; and just as in Mark the "authority" of Jesus connects, on the one hand, with the proclamation of forgiveness and with the deliverance of possessed souls from unclean spirits, and, on the other hand, shows itself in the setting free of His followers from crippling legal traditions (Mark i. 27, ii. 10, ii. 24, iii. 4), so the Sermon in Matthew begins with gospel in the form of Beatitudes, and passes on to tell how Jesus superseded the legal tradition and even the Law itself (Matt. v. 21–48). But here arises *our problem,* for from the offer of the Gospel in the Beatitudes the Sermon passes to the demand of a "righteousness", stricter in its rigour than that of the Law, which Jesus asks of His followers and which conditions their entrance into the Kingdom of Heaven.

(1) We begin with the *Beatitudes* which represent the Gospel and which offer the blessedness of the Kingdom of God and the Messianic salvation to a certain order of spirits. In the Aramaic original the literal sense of the Beatitudes would be "O happiness of those (or of you) who are poor, sorrowful, hungry!" In *Luke* the sayings are stated in the second person, so that the Beatitudes point to a recognizable, existing group of persons who possess the characteristics in question: in other words, they are addressed in Luke to the body of *disciples* or, as we might say, to the Church. In view, however, of two things, (i) an Ebionite strain exalting poverty in the Judean church in which Luke collected a part of his tradition, (ii) the tendency of this church on the strength of its material poverty to proclaim itself heir to the promises given to "the poor' in the Old Testament and in the Gospel of Jesus, it will be unwise to stress the Lukan form of the words. It is more probable, considering the Isaianic prediction "He hath anointed me to preach glad tidings to the poor" (Isa. lxi. 1), that Jesus offered the blessedness of the Kingdom to the poor generally and with reference to the religious or inward connotation of poverty. This application *Matthew* fixes by adding to "the poor" the qualification "in spirit". According to him Jesus in this and the succeeding Beatitudes is offering the Messianic Kingdom with its consolation and satisfaction, not to any definite group or society already existing and claiming to be "the poor", but *universally* to all persons who exhibit in conduct or in spirit the qualifications named. As soon as the Messianic Kingdom is apprehended as "near", the type of spirit for which it is destined at once comes to light, and these are the blessed. So Matthew.

But here a question arises which is important for our present purpose. Those qualifications of spirit which the inheritors of the Kingdom are seen to exhibit, do they refer to antecedent virtues or excellences or *conditions of character* on the part of the persons in question? If so, we shall have to say either (i) that the Kingdom of God, the Messianic salvation which Jesus preaches, is something which the blessed *win* or acquire by title of their own, in which case the Gospel of Jesus will have nothing to say to those others, to whom nevertheless He offers it, the outcasts and the sinners; or (ii) we shall have to say that Jesus thought of a predestined elect which was inscrutable to human vision, and which, because it was inscrutable, justified His offering of the Gospel to all, saints and sinners alike. But the fact that in neither of these cases is Jesus' call to sinners fully real should make us hesitate before adopting either of these explanations. (i) "*Personality-value*", the thing on which so much stress is laid in Greek and in modern ethics, and which makes moral worth depend upon acquired excellence or culture of character, has no place in Biblical or Jewish-Christian thought. There men are righteous, holy, pure in virtue not of some acquired state or habit of character but in virtue of their *obedience* to the Will of God. Not only so, but what the Beatitudes indicate in every case is not the presence in the blessed of "personality-value" but the very opposite, the total absence of such value. The "poor in spirit", the "sorrowful", the "meek", the "hungry", are those who in real truth have not a stiver of personal claim as they come before God, who indeed are stricken by their lack of goodness, the impotence of their own striving, the starved condition of their souls. (ii) While we cannot say that *predestination* has no place at all in the thought of Jesus, the way in which He stresses man's will and responsibility in this Sermon and elsewhere, suggests that the qualities or reactions described in the Beatitudes are not independent of *moral will* or *choice*. What then is the situation? We exclude the personality-value theory because it renders meaningless the offer of the Gospel of Jesus to sinners. We exclude the predestination theory because it leaves no proper room for man's responsibility as moral agent. Is there anything left by way of possible explanation? We come here to what, I think, is the real core of the whole matter.

Jesus in the Beatitudes is characterizing and pronouncing as blessed not those who possess antecedent states or qualities of character but those who exhibit certain responses or reactions when the Gospel of the Kingdom is presented to them. The sense of need, the sorrow, the humility, the soul-hunger of the Beatitudes are results produced by the gospel-message. In other words, Jesus regards the Gospel itself as the true reagent which brings out the basic character of the individual.

Jesus trusted the vision of God in His forgivingness, mercy, and love to convert the soul, to give strength to the will, to change the life of men. He trusted the Gospel itself to raise men to a new level of power. We see by the same Beatitudes what Jesus preached as the content of the *Gospel* of the Kingdom: God would wipe away the tears from off all faces: He would make the life of the defeated a life worth living: He would still the spiritual hunger of men's souls: they would experience His mercy: they should see His face in purity: they should be called the sons of God. All that follows—the new nature—is reaction to this gospel.

(2) We come now to the second, and perhaps more difficult part of the Sermon, but here possibly the results already won may help us. From the gospel proclaimed in the Beatitudes the Sermon passes to Christ's *demand* of "righteousness' as defined in the section on the Law (Matt. v. 21–48). The Old Testament religion and revelation had shown that, while God's purpose for the world expresses itself in other regions also, it is in the sphere of human life and conduct that it can be most adequately and confidently regarded as fulfilling itself. The love of God to the world has this purpose ever in view. And here in the Sermon we see the true order of things. From God's redeeming love and grace we move on to God's "ought-to-be". The coming of the Kingdom of God means the *radical* apprehension of both these things, both God's love and God's moral requirement. The nearness, the coming of the Kingdom means that *both His love and His moral will are to be in possession.* That they shall be in such possession is God's affair, God's business. He means that His will shall come into force because it is His pleasure to give the Kingdom to the little flock. Man's part is his proper reaction to this Will, radically believed in: in other words, it is his acting upon it by *faith.* Rightly, therefore, Jesus in the section on the Law is addressing His followers, those who already know Him through the Gospel, and whom He now means to perfect in holiness.

Here are three points:

(i) Over against the mere text of the Law, as interpreted by itself or by the tradition, Jesus sets an interpretation of God's Will which takes in the whole province of a man's inner life, his thoughts, desires, motives, everything. It is not enough not to kill, or not to commit adultery. God's demand of righteousness extends to our inmost thoughts. The Jew, keeping to the text of the Law, holds to a *limited* conception of Divine obedience. When he has obeyed the literal command, he thinks he can keep the rest of himself to himself, or, if he goes further than the text requires, he thinks he earns merit with God. Thus the Law becomes for the legalist a roof or a screen over him which cuts him off from the searching light of God. This is the damning sin of Judaism that it has made the Law a screen against God, and this is our damnation when we become content, or shut up in our own tradition, our own cultus, our own claims or history. Jesus, who has already brought us face to face with God in the Gospel of the Kingdom, in the Beatitudes, will have us henceforth live under no sheltering roof of law or system, but in the absolute open where God searches us and knows us, discloses our hearts, our wickedness, to us, and leads us in the way everlasting. We must live in that light, and go on *through* that light, even though it kills us. It has been represented that what Jesus does in the Sermon is that over against an external conception of duty He sets an inward conception, over against the letter He sets the spirit of the command. It is in no such analytic spirit that our Lord proceeds. What He really does is, over against every partial or limited conception of God's service, to set an *absolute* or *unlimited* conception, in which nothing of man is left to himself, and Jesus trusted that such a vision of God, which throws a man entirely upon God, and demolishes for ever his contentment with himself, would set the springs of a wholly new life in motion.

(ii) Rabbinical thought distinguished in the Law between what it called the element of the "measured" and the element of the "unmeasured" or "committed to the heart of conscience" (*Masur-la-leb*). Duties appertaining to vows or sacrifices represent the kind of thing that is measured or defined. But the command of *love,* of charity, of goodness is unmeasured, left or committed to the heart. Now what Jesus does in the Sermon on the Mount is to elevate the latter to supremacy. Love's demand cannot be circumscribed. It extends even to enemies. But in Judaism *all* parts of the Law were equally Divine and obligatory, and therefore Love is restricted to a *compartment* of life by the equal recognition of other claims, as for example when the love due to parents is restricted or excluded by the sanctity of the Korban-vow. This was legitimate Judaism. For if all parts of the Law are equally holy, then each has only a restricted province. When Jesus, on the other hand, raises the unmeasured command of Love to the sovereign position, He makes it no longer possible for Christian life to settle down again on the plane of the Law. Religion is raised to a new level at which it must remain. An "Überwelt" or higher world with its law, the law of the Kingdom, has appeared, and Jesus teaches that, with the *acceptance* of the new world, the power also of that world, the *power* of God, will become a living reality, transforming and inspiring human life.

Men ask today, But is the ethic of the Sermon on the Mount practicable or possible for us? The reason why we ask the question is that we insist on standing with both feet on the present world-plane. We have accepted certain limited conceptions of ethical possibility from the standpoint of which we judge Jesus, instead of being judged by Him. But in real truth the question what is possible for us is not the *first* question which we need to ask. The first question we need to ask is, *What is the Will of God?* The whole life of religion is in the end a reaction to that, and even if this knowledge humbles us, and overwhelms us in the dust, and turns every claim and boast of ours into a mockery, it is still the only starting-point for the soul's true history. And our Lord would seem to trust not only that the vision of God, as He comes to reign, will make an end of legalism but that the full presentation of God's will in all its height and depth and breadth is *the* means of at last setting up in the soul of man the ferment and the forces which will change him.

(iii) "You shall be perfect, as your heavenly Father is perfect." Here at last we come to the inner penetralia of the Ethics of Jesus. His imperative, His ethic is based not on man's nature or constitution or reason or claims, or on his autonomy or personality-value, or social-relations or anything of that kind, but on the vision of God and on the power of that vision to kindle a likeness to itself in the redeemed soul. That is why the problems connected with the Sermon cannot be settled within the ordinary province of morals, but only within the religion of earnest and humble spirits.

And this is where all the ethic of Christ begins. He does not speak of power but rather of insight. Jesus seeks to place man where he will at last really see what it means for God's Kingdom to come. The Jewish people had followed that vision, but in their case, because they failed to grasp *radically* what it meant as regards sin, and as regards the demands of God's holiness, they had relegated it to the future, and it had eluded them as a rainbow eludes the traveller. But Jesus, proclaiming it "near", makes the individual stand face to face with God's eternal will both in its love and in its searching holiness, and look into the eyes of eternity. At this closeness of approach, in the white light of God, all else, the whole circle of earthly interests, is in shadow, thought away, done with. And man, instead of drawing back, is to go forward into that light. He must *love*, must love even his enemies, as the duty will present itself. Jesus trusted this vision to produce the true righteousness. And what He requires, as love, is not a condition of soul, or state of emotion, or personality-value, but *obedience*. "Ye shall be perfect," not as though ever attaining or ever being without sin but at least as knowing what the norm of the ethical life is.

So the Gospel with its vision of God, as Jesus presents it, produces the ethic. The latter is reaction to the Divine forgiveness, love and holiness. It is as St. Paul puts it, "the love of God is shed abroad in our hearts through the Holy Spirit which is imparted to us" (Rom. v. 5). And as it is through Jesus Christ we thus see God, the Christian life is no longer ἐν νόμῳ or ἐν τῷ 'Αδάμ but ἐν Χριστῷ.

Is this Interim-Ethic? No, not alone, for God's perfection has no relation to a mere interim. Is it, then, Kingdom-Ethic? No, not alone, for its obligation dates from the moment that Christ takes hold of us. Rather is it *Christ-Ethic*, the Messianic Ethic, which links present and future together. Christ's principle is that because God wills that His Kingdom should come and His will be done, man is able to obey. And it is actually the case that in many a humble soul the imperative of Jesus—whatever questions it may raise for an ethical philosophy—is daily realizing itself by simple acts of faith, not fully or perfectly, but nevertheless sensibly and really in all our communions.

CHAPTER 4

The Purpose of the Parables: A Re-Examination of St. Mark iv. 10–12[1]

Chapter 4 of St. Mark's Gospel records a number of parables which Jesus, speaking from a boat on the Galilean Lake, addressed to a thronged audience on the shore. The chapter is a construction. After the Parable of the Sower, which begins and ends with words inviting attention, there occurs an interruption: an inner circle of disciples puts to Jesus the question of "the parables". As this is said to have taken place when Jesus was alone (iv. 10), whereas in the rest of the chapter He is publicly engaged with His lake-shore audience, it would appear that the episode Mark iv. 10–12 represents an insertion into the record, at this point, of material from another context. In fact in this chapter of Mark it is usual to distinguish three strata of source-tradition: one consisting of parables, another supplying an "interpretation" of the story of the Sower (iv. 13–20), a third represented by the disciples' question and our Lord's answer. As it is with this question and answer we are to be engaged in the present inquiry, the primary task must be to determine whether the tradition here recorded embodies authentic language of Jesus and if so, what its meaning was.

I

The statement that it was an inner group of disciples who raised with Jesus the question of the parables suggests that in St. Mark's time obscurity had fallen over certain elements in the tradition at this point, and the teachers of the Church were concerned to dispel the perplexity. A generation had passed since Jesus had proclaimed the Kingdom of God as not merely impending but as already actualizing itself in His word and work. He had used the analogies of the seed sown in the ground and the lamp brought into the room, but what

[1] Reprinted from *The Expository Times*, Feb. 1957, Vol. LXVIII, No. 5, pp. 132–5.

did these figures of speech, each with its Old Testament *aura*, signify on His lips? Parables like the Seed Growing Secretly, the Mustard Seed and the Leaven had no appended moral, and in the Hellenistic Church this tempted to allegorization, while, as the variant Synoptic applications of the word show (Mark iv. 21, Luke xi. 33, Matt. v. 15), the metaphor of the lamp could be referred to subjects so diverse as the Person of Jesus, the content of His message, and the behaviour of His disciples. Scripture *testimonia* also could be cited which made speaking in parables equivalent to the utterance of *hîdoth*, "riddles" kept secret from the world's foundation (cf. Matt. xiii. 35).

Moreover, in the tradition there were words of Jesus which spoke of His message as divinely concealed from the wise and as revealed only to children (Matt. xi. 25, Luke x. 21) or only to the first generation of disciples (Matt. xiii. 16–17, Luke x. 23–4). In addition, there had arisen in the Hellenistic Church by St. Mark's time a strain of theology which attributed Israel's rejection of Christ to Divine causation. The principal witness here was St. Paul who averred that, though the Jews had had the Gospel of Jesus preached to them (Rom. x. 18), God had inflicted judicial blindness upon them, "a spirit of stupor, eyes not to see and ears not to hear, down to this day" (Rom. xi. 8). The same theology, quoting like St. Paul from Isa. liii. 1 and vi. 9–10, was later to appear in the Fourth Gospel as the explanation of the incurable unbelief of the Jewish people (John xii. 36–41). Indeed so strong was this current of thought in the Apostolic Church that in the judgement of many scholars no other origin need be sought for the saying attributed to Jesus in Mark iv. 11–12. The passage represents, as they consider, not Jesus but the Paulinism of St. Mark. This theory is not, however, as plausible as it looks. If the common tradition of the Church bore with it words of Jesus so indubitably authentic as those mentioned in the first sentence of this paragraph, there is no reason why the theology of Paul, John, and the Hellenistic Church should not have started from *Jesus*, and why utterances like Mark iv. 11–12 should not be genuine, though indeed their original *sense* has yet to be explored.

II

The Markan passage runs as follows: *When he was alone, those who were around him with the Twelve put to him the question of the parables. And he said to them: to you* (disciples) *the mystery* (revealed secret) *of the kingdom of God has been given, but to those outside* (i.e. non-disciples, half-hearers, opponents) *everything is in parables* (i.e. is figuratively expressed and appears and remains enigmatical), *in order* (ἵνα. Jesus, employing words that recall the prophet Isaiah's commission, Isa. vi. 10, says that the purpose of the parables is) *that seeing they may see and not perceive, and hearing they may hear and not comprehend, lest* (μήποτε) *they turn and are forgiven.*

Two things may here be affirmed regarding this Markan passage.

(1) The text is ancient. The Isaiah quotation has features which align it neither with the Hebrew nor with the LXX text of Isaiah but (as T. W. Manson has shown) with the Aramaic Targum employed in Palestinian synagogues and with the Peshitta version. Whereas in Mark, as in the Targum and Peshitta, the closing phrase refers to *forgiveness*, in the Hebrew and LXX of Isaiah and in St. Matthew and St. John the reference is to *healing*. This gives the Markan tradition a definitely Palestinian background and suggests an early rather than a late date for its formation.

(2) St. Mark's is the primary Synoptic version of the saying, for it exhibits the hardest features. Matthew has replaced Mark's "in order that" by "because", thus making the parabolic teaching of Jesus an accommodation to the ignorance of the outsiders (Matt. xiii. 13). This softening is manifestly a secondary feature, as is also the Evangelist's expansion of the Isaiah quotation (xiii. 14–15) by which incidentally he has gone far towards cancelling out his own accommodation theory. Luke for his part has dropped Mark's "lest they turn and are forgiven", and has cut down Mark's "that seeing they may see and not perceive", etc., to the bare stump "that seeing they may not see", etc., thereby dismissing what, as I shall contend, is a cardinal feature of the Markan representation. But if Mark's is thus the basic Synoptic account, is its meaning that Jesus used His parables to *conceal* the truth, putting the people off with stories and precluding their conversion?

This interpretation is so repellent that not only Matthew and Luke but exegetes in every age have sought to extenuate its force. (Thus T. W. Manson proposes that in the original Aramaic a grammatical particle, standing for the relative pronoun "who", was, when translated into Greek, mistakenly given its alternative sense of ἵνα; what Jesus said was: "Everything is in parables for those outside, *who* seeing see and do not perceive"). This, however, is conjectural, and is not Mark. Again, Vincent Taylor and Joachim Jeremias propose that the saying, though a genuine dominical word, did not originally refer to the parables but to the teaching of Jesus in general. But this, too, is to abandon Mark who expressly links the word to *the parabolic teaching,* and may be trusted to have made sense of it as such, a sense not inconsistent with the parable he next reports: "Does the lamp come in to be set under the bushel? . . . Is it not rather to be set on the lampstand?" (Mark iv. 21.)

The same connexion of the word with those parables makes, in a different way, against those who, so far from finding the saying insupportable, welcome it as a veridical statement of the judgement-function of the Son of Man on earth. Taking their stand on the apostolic theology already mentioned they find no reason why Jesus should not *intend* to reserve the truth from the unreceptive. The objection to this is twofold. (1) Neither in Isaiah, nor in Paul or John is there any reference to parables being used. (2) Why should *parables* be the chosen means of vindicating the righteousness of God against the unbelieving? When we think of the simplicity, directness, human appeal, and exquisite art of the parables of Jesus, can we think of a really negative purpose being served?

The question therefore arises whether *another* interpretation is not possible, one which, while doing justice to the Evangelist's Greek, answers better to the situation of Jesus and to the character of His evangelical purpose.

III

The word about people having eyes to see but not perceiving recalls the Old Testament account of the prophet Isaiah's commission (Isa. vi. 1–10). That commission emphasizes the obtuseness of the contemporary mind, which the prophet's teaching will only aggravate. He is to deliver his message, but its effect is to be negative: "lest they see with their eyes, and hear with their ears, and understand . . . and turn, and be healed." God intends His word by the prophet to be one of *judgement*. He says to Isaiah in effect: Go, and fail!

Jesus had the Isaiah passage in His mind, and He is conscious of fulfilling Isaiah's task. But does this fulfilment mean that He is to repeat Isaiah's experience? What does it mean for Jesus Christ to *fulfil* Isaiah or, for that part, to fulfil the law and the prophets? Merely to do what they did or—to prosper where they failed? Surely, as regards both Moses and Isaiah, allowance must be made for the sovereign freedom of the Messiah's action. God's servant (Isa xlii. 4) is not to fail or be discouraged.

Now nothing in Isaiah's commission is said about the use of parables, whereas the Jesus of St. Mark applies the Isaianic words expressly in that connexion. May not the use of parables be the new thing by which the message of Jesus is to transcend the teaching methods of the prophets? Where Isaiah failed, Jesus by the adaptation of His message to the universal intelligence proposes to succeed. In that case He speaks in parables not to repel the many but to engage them, that what happened in Isaiah's case may never happen again.

IV

Such an *a priori* approach, which allows of a word spoken to a prophet becoming plastic to the mind of Jesus and receiving a meaning closely related to His function in *Heilsgeschichte*, is not incompatible with the Greek language of Mark. We are accustomed in reading the passage to lay the stress on the people's "not perceiving" and their "not comprehending", whereas on closer scrutiny it may be found that the real emphasis is on their "indeed seeing" and "indeed hearing". In the Hebrew language the use of the infinitive absolute to reinforce a verb has the effect of accentuating the notion or action or state denoted by the verb. In the LXX text of Isa. vi. 9 and in Mark iv. 12 this Hebrew idiom is reproduced in Greek by the use of the participle in conjunction with the verb. Consequently the Markan word is patient of the meaning: "that they may indeed [or surely] see and not perceive, and indeed [or surely] hear and not comprehend," the emphasis falling on what comes to the people's eyes and ears. Further, the paratactic syntax is interesting. The paratactic structure native to Hebrew and other Semitic tongues admits of things being co-ordinated which in our more logical idiom would normally involve the use of main and subordinate clauses. For example, when our Lord says (Matt. xi. 25, Luke x. 21): "I thank thee, Father, Lord of heaven and earth, that thou hast hid these things from the wise and understanding, and hast revealed them to children," need it be supposed that the concealing of the truth from the one class and the disclosing of it to the other stand on an equal level of Divine intention as the paratactic syntax seems to suggest? Is not the actual meaning rather: "I thank thee, Father, that while [or though] thou has hid these things from the wise, thou hast revealed them to children"? Reverting to the

Markan passage, can we not take the words analogously to mean: "that they may indeed see, *though* they do not perceive, and indeed hear, *though* they do not comprehend"?

In that case, the final clause, "lest (μήποτε) they turn and are forgiven," will admit of being connected up with the part of the sentence which bears the accent, so as to yield the meaning: "indeed see . . . and indeed hear . . . *in case* they yet turn and are forgiven." μήποτε, on this construction, will embody the usage of μή in cautious assertions which Dr. Vincent Taylor does wrong, I think, to exclude. What the idiom expresses is *a still open possibility*: "Is there a chance of their turning?" Implied answer: "There is."

On this understanding our Lord is not foreclosing the issue. Though non-disciples are at present blind to the spiritual meaning of His message, He will nevertheless by His parables lodge something in their minds which they can grasp and carry away with them. A picture will be set before their eyes. A story will be impressed on their imaginations. The seed will be planted in the ground. The Sower's word will prosper, it will not return to Him void. Something will get inside the door which mayhap will hold the door open to Jesus and eventually lead the non-disciples to conversion.

V

If the claim of this interpretation to a sympathetic hearing should be admitted, what results follow for Christian truth in general, and in particular regarding the use of the concrete illustration, the presentation of the truth in parables?

First, Christian truth, the revelation of God in Christ, comes to us on two levels of life.

> *Not first that which is spiritual but that which is natural; afterwards that which is spiritual* (1 Cor. xv. 46).
>
> *If I have spoken to you of earthly things and you believe not, how will you believe if I tell you heavenly things?* (John iii. 12).

While we may not posit a natural theology, nature and the structure of human life offer analogies to the redemptive order of God.

(1) There were in the days of Jesus those to whom He was strange and alien, a Galilean visionary, a reputed wonder-worker, a preacher who at street-corners spoke about the Kingdom of Heaven and the coming of the Son of Man, but to whom they could lend no credence

because His ideas differed from theirs. He would not share their nationalistic ambitions nor indulge their apocalyptic dreams. So they stood off from Jesus and remained "outside" His counsel.

(2) There was, on the other hand, the inner circle of disciples who had entered into personal relations with Jesus and had come under the power of His word, from whose eyes He had removed the scales, and to whom He became revealed as the Messiah. These were they who were in time to say: "Lord, to whom shall we go? Thou hast the words of eternal life." For this inner circle God's salvation has actualized itself in Jesus. The reign of God, once politically or apocalyptically envisaged, has revealed its spiritual meaning to their souls. Their lives have come under its instant sign and claim. Without ceasing to be eschatological and transcendent the Kingdom has been interiorized. *Jesus has demythologized the Kingdom for this group, He has unveiled the mystery.*

So today, side by side with the committed Christians of the Church for whom the Kingdom of God has become identified with the Lordship of Christ, for whom life means being "in Christ", having Christ for the ground, the sphere, the substance, and the goal of life, there are in the world (and sometimes also in the Church) those to whom this higher realm of existence, experienced as the New Creation, remains inscrutable. For them Jesus Christ is, at the most, an ethical teacher or social idealist or religious mystic. They are prepared to listen to His teaching, though as they listen they keep a critical eye on the preacher, and give only a qualified attention to what he says. For such hearers Jesus is not, or not yet, Incarnate Redeemer, Word of the Father, Mediator with God, the Second Adam, our true Life, the Overcomer of the world. What has Jesus Christ to offer on those two levels of existence?

To the first group, as we have seen, He offers the open "mystery" of the Kingdom as centred in Himself, the demythologized Kingdom, the New Creation of human life in God. To the second group He offers His *parables*.

A final word, then, about the *matter* of the parables.

VI

The parables are not all and only for the non-disciples. Some are addressed to the Apostles, and not always understood by them; cf. Mark vii. 17–18 and again Mark viii. 17–18. Clearly Jesus used this instrument of teaching not *only* to call uncommitted hearers to attention but to interpret to engaged followers the nature of the life on which they have entered. Yet, by and large, the parables are propaedeutic, and fall into two types.

(1) There is the recognizable group represented by the Sower, the Seed Growing Secretly, the Mustard Seed, the Leaven. Mostly the tradition introduces these in such forms as "the kingdom of God is as if . . ." or "how shall we liken the kingdom of God?" Here the deliberate choice of analogy from the *natural world* is characteristic. In His wilderness temptation Jesus, revealed to Himself at His baptism as the beloved Son of God, had become exposed to Satanic solicitations that aimed to divert the course of His calling from nature to *super-nature*. Turn stones into bread! Give the people signs from heaven! Seize the promised Kingdom by the use of force! The naming of the Messiah at the Jordan had brought the Power of Evil to its feet, and Jesus is allured to interpret His empire in terms not of the Divine but of the demonic order. May we not see in this group of parables His rejection of the demonic principle and His steady affirmation of the providential natural order as affording the true analogy to the energy of the Divine grace in redemption? It is significant that none of these parables speaks of stones being turned into bread, or of signs being given from the skies. Instead we have the analogy of the seed being sown in the ground, and of bread, harvest, and the Divine *synteleia* springing from the earth through the semination in it of a transcendent spiritual life. By contrast, the "force" and "forcers" alluded to in Matt. xi. 12 as aggressors of the Kingdom of Heaven are the powers of demonic disorder. In this way the Gospel of Jesus and His use of parables stand in positive relation to the principle of the Incarnation. Jesus is on earth *Messias Absconditus,* not *Revelatus,* and His word to the many clothes itself accordingly in images drawn from lowly things on earth.

(2) There is the mass of general parables deriving their symbolism from the variegated experience of *human life* in the home, the street, the market, the law-court, the vineyard, the shop, the wedding-feast and so forth. Here the method is by suggestion of the moral issues involved in the common intercourse of life between man and man, master and servant, debtor and creditor, rich and poor, wise and foolish, to focus at one particular point the bearing of the existential claim of God on men. Take, for example, the Parable of the Good Samaritan. Here is a story through which the principle of mercy in-

tegral to God's will to bring in His Kingdom, and embodied in the incarnate life of Jesus, confronts the ordinary wayfarer on the roadside of life with power to shatter the complacency and self-defence which he has erected against the love of God. Here then, as also in such parables as the Rich Fool or Dives and Lazarus or the Guest without the Wedding Garment, Jesus stands and knocks at the common street-door of life, but leaves some truth with the inmates of the house which may lead eventually to the house being thrown open to Him: "O fool, this night thy life is required back from thee. Whose then shall those things be which thou hast got in readiness? So is it with him who lays up treasure for himself and is not rich towards God," or again, "Friend, how didst thou come in here not having a wedding garment?"

If Jesus thus speaks in parables to the man in the crowd, evangelism has to begin on the same level and by the same methods but also with the same hope that the man who has been disturbed in his complacency will open his heart to God. For the only future of arrested man is God.

CHAPTER 5

The Son of Man and History[1]

In an age like the present, when the good will to establish a reasonable order of international life on earth is beset at every turning by impediment and frustration, there exists a temptation, if not to think of history as irredeemable, at least to moderate considerably our confidence in the relevance of Christianity to mundane affairs. We should not be surprised to find an increased tendency to mysticism, or if the hold of external reality over the mind is too strong to permit such withdrawal of the soul into itself, a lapse may set in towards an apocalyptic judgement on history with a hardened sense of the opposition of God to the world. In evangelism the effect may be to give preference to the Home Mission task of the Church over its Foreign Mission and ecumenical commitments. Certainly a change has come over the face of things and over our own temperaments since the Edinburgh Missionary Conference of 1910. There has been a screwing down of the lights. There has been a retraction of many hopes. In 1910 the Christian Churches stood on the tiptoe of missionary enthusiasm. The doors were swinging open in all lands to the entrance of the Christian Gospel. The day of the Son of Man was believed to have come near. Optimism with relation to history was of the order of the day. Today the world-scene has grown clouded and ambiguous.

But does the change *justify* a reduction of the Christian hope for history? Should the greater realism of our present world-outlook encourage a trend of mind which is negative to that hope? *Is there a New Testament philosophy of history, and, if so, what is it like?*

In proposing to treat of this question the writer regards it as not insignificant that numbers of men who, a few years ago, were disposed —partly under the influence of the prevailing direction of theological opinion—to be pessimistic and apocalyptically minded with regard to the world-outlook, have come to speak a different language, not because the facts of history have altered for the better, but because these

[1] Reprinted from *Scottish Journal of Theology*, Vol. 5, No. 2, 1952, pp. 113–22.

persons have come to a maturer understanding of the character of the Gospel.

I

We find in the Gospels a series of words of Jesus which relate to the mission and destiny of the "Son of Man", and which in style and character stand out in high relief from the mass of His recorded utterances. These sayings are *oracular* in tone in that their subject, the Son of Man, is introduced without explanation or mediation in the context. They are thematic in form and didactic in substance as laying down what the Son of Man is to do, to experience, or to be. They are kerygmatic in intention, revealing a design to bring together and to think together the calling of the Son of Man and His historical manifestation. In view of these features and the circumstance that in the Gospels the term "Son of Man" occurs always and only on the lips of Jesus, the conclusion to be drawn is that these sayings, so far as their original form and text can be critically established, represent authentic revelation of our Lord Himself. Consequently it is not surprising that a modern German theologian should propose to take these utterances as *the* historical kernel of the gospel. "Of the wrath of God," writes Ethelbert Stauffer, "of the kingdom of God, of the people of God, and of the eschatological Redeemer, the Baptist has already spoken. Jesus first speaks of the Son of Man and of His Way."[1]

Whether or not Stauffer is right as regards his main contention, it is impossible not to agree that the Son of Man sayings have a place within the *penetralia* of the gospel revelation. Clement of Alexandria quotes a word of Jesus from a certain (probably a Hellenized) Gospel in which Jesus speaks of His "mystery": μυστήριον ἐμὸν ἐμοὶ καὶ τοῖς υἱοῖς τοῦ οἴκου μου.[2] Whatever this *mystery* may have been, it cannot but have included in it the truths set forth in these sayings about the Son of Man. So that we may regard these words as clustered lights situated to left and to right, so to speak, of the chancel steps leading to the innermost shrine.

To left and to right! For these Son of Man sayings fall into two groups: first, a group which bear on His *humiliation*, which associate the fortunes of the Son of Man with the condition and experience of humanity, or bring Him into action or involvement in its tragedy:

[1] *Die Theologie des Neuen Testaments*, pp. 10 ff.
[2] Cited in Huck's *Synopse*, p. 72.

The Son of Man came eating and drinking.
The Son of Man hath not where to lay His head.
The Son of Man came to seek and to save that which is lost.
The Son of Man hath authority on earth to forgive sins.
The Son of Man must suffer much . . . and be rejected . . . and slain.
The Son of Man is delivered into the hands of men.
The Son of Man came not to be ministered unto, but to minister and to give His life as a ransom for many.
The Son of Man goeth as it is written of Him, etc.

In all the sayings of this class we have an *integration* of the Son of Man with the condition, necessity, contingency, pathos, shame, sorrow, and sin of human life in history. Over against these there is, secondly, the group of sayings which present the Son of Man in the *transcendence* and glory of His risen and victorious life. *Is this the same Son of Man?* By all the evidence of the Gospels and of the New Testament He *is* the same, though some critical expositors, unable to support the paradox of the position, have proposed on theoretical grounds to declare one or other of the two classes of sayings unauthentic. Examples of the second group are:

The Son of Man must . . . rise again.
The Son of Man shall rise again from the dead.
They shall see the Son of Man coming in clouds with great power and glory.
You shall see the Son of Man sitting at the right hand of power, and coming with the clouds of heaven.
In an hour that you think not the Son of Man cometh.
As the lightning . . . so shall the Son of Man be in His day.
When the Son of Man shall come in His glory and all the angels with Him, etc.

Here we have the ultimate *sublimation* of the Son of Man in contrast with His earthly humiliation. But it is significant that *this transcendent regnant life of the Son of Man does not pass out of relation to, or cease to have meaning for, the terrestrial sphere of His historical manifestation.* Apart from the fact that the Son of Man has His adherents and followers here, whose "way" on earth is to be conformed to His way, and whose norm of life is to be the example of Him who "came not to be ministered unto, but to minister", the glory of the Son of Man is to be made visible to "this generation", and He is destined to "come" again in history. In other words, the focal point from which the graph of this transcendent destiny of the Son of Man is described lies on the plane of this world's history.

Whereas in the Book of Daniel the figure depicted by the seer as having the likeness of a "son of man" goes to the Ancient of Days to receive an everlasting dominion, *but does not return,*[1] in the New Testament revelation the Son of Man, the Lord from heaven, comes back to the world, bringing His kingdom with Him.

> Though now ascended up on high,
> He bends on earth a brother's eye;
> Partaker of the human name,
> He knows the frailty of our frame.

The line which runs from His suffering to His glory does not in the New Testament presentation lift from the plane of the world's history and soar eternally into the blue, but curves back again to that history, and meantime enfolds that history, remains in touch with that history, and finds its completion in that history. *The recession towards eternity of the movement which begins in the Incarnation does not cut out the earth, or by-pass its process, but takes the world and history up into itself.* As St. Paul's teaching puts it, Christ "must reign till He has put all His enemies under His feet". Surely at this point the New Testament teaching has something to say to us with regard to our present world besetment and predicament!

II

From these two classes of Son of Man sayings there start the two great engagements of Christian thought within the mind of the New Testament Church. These are *the Parousia-hope* and *the Church's sense of mission to the world.* It was the apocalyptic determination of mind that first asserted itself not only at Jerusalem but at other centres of Christian evangelism, such as Thessalonica. The question "Lord, is it Thy will at this time to restore the kingdom to Israel? was asked before the intimation came from the risen Lord of the Church's mission to the world, and from the record of the Book of Acts it would appear that the latter engagement first came to clearness in the consciousness of the followers of Stephen.

The present writer has elsewhere dealt with the part played by St. Stephen in this remarkable evolution, and the story need not be repeated here.[2] At the heart of the evolution was the immediate presence to Stephen's mind of the Son of Man as already at the right hand of God. To this enthroned Jesus Stephen commits his spirit.

[1] Dan. vii. 13 ff.
[2] See the writer's *The Epistle to the Hebrews* (1951), pp. 25–46.

For this man, on whose lips alone after Jesus the name "Son of Man" appears, Judaism with its law and its cultus was a thing of the past. What dominates his world, regnant over history like the Morning Star in the sky, is the *Christus Victor*, the Lord Jesus, to whom the whole world and the whole future now belong. What would be Stephen's *gospel* as, with Israel and its institutions dropping behind him into the past, he faces towards the glory of the Son of Man and the dawn of a new day? What but this: "Because He lives, we shall live also"? To this Son of Man Stephen commits his spirit. Life, salvation, shapes itself now as Christ-grounded and Christ-enfolded. Undoubtedly by its circumstances Christianity would now, if not before this point, be thrown on mysticism, on a dependence upon the invisible world such as Judaism under the law had never known, on life "hid with Christ in God". Yet not on mysticism pure and simple, rather on *historical mysticism.* The law and the prophets were ended, but the Son of Man had been "made under the law". He had "risen out of Judah". The salvation which He offered was "of the Jews". The Christian Saviour was not a bolt from the blue like Marcion's Saviour, nor was His God like Marcion's God. There comes, therefore, a solidifying of Christian thought and theology around the historical significance of the Redeemer.

For one thing, He is now preached as "*the light of the nations*". This expression had been used of the Servant of the Lord in Second Isaiah, and it was later taken over for the apocalyptic Son of Man in the First Book of Enoch. Now it serves to assert the world-significance of the Jesus whose dominion as the Son of Man embraces all nations, peoples, and tongues. He is preached as "*the Wisdom of God*", as "*the Logos*", the historical expression and instrument of the activity and the mind of God in creation and history as well as redemption. He is the answer of God to a world which in its Jewish sector has asked for signs and in its Greek sector has sought for wisdom. He is proclaimed as God's response to both sectors and in relation to both demands. He is the sign of the omnipotence of God and He is God's paradoxical yet real provision for man's demand of rationality. Judaism had looked for a Messiah and at Alexandria it had pondered the significance of divine wisdom in the cosmos and in *Heilsgeschichte.* But Judaism had not, so far as I can see, fused the conceptions of the Messiah and the Wisdom of God. On the other hand, in the literature of the Christian world-mission the identification is complete.[1] It is

[1] See the writer's *The Epistle to the Hebrews,* pp. 93–7.

present in St. Paul's Letters, it is present in Hebrews, it is present in the Johannine Gospel and First Epistle. The Son of Man as Wisdom of God and Word of God stands organically related in all these writings to the world and to human history. The only explanation that can be offered is that the crystallization of ideas in question arose spontaneously with Christianity at the very beginning of the world-mission. While neither St. Paul nor the writer to the Hebrews expressly designates Jesus Christ as the "Son of Man", His image and idea are present in the Pauline Second Adam, the Man from heaven, the One who laid aside His glory to assume our nature. Equally they are present in the Man of the Eighth Psalm to whom, as the writer to the Hebrews sees, universal dominion is given. In the Johannine theology the Son of Man is expressly named. He is the One who has descended from heaven, the Logos who has become flesh. And the supreme point in every representation is that He who came to claim dominion in our nature is regnant now in history and shall come again in glory.

III

He who came to claim dominion in our nature is regnant now in history and shall come again in glory!

It is in the light of this supreme New Testament confidence that we have now, as we revert to our primary question, to orient ourselves to the world-situation today, and to consider our attitude to the world-mission task of the Church. How very different is *this Christian mystery of the Son of Man* from an apocalypticism which sways away from history, which conceives the Church as merely an Ark on the water-floods, which regards Christians as brands plucked from a world-burning! In the Jewish "Similitudes of Enoch" we find a Son of Man, the representative of the people of God, who is a lay-figure. He is exalted perhaps and glorious, but he is not a redeemer. He does not stoop to earth, nor integrate himself with history. He bears no sins or sorrows. He lays no transforming law of love on a reclaimed humanity. He merely waits in heaven to receive an elect who come to him at the end of days when he shall reign among them. It is another mystery altogether which is unfolded to us in the gospel. It is *the mystery of a transfigured apocalyptic which takes history up into its process, which indeed apocalyptizes history*. It presents the fulfilment of the Son of Man in history, the taking of man into Christ, the sublimation of the human process by the "recapitulation" of it in the Redeemer. The resulting substance is *the Body of Christ on earth*, a body formed in humanity by the indwelling Redeemer. While the vision of the *final* glory of the Son of Man continues to soar overhead, it is never in essential Christian thought dissociated from the Church, which is the pillar and ground of the truth.

The New Testament says that this Son of Man "shall come in like manner as you have seen Him go". How, then, did He go? By what process did He fulfil the mission which was written of Him? The New Testament answers by saying: "This is He who came by water and blood; not by water only, but by water and blood", in other words by baptism and by crucifixion. If, then, His going and His coming are to be "in like manner", it is plain that *the Parousia, whatever it may signify in its eternal dimension, is not to be understood in separation from the Incarnation and from Calvary.* It is not discontinuous with the latter but is their consummation. And there is a peculiar proof of this in the New Testament. While the star of the Parousia-hope burns above history, it stands always directly over the Church, and it keeps moving forward as the world-mission of the Church advances. The Second Advent *is never allowed to become identified with any contingency in contemporary events, however earth-shaking and portentous these may be.* Apostles and evangelists say: "Not yet the end!" "First must the gospel be published among all nations!"

The successors of Stephen and the other leaders of Christianity, who went out with their passionate proclamation of the Second Advent, could not find in any contemporaneous happenings the sign of its fulfilment. In this they differed from the mass of Christians who, once and again, when persecution came upon them, or later when Judea went down before the Roman legions, were sure that the End had arrived. How do we explain this singular fact that, despite everything that happened in these first generations, despite even the destruction of Jerusalem in A.D. 70, the expectation of the Parousia is put off and off by the responsible leaders of the Christian Church? It was not that the alleged outward signs of the End were not sufficiently *critical.* What could be more critical, in an external point of view, than the Neronian persecution at Rome and the desolation of the Holy City? Yet a strange constraint lay on the Apostles not to accept these events as final. Something existed at the heart of Christianity which resisted any too near an expectation of the End. Nor in the light of the considerations which have been before us in this study is the nature of the restraint difficult to recognize. *The Saviour had laid*

hold on history to claim it for Himself. And the Church had its world-mission which it must pursue to the last issues.

For example, when the Thessalonian Christians, fed by St. Paul on hopes of the near Parousia, leapt to the conclusion, the moment that persecution swooped upon them, that the predicted end of the world had arrived, St. Paul entreats them, for the sake of the real Parousia-hope, not to give way to the excited idea, whencesoever derived, whether from "spirit, or word, or alleged letter from himself", that "the day of the Lord had set in". He tells them that much must happen before that time, and meantime he asks them to *go on with their work.* He saw that apocalypticism threatened to paralyse the life of the Church and its mission to the world, and he had his answer ready.[1]

So also in the Gospel of Mark, chapter 13, the evangelist, writing after the Neronian persecution of the Church and before the Fall of Jerusalem, dwells with unusual fullness on the tradition existing in the Church with regard to our Lord's predictions of His Parousia, and underscores certain features. The readers are warned against premature reports that the Lord has come. There will be wars and rumours of war, but "the End is not yet!" There will be secular upheavals and commotions, but "these things are (but) the beginnings of the throes" through which the Messianic age is born. There will be persecutions, for "the gospel must be published to all the nations", but "it is he who stands firm to the end who will be saved". Even the Hand which shows itself in the profanation of the Holy Place at Jerusalem and in the intolerable sufferings which will follow, even that Hand of judgement is not to be interpreted as writing *Finis* to history, for only afterwards, and beyond these events, will the Son of Man appear.[2]

According to the New Testament consciousness, therefore, the sign of the Parousia lies beyond any world-events which can be imagined! Nevertheless it stands right over the path of the Christian mission to the world. The Son of Man has chosen the integration of Himself with sinful men as the way to His glory. This "Not yet the End!" of the world-evangelism of the Christian Church is the thing in the New Testament religion which *leaves the door of hope open to history* as the province of the Divine working and of the Divine design of salvation. The line which links Bethlehem with the Second Advent runs through history, not overhead of it. History comes into eschatological estimation and determination.

[1] 2 Thess. ii. 1–12, 15–17. [2] Mark xiii. 1–27.

The mysticism which flees history and the pseudo-apocalypticism which looks askance at it are equally excluded from the New Testament point of view. The apocalyptic attitude which leans away from history represents not a Christian, but a sub-Christian determination of mind. But let us remember that the Christian disposition to wait quietly and hopefully for the salvation of the Lord must take account not only of the word of Christ to mankind but of the character of its *preachers*. These are to see by the Son of Man Himself what manner of men they are to be:

> as unknown, and yet well known;
> as dying, and, behold, we live;
> as chastened, and not killed;
> as sorrowful, yet always rejoicing;
> as poor, yet making many rich;
> as having nothing, and yet possessing all things.[1]

The apostles and ministers of Christ are to integrate themselves with humanity. Their way is the way of the Son of Man who goeth and also cometh as it is written of Him.

A few years ago a young missionary returning to India after his first furlough set down for the rest of us the thoughts which were in his mind. It is the stage when one is no longer sailing for the first time over blue seas to a new enchanting land, or drifting up romantic rivers through a rapturous mist of jungle and rice-fields, but when all that is over, and the man is face to face with the facts, the poverty and apathy and hopelessness of depressed millions, and the pride and prejudice of the higher orders, and when one has the task of making the love of God in Christ real under such conditions. What shall one do then? And little by little he shows us how the missionary has to learn patience and lowliness and sacrifice, all of the order of self-extinction, until in the end he has nothing behind him but the Crucified. India has had enough of systems and doctrines and ideologies. If the love of Christ is to be made real and to have an impact on society, it must be by becoming incarnate in His representatives. They are "crucified with Christ", and it is no longer they who live, but Christ liveth in them.

But then this missionary, who has told us of the difficulties of the work, turns over a leaf, and tells us that Christ is coming in India. He sees visibly the signs of His coming. Just as of old the message came, "Go, tell His disciples and Peter that He goes before you into

[1] 2 Cor. vi. 9–10.

Galilee. There shall you see Him," so now it speaks of India. There, in the old days, were the Apostles, and when Jesus died upon the cross, all their *pre-conceived* ideas perished with Him, nailed to the cross. And then, when they had nothing of their self-assertion left, when the stage had been swept clear of all this, He lifted His hands upon them, and said: "All power is given unto Me in heaven and on earth. Go ye, therefore, and teach all nations . . . and, lo, I am with you all the time, even to the end of the world."

CHAPTER 6

Principalities and Powers: The Spiritual Background of the Work of Jesus in the Synoptic Gospels[1]

I

That the revelation of God to Israel stood in the most intimate relation to a supernatural conception of the universe is apparent on every page of Holy Scripture. Angels, spirits from Jahweh, Satan, and demons bearing various names figure in the record. They appear in the oldest strata, and are to be accounted indigenous, aboriginal elements in the religion of the Hebrew people. More important is it to notice the development which, under the influence of later Babylonian and Iranian ideals, the conception of the spirit-world underwent within the Bible itself and to a still higher degree in post-Biblical Judaism. In the Rabbinical theology we find ourselves in a tropically luxuriant world of supernatural powers and forces, divine and satanic, angelic and demonic, a world of intermediary spirits, whose influence, beneficent or malignant, extends and is experienced over the whole domain of nature and life. This development of ideas appears to have synchronized with the rise of apocalyptic eschatology in the period between the Old and the New Testaments. This had sublimated the Reign of God, and had elevated the Messiah or the "Son of man" to a position above the gods, "lords", angels, "elements", and demons of the spiritual world.

It is instructive to note some examples of this sublimation. In older Israel Jahweh is king, and Jahweh's reign means primarily the subjugation of Jahweh's enemies to Jahweh and to His "Son", the king of Israel (Psalm ii, Psalm cx). At this stage the "enemies" are the nations of the earth which oppose themselves to God and to the king whom He has set on His holy hill of Zion. A conception of resistant powers, mythological in its origin as may be inferred from the early Babylonian forms of the Creation story, has been historified by be-

[1] Reprinted from the *Bulletin of Studiorum Novi Testamenti Societas*, 1952.

coming linked with Jahweh's act in the redemption of His people from Rahab-Egypt and the maintenance of His righteous rule over that people. In the later Israel these enemies of the Lord have become the supernatural potentates of the invisible world. Thus, while we read in Psalm cx that Jahweh has said to the reigning prince in Israel: "Sit on My right hand, until I make thine enemies thy footstool," St. Paul, who has the later Jewish world-background behind him, explains that the Christ of God must indeed reign until all His enemies are under His feet, but he adds significantly that the last enemy to be destroyed is "death" (1 Cor. xv. 24–7). So in Isa. xlv. 22–3 the God of Israel, in words addressed to "all the ends of the earth", is represented as saying: "By myself have I sworn that unto Me every knee shall bow." St. Paul applies this passage to the exalted Christ and says indeed that in the name of Jesus every knee shall bow, but he supplements the statement by appending the words, "of things in heaven and things on earth and things in the world below" (Phil. ii. 9–11). In this manner the spirit-world has been filled out. It has taken on new dimensions and acquired a cosmic range and character. Once more, while at the early Old Testament stage the angels are undifferentiated in their office or function, in later Israel they are distributed as archons over the various ethnic peoples (Deut. xxxii. 9, LXX). Angel-princes of Persia and Greece are met with, over against whom Michael appears as the heaven-appointed guardian of Israel (Dan. x). And these angelic archons, whether associated with the world-empires or with the stellar "heavens" or with cosmic "elements" or with the pagan religions in which they are worshipped as "lords", have, together with the principalities assigned to them, fallen to the wrong side in the cosmic dualism which now dominates the picture. They are the "powers" which, though with Satan they have suffered a reverse at the hands of the New Testament Redeemer, are still active, and we wrestle against them: "not against flesh and blood, but against the principalities, against the powers, against the rulers of this dark world-age, against the spirits of wickedness in the heavenly places" (Eph. vi. 12).

This development in the conception of the spiritual world did not indeed exert its influence uniformly over the whole area of Jewish and early Christian religion. In the synoptic Gospels we find a simpler representation. We do not encounter the forces of darkness in the "heavenly" places, nor are they organized after the pattern of St. Paul's grandiose hierarchy of cosmic spirits, but we meet them on the earth-level of popular demonic belief, in the form of malignant and ghoulish beings which, under Satan as their head, invade and occupy the souls of men to their ruin and to the frustration of God's will to establish His reign. It was in the context of this popular conception of the spiritual order that the Christian gospel was first formulated and invested with the character of a message of redemption.

In modern times the application of rationalistic or, as we would now prefer to say, scientific criteria to the observation of reality has led to an abstraction from all such supernaturalism. The scientific mind through its immediate preoccupation with the observed sequences in the physical world of what we call cause and effect has rejected spiritualistic causality in every shape and form. Christian theology has retreated from large areas of the older supernaturalism, and the question cannot be held back whether even in the substance of what it has conserved, in the doctrines of the Incarnation of the Son of God, the Atonement, and the Christian redemption generally, it has not abandoned insights which were organic and fundamental to these doctrines as originally preached by apostles and others to the world. Since the Renaissance a transference of interest from the outward to the inward world has taken place, the process being assisted by the very inwardness of Reformed religion. We have turned to the study of the soul of man, and propose to compensate by psychology for the abandoned insights of the older theology. It has, however, to be recognized that in this realm of psychology phenomena confront us of which the causes are just as inscrutable, just as much withdrawn from observation and understanding, as any postulated by the spiritistic world-view of the Bible. It is coming to be realized that the mysteries which are left on our hands—mysteries like the origin and malignity of error, the incidence of mental, nervous, and psychophysical disorders, the strength and virus of the forces making for moral contamination and ruin, and the inordinate influence exercised by the *Zeitgeist* over men in society—are all the greater because the spiritual agencies once invoked for their explanation are no longer available for that purpose.

It is, therefore, not surprising that in modern times there has been a return to a deeper recognition of the mystery of man's spiritual environment. The way was prepared for this by the rise of the Romantic Movement in literature, which threw open the windows of the soul again to the world of imagination, feeling, and will. The movement has been powerfully reinforced by the new science of Psychology, which has disclosed the existence of multiple levels of consciousness within the human personality, and has thereby rendered plausible the hypothesis of diverse strata within the structure of reality. With this has gone the development of social Philosophy in the modern world, which has forced to the front the part played by hysteria and other irrational elements in mass psychology and ethics. And there has been a revolution in Physics, as the result of which the bonds of the materialistic hypothesis in its older forms have been broken, and we are faced by energies and agencies in the universe which are more akin to the nature of spirit. Atomic science has picked the locks of the physical sub-structure of the world and has been opening underground cellars in which it is not strange if spectres are seen looking through.

There is sufficient reason, therefore, for focusing attention today on certain questions regarding modern theology and modern preaching, at least to the extent of inquiring into the relevance of the latter to the physical nature and needs of men. While it is not my business now, even if it were within my competence, to discuss ontological questions regarding the nature of the invisible world or even regarding the relation in which the Biblical language may be conceived to stand to that reality, it is not only pertinent but, as I feel, urgent to ask whether justice is done in our theology and in our preaching to aspects of man's spiritual make-up and predisposition which were vividly present to the mind of Jesus and His apostles and were by them attributed to preter-natural causation. One has only to run the eye over the synoptic Gospels to be aware of the features of the human predicament on which the evangelists, and the tradition on which they drew, chose to dwell as reflecting most characteristically and most profoundly the work of Jesus as Redeemer of men.

II

No one will desire to question the great and permanent debt under which we stand to the great classical works on the interpretation of the Gospels by which in our modern age the limits of a reasonable historical understanding of these documents have been laid down. In recent months this debt has been notably increased by the publication of Dr. Vincent Taylor's long-awaited Commentary on St. Mark which, following in the wake of Swete but incorporating the results of an immense and discriminating review of all work done on the Gospels in the last half-century, will now take its place as the essential authority on the subject for a half-century to come. But just because this work has been done, and done so thoroughly, and at so sacrificial a cost on Dr. Taylor's part, it may be asked whether under the protection of the great guns of the fortress which he has erected, and within the safety-zone which he has created, it is not permissible now to let off some of our popguns, here and there, at this or that exegetical or theological target. If this is conceded, a place may be found for some of the questions which it is now proposed to raise.

In Mark 1 John Baptist is introduced as fulfilling a mission to prepare "the way of the Lord". Over what kind of terrain or world—human or demonological?—was this "way" of the Lord to be driven? And the "forgiveness of sins" which the Forerunner put in the foreground, from what doom was this amnesty to deliver the hearers? Was it from the judgement of God on the characters of men *simpliciter*? Or was it from the judgement of God on the cosmos, Satan and his minions included? Again, the word about the "Mightier" who was to follow John. What was He mightier for? Does the name "the Mighty" reflect the *El Gibbor* of the Messianic passage, Isa. ix. 5, where some of the LXX texts have the reading *ischuros exousiastes*? In any case, who is it against whom this Hero, this Prince with God, is out to measure His strength? Against men? Surely not this primarily or alone. Against the nations of the world? John does not speak of these nations. Against the powers of darkness in the invisible world? The passage does not say, but significantly enough it is related presently that Jesus, being baptized of water and the Spirit, is impelled by the Spirit into the wilderness where He is assailed by the "devil". He dwells with the wild beasts, who are symbolic not of the homes and haunts of men but of the demonological waste.

In the same chapter, at verse 15, Jesus comes into Galilee, preaching the gospel of God in the form: "The time has fully come, and the Reign of God has drawn near." We remember that in the Psalms and the Prophets the reign of God is regularly set in relation to the overthrow of the "enemies" of God, and we ask, who are the enemies who are now to be overthrown? A verse or two further on, we are told that Jesus, teaching in the synagogue at Capernaum, astonished His hearers by His "authority", and it at once appears that this authority or power has to do with psychical factors conditioning human existence, for the first and most eloquent demonstration of it is an exorcism!

In the exorcism in the synagogue in Mark i. 23 ff. Jesus comes into direct contact with demon-belief and its attendant phenomena, and the cry of the possessed man, "Avaunt!" or "Interfere not here!", followed by "Hast Thou come to destroy us?", declares that there can be no truce between the Messiah and the demons. Jesus expels the "unclean spirit", and that evening they bring to Him all the possessed —Matthew adds "and the epileptic"—and Jesus drives out many demons, not permitting them to speak.

In Mark ii. 1 ff. there comes the story of the paralytic. The word of Jesus, "Thy sins are forgiven thee", stands in pointed relation to the man's physical prostration, and the right of the Son of Man to forgive sins on earth is made to turn on His power in the psycho-physical realm. Forgiveness of sins clearly goes with release from bodily inhibition, and though supernatural expressions are not employed in the narrative, there can be little doubt that demonological causation is assumed. In any case, forgiveness of sins by its double bearing implies the relevance of the work of Christ to the whole domain of the psycho-physical.

In the interpretation of the master-parable of the Sower in Mark iv it is stated that Satan catches away the "word" from the souls of some of Jesus' hearers, and the same demonic character may be ascribed to the other causes which are named there for the failure of men to respond to the gospel, such as "distress", or "persecution" because of the word, or the "cares" of the present "aeon", or the illusion produced by "riches" and other secular concerns. A demonological character clearly attaches to the kindred term "Mammon", and we remember that the New Testament speaks elsewhere of covetousness as "idolatry" (Col. iii. 5; cf. Eph. v. 5).

Mark v contains the full-length story of the Gerasene demoniac, where the deranged man, being asked his name by Jesus, answers "We are a legion". This is a revealing word which, while it illustrates the popular belief that a host of demons may enter into a man, reflects also the psychopathic conditions, the pathology of an occupied country, where historical causes have played a part in producing mental derangement, distorted passions, and so forth. We notice also in chapter vi that the commission of Jesus in sending out the Twelve on their campaign in Galilee expressly includes authority over the "unclean spirits", and exorcisms by the Twelve of many demons are reported.

In vii. 21 it is to be remarked that Jesus teaches that the "evil thoughts" and sins which make men "unclean"—there is at this point a clear reference away from ritual standards to the underlying facts of psycho-physical reality—are "from within, from the heart". Similarly in Matt. v. 29 f. Jesus speaks of the offences that destroy the body as exercising their baleful influence through the body, through offending eye or hand. Thus Jesus over wide areas of His teaching, as for example where He is criticizing scribes, Pharisees and others or, as here, is instructing His disciples, does not carry the motivation of sin further back than to men's "hearts". But this, while affirming the complicity of men in the evil which corrupts their natures, does not settle the question how these evil desires have come to arise in men's hearts, nor whether the responsibility and guilt of men can be dissociated from their position in a fallen and Satan-dominated world.

We may leave aside a number of other passages dealing with exorcisms and the demons, such as the healing of the epileptic boy (Mark ix. 14 ff.), the exorcist outside the ranks of the Twelve (Mark ix. 38–40), and the uncanny warning about the return of the demons to unguarded hearts (Matt. xii. 43–5, Luke xi. 24–6), and we shall take up for consideration certain oracular utterances which have come down in the tradition of the teaching of Jesus.

In Matthew and Luke there is the petition in the Lord's Prayer: "and lead us not into temptation, but deliver us from the evil". A recollection of the temptation of Jesus in the wilderness makes plausible the assumption that the reference of the words is to the devil. With this agrees the colour of the word meaning "deliver", for the use of which compare 1 Thess. i. 10. In another passage also, if allowance is made for the general apocalyptic background of the thought of Jesus, a strong case may be maintained for taking "him that is able to destroy both soul and body in Gehenna" (Matt. x. 28) as an allusion to Satan, though the point is not certain.

In Matt. xvi. 18 ff. the statement that "the gates of Hades will not prevail" against the Church brings out the supernatural overtones of our Lord's conception of the believing company. The Church is exposed all the time to the assaults of Satan-Hades, but will stand because it is founded on a rock. Here we remember that Jesus at the outset of His ministry had successfully resisted the solicitations of Satan though the latter claimed that the "power" and the "glory" of the kingdoms of the world belonged to him. So in His answer to the Beelzebub-charge made by the scribes Jesus represents Himself as the "Stronger One" (cf. John Baptist's prediction) who has broken into the "house" of the Destroyer, and by expelling the evil spirits in the power of the Spirit of God has confronted His accusers with the supreme evidence of the Reign of God. This is a present actuality in history (Matt. xii. 28).

In the light of these facts we are encouraged to give to one very difficult saying of Jesus what is not improbably its right interpretation. It is the unglossed mysterious word occurring in Matt. xi. 12: "From the days of John the Baptist until now the Kingdom of Heaven suffers violence (*biazetai*), and the "violent" (*biastai*) take it by force." Are these violators the demons, the underlings of Satan, who since the temptation directed at Jesus after His baptism by John have entered on an intensified campaign of hostility to the Reign of God? We remember that in Luke iv. 13 the Tempter is said to have departed from Jesus but only "until a fitting time". Has the time there hinted at now set in? When the Seventy at their return from their mission report that even the demons are subject to them in the name of Jesus, Jesus makes the reply "I looked to see Satan drop like a lightning-brand from heaven". The development of the conflict to a high point of crisis seems to emerge from these words, and with this agree the asseverations of Jesus which follow. While He has given the Seventy authority over the forces of the enemy, He bids them rejoice not because the powers of darkness are under their control, but because they have themselves been delivered from the guilt and condemnation brought by these powers on the world. The books of the citizenship of the Kingdom of God have been opened, and the names of the disciples have been registered there (Luke x. 20). The best parallel that can be suggested to this difficult word is the Pauline passage, where Christians are asked to give "thanks to the Father who has qualified us for a share in the inheritance of the saints in light, who has delivered us from the power of darkness and translated us into the kingdom of his beloved son" (Col. i. 12–13).

Helpful light falls also on another very mysterious word of Jesus. It is the word (Luke xii. 49–50): "I came to cast fire on the earth, and how I would it were already kindled! But I have a baptism to be baptized with, and how embarrassed I am until it is accomplished!" We remember that John the Baptist had said that the mightier One would "baptize" with the Holy Spirit and with "fire". Jesus has come to set this fire alight and so to fulfil His task of baptizing with the Spirit. But at present something is opposing and frustrating that purpose. What is this something? In the light of the central issue elsewhere confronting Jesus there can be little doubt about the answer. The frustration is from the invisible powers of darkness and from the men whom the demons still control. If Jesus is to fulfil His baptism and to bestow the Spirit, it must be through accepting the last conclusions of the conflict with the demon-world into which He has been drawn. "See", He replies to Herod Antipas, "I am casting out demons". This task Jesus must go on pursuing to the end, despite the fact that He is now proscribed in Galilee. In Galilee, for the moment, He is inviolate, for "in the nature of things no prophet can possibly meet his doom except in Jerusalem" (Luke xiii. 31 ff.). It is in Jerusalem that "the power of darkness" (*he exousia tou skotous*) will finally attain its "hour". This may help us in turn to understand a third mysterious word (Mark x. 45), where also there is a reference in the context to "baptism". It is the word spoken to the Twelve after the ambitious request of the brothers James and John: "The Son of Man came . . . to give His life as a ransom-price for many". A ransom-price! To whom paid, and for whom, and why, and in what coin?

Finally, in Mark xiii. 6, in the Parousia discourse, there occurs the perplexing statement: "Many will come in My name, saying *Ego eimi*, and will mislead many." It has always been difficult to explain how any Christian in his right mind could wish to impersonate his Master and deceive his brethren. But the difficulty disappears if the thought is of Satan or other spirit of evil speaking even through Christians, as for example through Peter when Jesus had to say to him: "Get thee behind me, Satan" (Mark viii. 33). This did not mean that Peter was Satan, but it does mean that Satan without loss of identity was making use of Peter at the moment (cf. Eph. iv. 27).

It is not necessary to extend the survey further. We may simply notice the promise given by Jesus to the Twelve at the Last Supper, where He addresses the Twelve as "you who have stood by Me in all My trials" (Luke xxii. 28); also His warning to Peter on the same occasion: "Simon, Simon, Satan has asked for (all of) you, to sift you (all) like wheat, but I have prayed for thee" (Luke xxii. 31); finally, the pathos of the word with which He surrenders to His captors at the end: "This is indeed your hour and the power of darkness" (Luke xxii. 53).

So the *exousia* of Jesus the Messiah comes to last mortal grips with the *exousia* of the demonic world. And the apostolic gospel from its illuminated standpoint will tell us the rest of the story. The "archons" who dominate this present world-age, writes St. Paul, did not recognize the hidden wisdom of God, for "had they known it, they would not have crucified the Lord of glory" (1 Cor. ii. 8). Christ, he writes again, "having disarmed the principalities and powers, made a public spectacle of them, when He triumphed over them on the cross" (Col. ii. 15). God, we read further, by the power exerted in the raising of Christ from the dead, "has made Him sit at His right hand in the heavenly world, far above all rule and authority and power and dominion, and above every name that is named, not only in this world, but in the world to come" (Eph. i. 19–21). From the Pauline, and indeed from the whole New Testament standpoint, when the Christ bowed His head on the cross, all the powers of darkness, all the demonism of the cosmos, affronted Him and closed with Him in mortal combat. Behind all "the fearful enmity of the carnal heart of man towards God" which arrayed itself visibly against Jesus at His trial before the Sanhedrin and at Calvary, stood the embattled hosts of the invisible world, hazarding all on a last trial of strength. And Jesus, when He faced and accepted that challenge, was taking upon Himself all that hatred, all that guilt, and all that judgement of God which lay upon it, in order to complete His "baptism", His work of delivering men from the power of the Enemy and so restoring them to forgiveness and to God.

III

That here we have the classical or early patristic approach to the Christian doctrine of the Atonement is generally allowed. But does it represent a phase of thought or form of language which we can now leave behind? There is more in the New Testament teaching about the death and resurrection of Christ than is comprised in this theology. Jesus Himself in His teaching about man and sin does not always bring in the dark supernatural background of life, but is often content to present the mystery of redemption in terms that do not go beyond God and the reasonable soul. The heavenly Father calls and His children return to Him. But behind this teaching, all the time, something else is latent, and in flash after flash of profoundest utterance regarding His work for men and their salvation the apocalyptic background of the mind of Christ shows through. When the sun is in eclipse, the fiery corona which surrounds its disc comes into view, and when Jesus bowed His head before the hour and the power of darkness, the apocalyptic setting of His life flamed out in all its clearness.

Those electrical words of Jesus about the kingdom of heaven being "outraged" at the hands of the "outrageous"; about His coming to cast "fire" on the earth but having a "baptism" yet to be completed; about the Son of Man giving His life as the price of the deliverance of the many—words like these are not inventions of the Church or glosses added by interpreters. These words were there before the Church. They form the corona of the Incarnation. And they seem to have passed over the heads of their first reporters; only so do we explain why the word in St. Matthew about the *biastai* has come down to us unglossed. But if this is so, the supernatural demonological element in the gospel is not a mere veneer. It is not a temporary trapping which can be stripped away from the gospel. It is engrained in its very substance. It is needed to bring out its sense.

In a recent book, *The Cosmic Christ* (1951), Dr. A. D. Galloway, who has much to say that is of great value with regard to the Biblical eschatology, proposes to transpose the demonology of late Judaism and early Christianity into the terms of a recognition of the impersonal and unmeaning character of external reality as it confronts the soul of man in its cosmic setting. It is doubtful whether this transposition of the Biblical material can be carried out without remainder and without serious loss to religion. Such a commutation of ideas hardly does justice to the specific nature of the problem with which our minds are faced when we turn to the moral nature of the human situation. As we look at humanity in its collective aspect, with its terrible exposure to hysteria and hallucination on a gigantic scale, those merely negative categories of the impersonal and the unmeaning do not fit all the facts. They are not adequate to the expression of man's whole experience of his moral environment. As we look at history, what we see is often not the merely impersonal and unmeaning but the irrational and *the mad.* The face that looks through at us is akin often to the insane. Certainly as Jesus looked at men, He saw them not always as rational moral units or self-contained autonomous spirits; He saw their souls as a battle-ground, an arena or theatre of tragic conflict between the opposed cosmic powers of the Holy Spirit of God and Satan. As Tatian in his *Oration* put it: "The demons who order men about are not the souls of men."

The question which most presses on us here, however, concerns the relation of Christian evangelism to this human situation, and here it is instructive to watch the attitude of Jesus to the possessed to whom He ministered. We see the place He gave in His ministry to these unbalanced minds. We see Him speaking to their condition, calming their terrors, speaking reasonably to their minds where that was possible, recalling them to themselves and to God. He distinguished between the men and the "spirits" which had seized control of them. This is important because it shows how the dangers latent in the recognition of a "demonic" element in human life are to be avoided in the Christian approach to the problem.

But in the worship and in the preaching of the Church today are we allowing sufficiently for this mysterious background to human existence which the Lord recognized and accepted as real when He came and preached to the spirits? These nameless fears, the terrible insecurity of soul, the sense of exposure to physical forces of one or another dread kind which oppress the minds of men, so that while they sit in the pews of our Churches they are trembling sometimes on the verge of some dark abyss—is there enough religious realism in the atmosphere of our worship and in the terms of our doctrinal teaching to take a grip on these minds? Or are we speaking to them in the abstract, impersonal terms of a purely rational moral paraenesis, labouring ethical points which have not perhaps a primary relevance to the existential situation of the hearers, and forgetting their fears, their appalling insecurity, and their despair? For it is not enough to believe and to know that Christ has dethroned the spirits, and to regard the demonological element in the New Testament as a sub-Christian survival. For St. Paul, who knows that from the love of God in Christ there is nothing that can separate us, "neither angels, nor principalities, nor powers", is most painfully insistent that these forces of the spiritual cosmos are still active in man's life. As we might say, the psychical phenomena which accompanied the Biblical belief in interfering demonic spirits are still present, still recognizable, even where the belief itself is absent. When health is good, and happiness is unimpaired, and strength is firm, and hope abounds, men are rational, and their religious need is rationally moral. But let there come some breakdown in these defences, their souls cry out for life, for security, for peace. The apocalyptic background of the Bible comes again into relevance to life, at least for the preacher, and we to whom the Word is committed are summoned to remember the psychical context in which the work of Jesus was wrought when He came into Galilee, preaching the Kingdom of God.

PART II

The Christian Life

CHAPTER I

The Expression of Christian Life in the New Testament Literature: An Analysis of Religious Reality

I

Introduction

The New Testament reader will recollect that at a number of places in the Acts of the Apostles the Christian religion is referred to as "the Way" (Acts ix. 2; xix. 9, 23; xxii. 4; xxiv. 14, 22). It happens that on all six occasions the term appears on the lips of St. Paul or has relation to St. Paul's activities, first as persecutor, and then as Apostle of the Church. What inference, if any, is to be drawn from this peculiar restriction of the Acts-usage it is not easy to say, and perhaps not important to inquire, the less so because the term "the Way" does not occur in the writings of St. Paul himself. Qualified forms of the expression, such as "way of God" or "of the Lord", "way of righteousness", "way of salvation", "way of faith" and "way of life" are normal New Testament usage, and we may note the Jewish habit of giving the name *derek,* which means a road or path, to the principles governing the common life of any religious sect. To the absolute Christian use of the term *The Way* there is, however, no parallel, though clearly the term conveys the sense that distinctive beliefs and practices belong to the new society.

Externally the impression made by Christianity on the world is left by the Acts-narrative in no manner of doubt (Acts xvi. 20–1). At Philippi St. Paul and his associate Silvanus are dragged before the courts as Jewish disturbers of the public life, advocating customs not lawful for the patriotic people of a Roman *colonia* to entertain or practise. At Thessalonica it is asseverated—this time by irate Jews—that "these upsetters of the world have appeared here also . . . and to a man they are opposed to the decrees of Caesar, alleging that there is another King, Jesus" (Acts xvii. 6–7). It should be remembered that in or about that very year, A.D. 49, the Emperor Claudius at Rome had ordered the expulsion of the Jews from the city owing to an outbreak of rioting in the Jewish synagogues caused in all probability by the introduction of Christian preaching (cf. Acts xviii. 2). This had set by the ears both the *Roman* authorities at Philippi and the *Jews* at Thessalonica, and accounts for their proceedings against the Apostle. At Athens (Acts xvii. 18–20), again, St. Paul is ridiculed as an importer of "queer ideas" and "foreign divinities", preaching as he does of "Jesus and Anastasis", a word meaning "resurrection" which the Athenians probably took for some feminine divinity! At Corinth (Acts xviii. 13; xix. 26; xxi. 28) the Apostle is accused of propagating an illicit worship, at Ephesus of teaching atheism, and at Jerusalem of defaming the People, the law, and the temple of God. Such was the face outwardly presented to society by the people called "the Way": as at Ephesus, so in the world generally "there arose no little disturbance over the Way" (τάραχος οὐκ ὀλίγος περὶ τῆς ὁδοῦ, Acts xix. 23).

Internally, Christianity is marked by the possession of certain theological beliefs and by the practice of certain rules of life, and, as such, it must now be subjected by us to the test of the general analysis of the structure of religious reality. What is *religion*? Or better, what is religion at that highest stage of the religious consciousness which we encounter in the *Bible*? We may answer in a word. Religion is response, the worshipping response of the creature to the *manifestation of God*. God reveals His presence, and the manifestation, arresting and subduing the soul, passes through it, like light through a prism, breaking into articulate conceptions on the one hand and regarding the character of God and on the other hand regarding the way of life for man. So is it at the deep levels of Old Testament religion depicted in the traditions of Jacob at Bethel, Moses in Midian, Samuel at Shiloh, Elijah at Horeb, and Isaiah in the temple (Gen. xxviii. 10 f.; Exod. iii; 1 Sam. iii; 1 Kings xix; Isa. vi). In these traditions, some of which had been preserved at local sanctuaries, God manifests Himself as the Living One, the *I AM* ('Εγώ εἰμι) before whose transcendent essence or mysterious purposes man prostrates himself, covers his face, builds his altar, confesses his sins. Perhaps the most wonderful of all the delineations is where Moses in the sacred tent asks to see God's "ways" and to behold His "glory", and receives answer that that cannot be. All the same, standing in his cleft of rock Moses is allotted an epiphany (Exod. xxxiv. 6–7). The Lord passes before him, and proclaims: "the Lord, the Lord, God merciful and gracious, slow to anger, and abounding in stedfast love and faithfulness, forgiving iniquity . . . but who will by no means clear the guilty."[1] And Moses bows his head and worships, and receives commandments from God (Exod. xxxiv. 8, 10 ff.). Here, then, is divine manifestation engaging the soul, and passing through the soul's encounter with it into theology and law of life. In this manner the episode becomes transparent of the structure of the religious relation.

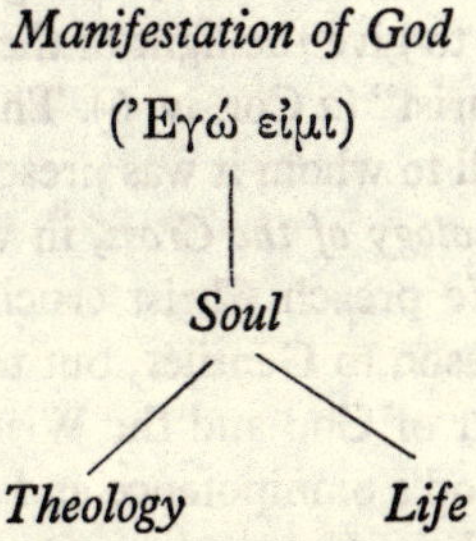

Cf. Psalm xxxvi. 9: "With Thee is the fountain of life; in Thy light shall we see light."

In the New Testament the Manifestation of God is *Jesus Christ*, the Son of the Father, incarnate, crucified, and risen. Jesus fills the whole sphere of God. Apart from Him as Mediator there exists no longer any access of the Christian soul to God, nor any communication from the divine side to us. Jesus is the *Way* (ἐγώ εἰμι ἡ ὁδός, John xiv. 6), and because He is the way, He is also the *Truth*—here the structure of religious reality comes very clearly to the light—and the *Life*. In other words, Jesus not only brings the revelation of God, *He is the revelation.*

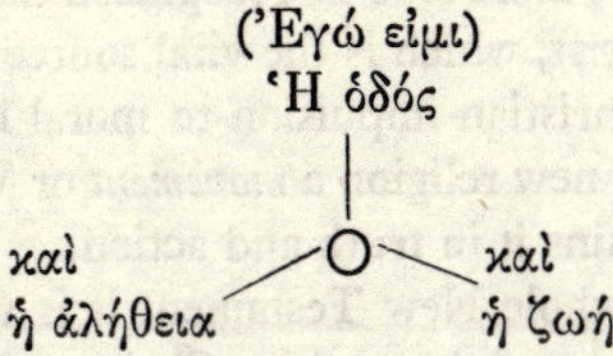

The concentration-point of the manifestation is His Cross (Gal. iii. 1; 1 Cor. ii. 2), and because it is here supremely that the soul meets with God, the resultant *theology*, the "truth" about God which breaks

[1] Cf. Mic. vii. 18–19, "Who is a God like unto Thee?" etc.

into and through the soul, is the theology of the cross, what St. Paul calls "the word of the cross" (ὁ λόγος ὁ τοῦ σταυροῦ, 1 Cor. i. 18), and the resultant ethic of "life" is the way of the cross. All these elements are present in every pattern of the Christian life which the New Testament presents for our analysis.

Thus (i) there is, as primary feature, the *Manifestation of God in Christ.* "The Word became flesh and dwelt among us, and we beheld his glory, glory as of the only Son from the Father, full of grace and truth" (John i. 14). "The God who said, Let light shine out of darkness, has shone in our hearts to give the light of the knowledge of the glory of God in the face of Christ" (2 Cor. iv. 6). This manifestation was not at first understood by all to whom it was presented.

(ii) There is the *Theology of the Cross*, in which the manifestation becomes *articulate.* "We preach Christ crucified, a stumbling-block to Jews and sheer unreason to Gentiles, but to those who are called a Christ who is the Power of God and the Wisdom of God" (1 Cor. i. 23–4), that is, who is God's omnipotence and God's answer to all our questions. So again, "Christ Jesus, whom God has made our wisdom, our righteousness and sanctification and redemption" (1 Cor. i. 30). Again, "the Son of God has come, and has given us understanding, to know him who is true" (1 John v. 20).

(iii) There is the *Way of the Cross*, which follows as the ethical consequence. "If any one will come after me, let him deny himself and take up his cross" (Mark viii. 34). Again, "to this you were called, because Christ also suffered for you, leaving you an example (ὑπογραμμόν) that you should follow in his steps" (1 Pet. ii. 21). Again, "You are dead, and your life is hid with Christ in God. . . . Put to death, therefore, what is earthly in you" (Col. iii. 3, 5).

Therefore, behind the doctrinal teaching and behind the ethical practice of Christianity, there is to be recognized that primary *engagement of the soul* by Christ, which is the vital source both of Christian doctrine and of the Christian impulsion to moral living. This is the thing which makes the new religion a *movement* or Way, which gets it going, and which sustains it in truth and action.

So throughout the whole New Testament it is with the nature of this primary engagement of the soul by Christ that we are occupied as we watch the rich and varied patterns of religious life which stem from the teaching of Jesus, and unfold themselves in the letters of St. Paul, the Johannine literature, and one or two other books of the New Testament. And already in *the Church of the early days* as it comes before us in the opening chapters of Acts, we see in miniature all the three constituents of religious reality.

(1) There is *the numinous background of the Church* in the manifestation of God which is made in the visions of the Risen Lord, and which is continually being renewed by the Holy Spirit. Here in the presence to the soul of the new glorified Christ we have the spiritual fountain of life from which everything else proceeds. ("Fear" we read "came upon every soul" (Acts ii. 43): "The place in which they were gathered was shaken, and all were filled with the Holy Spirit" (Acts iv. 31).)

(2) There is the *apostolic witness* to the meaning of the Christ-manifestation. This consists largely in testimony drawn from the Holy Scripture and contains in embryo the later theology of the Church. It may be said that in this earliest preaching, prophetic Scripture was the subject, and Jesus of Nazareth was the predicate, but this was because the unbelieving Jews contested the right of the Christians to appeal to Holy Scripture for their doctrines, and the Christians had to make good their claim.

(3) There is the Christian *way of life*, expressed very distinctively in the Church's community of goods (Acts ii. 44–7; iv. 32–7). Acts are mightier than words in the ultimate testimony to God, and that the apostolic society had its own way of solving the problem of "communication", and did it by deeds, not preaching alone, is scarcely to be questioned.

Nevertheless, the thing to which both this doctrine and this practice go back is very clearly the life and teaching of Jesus Himself. And the same is true of all the later norms of the Christian life in the Pauline letters, in Hebrews and First Peter, and in the Johannine writings. In all cases we find ourselves pointed back to the historical image and character of Jesus as He walked the earth among men. And this perspective applies very specially to the analysis of Synoptic religion to which we now turn.

II

Synoptic Discipleship: the Following of Christ

The Sower went forth to sow his seed, Jesus came into Galilee, "preaching the gospel of God, and saying: The time has fully come, and the kingdom of God has come near: repent, and believe in the gospel" (Mark i. 14–15). Heaven had opened over Jesus at His baptism. He had seen the Spirit descend upon Him, and had heard the voice: "Thou art my Son, the Beloved, on whom I have set my choice" (Mark i. 9–11). This initial *revelation* from God, conveyed in symbolic terms, now forms the numinous background of the first great expression of the Christian calling. Jesus summons men to lay their account with the revelation that has come from God, and to "repent" and "believe" the message.

The time (καιρός) that has fully come (πεπλήρωται) is the last time, the Age of the End, which is to witness the coming of the *Reign of God.* Prophets and Kings had looked forward to that time, and had not seen it (Matt. xiii. 16–17; Luke x. 23–4). Now its approach in Jesus demands that the hearers will orient themselves to the new situation.

It is *near,* this Kingdom of the End. But *how* near? So near that it is now to fill the whole horizon of the hearers of Jesus! So near that it lays immediate arrest on every life! So near that it no longer leaves a man any other option except the casting away of his life! No man can serve two masters (Matt. vi. 24; Luke xvi. 13). That proposition is stated theoretically, but it is not to be received theoretically but *existentially.* "Lord, suffer me first to go and bury my father." Jesus says: "Follow me now, and let the dead bury their dead" (Matt. viii. 21–2). So the Reign of God, hitherto only an apocalyptic hope, a dream, a vision that had flitted before men's minds as the rainbow flits before the traveller, becomes the single issue of life. Jesus makes it a *personal* issue. What does it mean for a man, for you, for me, for any person whatsoever, that God's reign should come *now* and come in the absoluteness of its holiness? Here is the real "nearness" of the Kingdom, the *existential* pressure of something which can no longer be set aside or put off to another day.

But repent! How can a man repent (μετανοεῖν), how change his mind, turn to God? Can a man give himself a new mentality, a new will, a new nature? The answer is that, of course, he cannot. The serious effort to do so, in the light of the searching ray of the divine holiness which Jesus Christ turns on to us, will only bring him to self-despair. On the other hand, the realization of this fact is perhaps the first thing that is needed. If the blessedness of the Kingdom of heaven is, first of all, for "the poor in spirit" (Matt. v. 3), it will follow that few others than the desperate will qualify for it or even want it. *In themselves,* that is. But if taken out of themselves, what then? In asking His hearers to "repent" Jesus adds "and believe in the *gospel.*"

The mental change-over which He demands is not to be effected in a vacuum but in association with that event which Jesus announces as at the door, and which is now to be the background of His followers' lives as it is of His own. *God wills* this event! God wills to establish His sovereignty and *to give* the life and righteousness of the Kingdom to those who cannot attain it of themselves. Jesus has stepped into the human situation, and it is not apart from but in fellowship with Him that repentance, the turning from self to God, the putting of God first, the recognizing that one has *no future except God*, is to be effectuated. Passing along by the Lake of Galilee, we read, "He saw Simon and Andrew, the brother of Simon . . . and said, Follow me" (Mark i. 16).

The first great expression of the Christian life in the New Testament shapes itself, then, as the *disciple-calling*, and it is to this curriculum and its requirements that we must turn for what remains of the present study.

(1) The men whom Jesus calls are from the start to be *sharers of His Life*. The manifestation of God, which now becomes the primary engagement of their souls, consists in the insistent hourly, daily, constant restraint of Jesus on their lives, an experience mediated to these first followers through the flesh of Jesus, but to others, including ourselves, only through the Holy Spirit working with and in the Synoptic Gospels. According to this pattern of the religious life, Christians begin, and indeed go on to the end, as *scholars* in the school of Christ. They are witnesses of His actions, hearers of His words, associates of His fortunes, companions of His way, and confidants of His mind on matters relating to God and human repentance and faith. All this constitutes a career of the highest privilege—it is "the gracious calling of the Lord"—but it is also a very searching and disturbing experience. Jesus refers to these disciple-followers as "friends of the bridegroom" (Mark ii. 19), guests at a wedding-feast. That is a very high privilege. It means that they belong, through their being with Jesus, to the new age of *the Messianic time*. But for the same reason, as the parables of the New Patch on the Old Coat, the New Wine in the Old Skins, and the Wedding-Garment make plain, they are to put on the life of *the New Creation*, and not go about in the old clothes of Judaism (Mark ii. 21–2; Matt. xxii. 11–14). The Messiah now takes precedence over the law, and the life of the "scholars" of Jesus is set above conventional Pharisaic righteousness (Matt. v. 20). Likewise these disciples have the honour, but also the responsibility, of

receiving *the "mystery" of the Kingdom* (Mark iv. 10–12). To those "outside", this Reign of God, as Jesus declared it, remains veiled in "parables"; in other words it remains, at best, a figure of speech, a colourful vision, or, as we might say, a religious myth. But not to those whose interior eyes have been opened, for whom the truth has been *demythologized.* These persons must know, with Jesus, the pain, as well as the joy, of the Kingdom.

It is indeed a very disconcerting experience, as well as the blessedest of callings, thus to have the manifestation of God made to them in *the daily walk* of life and to be taken within the veil of its mystery. It is not a very comfortable thing to be searched and known, and to discover daily just how wrong you are (Psalm cxxxix). It is not consoling to have your life ploughed up and ploughed under, and to realize continuously how far you are from God. And yet that is how this curriculum proceeds—and it is *life* that it should be so. It is not very pleasant to be told, like St. Peter, that you have a radically ungodly mind, that you have no sense of the things of God, and, when you feel at your cleverest, that you are Satan's dupe (Mark viii. 33). And it is not at all composing to live with the Sermon on the Mount, and to compare what is said there about *blessedness and love* with what you know yourself to be. Far easier to wish to back out of this kind of shattering realization, saying like Peter: "Begone from me, for I am a sinful man, O Lord!" (Luke v. 8). Easier, yes, but the way to life is *through the light,* not by circumventing it. So the Synoptic norm of the Christian life means that, from our calling onward, we come to serious terms with the life and with the teaching of Jesus. There is no by-passing this requirement.

(2) We pass to a second stage in the way. Hitherto the word to the disciples has been "Follow me!" But when Jesus becomes confessed as the Christ by His follower Peter, and is about to go to Jerusalem and to face the momentous issues of the last journey, He says to His disciples: "If any one will come after me, let him deny himself, and take up his cross and follow me" (Mark viii. 34). Hitherto it might appear as if the new knowledge of God and life gained by these scholars in the school of Christ was only an upper storey built upon the structure of their natural lives, a spiritual finish administered to their culture but leaving untouched the original instincts of their souls. But now into the synoptic representation of the calling of the Lord, there strikes the existential note: *Deny thy self!* The life which the disciple is called to live with Christ is not simply an improved

version of the life he has lived. It proves on experience to be the *contradiction* of that life. We may say that for the Christian in the school of Christ the life he is called upon to live will, sooner or later, and certainly in every situation of true self-discovery or crisis, reveal itself as the *opposite* of the life he has been, or is now living. Deny thy self!—that word means that the disciple must for ever tell himself that the truly Christian life is the life he has *not* got, and that he must be made over again, if he is to *go on* following Christ. It is also to be remembered that "self" here includes the world in its grip upon a man's life. "What is a man profited if he gains the whole world and loses himself?" (Mark viii. 36).

Jesus at the moment He made this demand was facing the final issues of His work. It is not strange that at that crisis the mystery and the paradox of His own destiny should throw its reflection on the calling of His disciples. In its original sense the demand of self-rejection and the bearing of the cross meant for these first followers the literal leaving behind of their homes and possessions and kindred in Galilee, and the taking of their lives in their hands to go with Jesus to Jerusalem. But the words have a more universal bearing. Sometimes in reading the Gospels we have difficulty in making out what part of the recorded teaching of Jesus, apart from the parables, was delivered to the multitude. Much, if not most, of the teaching which has come down to us is instruction given to the apostles. But at this point in the Synoptic record a remarkable feature enters.

The Evangelists—or at least two of them—say that Jesus' word about negating Self was of *general application* (Mark viii. 34; Luke ix. 23). St. Mark says that "He called to him the multitude with His disciples". St. Luke says that "He spoke the words to all". This implies upon the part of the recording evangelists a very definite sense that here, if anywhere, *the heart of the Christian calling* is to be looked for. Through the contradiction of the natural life, and not through the mere acquisition of spiritual knowledge and sensibility, lies the Christian way. The Son of Man is revealed as "the Suffering Servant". And it is under the sign of this profounder, graver, more existential under-standing of the manifestation of God in Christ that we go forward to the crowning stage of the Synoptic representation of the Christian life.

Let there be no misunderstanding about this matter. The natural life is not man's highest life. Yet the negation of Self demanded is not so much the renunciation of nature as the renunciation of the selfish principle of holding back, sparing self, fearing, hesitating, evading. And the way out is not asceticism, for that too may only be another retreat into the *Ego*. Rather does it consist in a *fuller outgoing* of our life to Jesus, a fuller sharing with Him as He goes forward to His passion, *letting Him, in effect, replace our Ego, so that life becomes life in Him, life from the dead, the emergence of a new personality* (cf. St. Paul, Gal. ii. 20–1, etc.). And this brings us to the final stage of our analysis.

(3) Up to this point Jesus and His disciples have been travelling as a team. And there have been those who have thought that when Jesus spoke of the *Son of Man* as intended for suffering, He was giving Son of Man a collective sense, and these disciples were included with Himself. They were all on the same road. But even if that were true regarding the term Son of Man, which is more than doubtful, the time was to come when Jesus was to draw apart from these followers, to put a *distance* between Himself and them, and to go forward to a single and indivisible destiny. Even at a point on the road to Jerusalem we read that "Jesus was going on in advance of them, and wonder came over them, and those who followed were afraid" (Mark x. 32). The separation was not yet, but the act of Jesus was premonitory, and in the Upper Room He was to say to all of them, "You will all be offended (πάντες σκανδαλισθήσεσθε), for it is written, I will smite the Shepherd" (Mark xiv. 27). The union of the Christ, the Son of Man, with "the Suffering Servant" is the supreme "scandal". In the Garden of Gethsemane even the most intimate three of the disciple-group were to be onlookers of His passion, not participants: Jesus "was withdrawn (ἀπεσπάσθη) from them" (Luke xxii. 41). At the arrest, they were all to forsake Him. And at Calvary where will they be? With the crowd. If not with those who are against Him, at least with those who wring the hands, who know that somehow they are implicated, but can do nothing about it!

In this last hour, there are not any of them over whose sense of their relation to Jesus there does not steal the consciousness that, despite the knowledge and grace they have received in the school of Christ, their *sin* has some part in that "fearful enmity of the carnal heart of man to God" which reveals itself around the cross. St. Peter's position we know, but is there a single one of these men whose moral consciousness remains intact in that existential hour? This, then, is the position into which the Synoptic way of life, the "gracious calling of the Lord", brings us before the day is done, standing afar, discovered to ourselves.

But before this separation and this discovery, what is it that Jesus, having loved His disciples and still loving them to the end, does to prepare them for the self-accusing depth of awakened moral consciousness into which they will be brought, and to ensure the permanence of the fellowship with Himself in seeking the Kingdom of God on which they had entered? What is it that He does to associate them with His sacrifice and to give that sacrifice a permanent relation to their lives, so that, functionally separated, they may still be one with Him? There is a faith that sometimes thinks in the naked strength of an unassisted spiritual comprehension to bear the weight of moral self-dicovery within the Christian life, and to dispense with *sacramental* aid. Such an attitude which, to a greater extent than those who hold it know, rests on a rationalistic or gnostic interpretation of spiritual reality rather than on dominical revelation, overlooks the infinite depth of mercy and compassion with which the Saviour, on the night on which He was betrayed, acted towards the so-soon-to-be-broken-and-dis-credited band whom He had gathered round Him. He was dealing with disciples to whom the *Word* had come, who had learned much about God and about their heavenly calling, but who had also come to know themselves and who could not, in separation from Jesus, support the weight of the discovered reality of the facts about themselves. At that moment Jesus took bread, and broke it, and gave it to them, saying: *This is my Body* (Mark xiv. 22–4). In the same manner He gave them the cup with words that spoke of *my blood of the covenant,* and they drank of it. There was an aspect of the ritual meal thus instituted according to which it was proleptic, an anticipating of the Messianic feast in the Kingdom of God. But the act did more than that. It associated the final consummation with Jesus' own sense of giving His life for the Kingdom of God. And by giving them the Bread and the Cup as something of which to *partake,* He was indicating by effectual signs their interest in His passion, consecrating them, in fact, for inheritance in the Kingdom.

Therefore, to complete the pattern of the Synoptic norm of the Christian life we must recognize as its final stage that it stands under the sign of the cross and of the Sacrament of the Body and Blood of Christ. To the two determinations of the Christian life already specified—"Live your life with Christ," "Deny yourself for Christ"—we must add the sense not only of inexpressible debt to the Redeemer but of *sacramental* dependence on Him. The Christian life is sacramental life. It is to be understood in the same sense as Isaiah understood his life: "Lo, this has touched your lips, and your iniquity is taken away, and your sin pardoned."

In the foregoing analysis of the pattern of Christian life in the Synoptic Gospels we have taken no account of the critical historical questions relating to these Gospels, nor has that been necessary. For we have been concerned not with the historical unfolding of the events of the life of Jesus, but with the conception of the Christian obedience as understood by the apostolic Church. And here undoubtedly we have the classical expression of the Christian way of life. This pattern remains a standard for all future time. The name "disciple" passed at an early time out of use. But the thing remains. In the Epistle to the Ephesians (iv. 20–1), do we not find the apostle saying, after words spoken about the sins which degrade the common life of men in the pagan world: "But you have not thus learned Christ (οὐχ οὕτως ἐμάθετε τὸν Χριστόν if indeed you have listened to him, and been taught in him (ἐν αὐτῷ ἐδιδάχθητε) as the truth is in Jesus"? Other assessments of the depth of meaning implied in the manifestation of God in Christ will meet us in the New Testament, but nowhere so rich, so concrete, so articulate, so moving a delineation of what it means to be a Christian.

III

Pauline Mysticism: "To me to live in Christ"

No greater contrast can well be imagined than between the Synoptic expression of the Christian life and the Pauline. For in the latter the manifestation of God in Christ is no longer in the flesh of Jesus but in His risen and glorified life. Therefore the tremendous emphasis in St. Paul on the element of the *Spirit*, which is now the medium of the communication. Again, in the Synoptic presentation it might appear formally—though the statement stands in need of some qualification—that grace works with nature; the new Christian life came to the first disciples of Jesus as something supervening on the old life in Judaism. In St. Paul, on the other hand, *grace* is set in opposition to nature, and it makes an end of legal religion. St. Paul speaks of himself, the zealot for judicial righteousness, as at the time of his conversion comparable to something "aborted", an ἔκτρωμα (1 Cor. xv. 8). He is clearly no product of any natural development in religion. Therefore his tremendous emphasis on the *transcendence*, and the paradox, of grace.

It is true that between St. Paul's religious experience and that of the first disciples of Jesus there exists a *continuity* in that it is the same "Son of God" who is revealed in both. St. Paul knows of two stages in the manifestation of the Son of God, a first in which He appeared κατὰ σάρκα as a descendant of David, a second in which He has been designated as "Son of God in power κατὰ πνεῦμα ἁγιωσύνης". This second stage has been inaugurated by the event of *the resurrection* (Rom. i. 3–4), and the distinction of this stage from the first stage is not qualitative merely but dimensional. Nevertheless, despite this continuity, there is an extraordinary difference between St. Paul's manner of speaking of the Christian's relation to Jesus and the language of the Synoptic Gospels. There is a *mysticism* in St. Paul which is new and startling. Whereas in the Gospels the Christian is said to "follow" Jesus or to come "after" Him or to be "with" Him, in St. Paul the thought is everywhere of the Christian as being *in Christ*: and to show the personal and absorbing character of the relation so described there are passages such as those where the Apostle says, "It is no more I who live, but Christ who lives in me" (Gal. ii. 20), or where he speaks of the Christian as having "put on" (Gal. iii. 27), or clothed himself with Christ at baptism (Rom. xiii. 14), or where he describes himself in an ultra-daring metaphor as suffering travail-pangs until Christ be "formed" (μορφωθῇ) in his converts (Gal. iv. 19). This is very remarkable language, especially when taken into comparison with the simpler terms of Synoptic discipleship, and it calls for explanation.

We may, if we will, connect the change-over in religious terminology with the transition to a new dimension of religious revelation which, as we have seen, St. Paul recognized to have come with the Resurrection of Jesus (Rom. i. 3–4). This numinous event marks the beginning of the *New Creation*, and therefore the Apostle can say: "If any one is in Christ, it is the new creation (καινὴ κτίσις): the old things have passed: look! they have become new" (2 Cor. v. 17). But while the New Creation opened the way for, and indeed demanded a new religious vocabulary, that does not explain why St. Paul should choose the term he does, and describe the Christian life as life *in* Christ. Stephen, we may believe, saw that the New Creation had come. Judaism had receded into the past, and the religious outlook of humanity was now centered and summed up in the person of the glorified Son of Man (Acts vii. 55–6). Yet neither Stephen nor his followers, so far as we know, spoke of Christians as ἐν Χριστῷ.

Scholars have, therefore, busied themselves in taking soundings over wide areas of contemporary religious thought in the hope of finding a clue to St. Paul's language.

Here we may, with Dr. Schweitzer, go back to the Jewish apocalyptic writings and see a potential mysticism in the conception of a predestinated solidarity existing between the heavenly "Son of Man" and the elect. Or we may, with the majority of modern scholars, and remembering that Saul was brought up at Tarsus in Cilicia, trace his language to a mental predisposition acquired by early familiarity with Graeco-Oriental *mystery-religion* and *gnosis.* St. Paul certainly does make use of words having a special currency in Greek mystery-religion and theosophy,[1] just as he makes use of words characteristic of the Stoic philosophy.[2] The influence of mystery-language comes out also in his interpretation of *baptism* as a "putting on" of Christ (Gal. iii. 27), and in the whole Pauline idea of *the death and resurrection of Jesus as a divine drama* (Rom. vi. 3–6; Col. ii) to be reproduced within the life of the believer, while the influence of certain forms of the Gnostic idea of the Revealer of God may be traced in his conception of Christ as the "last Adam", "the man from Heaven" (1 Cor. xv. 45–7). But while the Apostle may have found in these ideas a form in which to express certain sublime realities of the Christian faith, nothing in Greek mystery-usage or in gnosis is really parallel to his use of the term ἐν Χριστῷ. Nor is there any exact analogy to it in the rest of the New Testament. The Johannine expressions "Abide in me" and "I in you" refer to the fellowship (κοινωνία) existing between the Redeemer and His followers, which is itself a part of the fellowship which the divine Son has with the Father. In St. Paul, however, it is not so much the fellowship of the Christian with Christ that is suggested, as a union or interfusion of personalities. Christ is the new *Ego* of the Christian, and the Head or informing principle of the new humanity (1 Cor. vi. 17; Eph. v. 30).

It would seem, therefore, that the phrase ἐν Χριστῷ, as a category for the expression of the Christian life, is *a Pauline idiogram*, a unique product of the apostle's own religious sensibility. We say that "The style is the man", and that is true, but it was never truer than with reference to the man Paul, who in this plastic and creative way reveals the completeness, the all-outness of his personal response to Christ,

[1] E.g. μυστήριον, μυεῖσθαι, τέλειος, ἐμβατεύειν, φωτισμός, etc.

[2] E.g. συνείδησις, φύσις, ἐλευθερία in the ethical sense, τὰ καθήκοντα, λογικός, etc.

devotionally, theologically, and practically. While we cannot penetrate to the root of the phraseology in its first psychological ideation, we see clearly what the language is intended to express and cover. Christ is (i) the *ground* of the Apostle's faith. Christ is (ii) the *sphere* or milieu within which that faith is exercised. Christ is (iii) the *substance* upon which his faith draws and which it assimilates. In all these ways Paul is "in Christ", dependent upon, identified with and determined by Christ over the whole area of his being. Alternatively, Christ lives in Paul. There is an *interblending* of personalities, though it never supersedes the necessity of faith as the connecting-link between the redeemed and the Redeemer (Gal. ii. 20 f.).

(1) *The Manifestation of God in Christ.* Because by the very ardour of his Jewish legalism Saul had been carried into measures of extreme hostility to the Church of Jesus, the event of his *conversion* cut his life in two, and gave the expression of his Christianity a form very different from that of the Galilean apostles. These men had come gradually to the light and without the same sense of their past religious life in Judaism under the law (ἐν νόμῳ) having been at war with God and subject to the rule of sin and death. For St. Paul the change-over was critical and went to the root of the whole structure of reality. The experience could only be compared to the transition from chaos to order on the first day of creation. "It was the God", he writes, "who said, Let light shine out of darkness, who shone in our hearts to give the light of the knowledge of the glory of God in the face of Christ" (2 Cor. iv. 6). There we have the compactest and most luminous expression of the Manifestation which made Saul a Christian. Only, when we read the glowing words, let us be careful to understand them properly. The Apostle does not speak of an *inward* illumination which was merely *like* the coming of light at the creation. He means that on the Damascus road he became aware of the *objective* reality of the New Creation. The *New Creation* had dawned with Jesus Christ, but he, Saul, had been blind to it. Now, however, the dayspring from on high stood revealed.

The question has been raised in modern days whether the conversion of the Apostle had just that character of dramatic unpreparedness which is here ascribed to it. My own reading of the evidence leads me to conclude that it had. The passages in which St. Paul alludes to his career in Judaism before and at the time of his conversion suggest that that career was at the very height of its ardour and, as *he* thought, success. Thus he speaks of himself at the time of his crusade against the Church as "making progress in Judaism beyond the mass of my contemporaries among my own people, being as I was an unbounded zealot for the traditions received from my fathers" (Gal. i. 14–16). He writes again, alluding to the same acme of his persecuting zeal, that he was "in point of the righteousness which has the law for its standard, blameless" (Phil. iii. 6). In the same passage he speaks of his privileges and achievements in the Jewish religion as assets or "gains" (κέρδη) which he renounced, and treated as less than nothing, "for the sake of the surpassing worth of the knowledge of Christ Jesus my Lord" (Phil. iii. 7–11). Now if, as some people believe, his confidence in Judaism had been already internally shaken, would his accounts with the Law at the time of his conversion have shown so solid an entry on the credit side?

I feel, therefore, extremely sceptical about the rightness of regarding *Romans vii* as the record of a supposed period in St. Paul's pre-Christian life when he had come to despair of the Law and was in acute distress of soul.[1] The Greek Fathers, indeed, with their strong idealistic optimism, interpreted the state of soul depicted in the chapter as belonging purely to his *pre-baptismal* experience. Not so the Western Fathers, including St. Augustine, and the Reformers, including John Calvin. They with their deeper sense of the radical nature of sin give the spiritual analysis of Romans vii a *Christian reference*. It is the Christian soul which is placed under the microscope. Our modern age with its interest in biography, psychology, and psycho-analysis has reverted in some quarters to the idea that the chapter reflects an epoch in St. Paul's Jewish life. An example is Dr. C. H. Dodd's Commentary on Romans, but I find his arguments at this point far from convincing. One cannot think of a period in St. Paul's Jewish experience when he could, however dissatisfied with his own righteousness, have despaired of the *Law*. If he was inwardly convicted of moral insufficiency in himself, well then, to the Law—more study of its requirements, more fasting, more prayer! It is not possible, therefore, to think of Romans vii as the transcript of an actual stage of experience in Judaism. But just as little possible is it to regard the chapter as the *full* record of any real stage in Christian life, seeing that the chapter says nothing, till the end, about the grace of God in Christ.

In fact, if we take the chapter as autobiography, we are in the curious position of having to admit that it reflects either a Judaism, in which

[1] See below, pp. 146–159.

the glory of God had passed from the Law, or a Christianity in which the glory of Christ had not yet arisen on the Gospel.

I cannot, therefore, take the chapter, as it stands, as *history*, though it may embody fragments of St. Paul's experience both before and after Damascus. Rather is it, as I believe, a *dialectical analysis* of the state of a soul under Law. On the other hand, if we are to find an understanding approach to the conversion of the Apostle, we must look for it not in any internal breakdown of his Judaism, but rather in the contract into which, as the prosecuting attorney, he came with the Nazarenes, the people of Jesus. For it was then, for the first time, that the possibility of there being *a revelation from God higher than the Law* crossed his horizon and lifted its glory upon him.

(2) A revelation from God higher than the Law! This is what came to St. Paul in the manifestation of Christ at his conversion. We must now look into the content of the experience, and into the nature of the *theological* consequences which the Apostle was led to draw from it.

(a) The Manifestation of God to Paul was interpretable, in the first instance, as and only as an act of pure *grace*. Only unlimited goodness could account for a divine interposition which turned the persecutor of Jesus from error and blindness and opened to him the gates of a new life. God had intervened not in judgement but as one whose interest in a sinner had transcended the sinner's deformity, and that for the sake of reconciling him to Himself. *Why* had God not acted in *judgement*? Taking a word which was currently used in the Greek world to express the munificence or benefactions of emperors or provincial governors (χάρις), St. Paul sublimated it with reference to the mercy of God in salvation.

On the human side the correlative here was humility. "I am the least of the apostles," he writes, "unworthy to be called an apostle, because I persecuted the Church of God. But by the grace of God I am what I am, and His grace towards me was not ineffectual. I have laboured", he goes on, "above them all, yet not I, but the grace of God which is with me" (1 Cor. xv. 9–10). We note in passing: *not I, but the grace of God*. It was not merely that God had not rejected Saul. God had stooped to his *earth-level*, as he lay prone and helpless on the Damascus road, and had shaped an apostle out of him. Henceforth, St. Paul will take all religion first to this earth-level that, as grace, it may do its radical work.

With this emphasis on the primacy of grace we must associate the fact that the manifestation of God to St. Paul was a manifestation of

His "righteousness": compare Rom. iii. 21, νυνὶ δὲ χωρὶς νόμου δικαιοσύνη Θεοῦ πεφανέρωται, and i. 17 where, after asserting that the power of God to effect salvation is the content of the gospel, St. Paul explains by saying: δικαιοσύνη γὰρ Θεοῦ ἐν αὐτῷ ἀποκαλύπτεται ἐκ πίστεως εἰς πίστιν. No grace could be real for sinful man, and no power of God could be effective for "salvation" which did not reveal the *righteousness* of God as the source and power of the Christian redemption. Therefore it was not only the grace or mercy of God that stooped to St. Paul in his conversion experience, but God's righteousness, and therefore the man who says "it is by the grace of God that I am what I am" can also say that his supreme aim henceforth is ἵνα Χριστὸν κερδήσω καὶ εὑρεθῶ ἐν αὐτῷ, μὴ ἔχων ἐμὴν δικαιοσύνην τὴν ἐκ νόμου, ἀλλὰ τὴν διὰ πίστεως Χριστοῦ, τὴν ἐκ Θεοῦ δικαιοσύνην ἐπὶ τῇ πίστει, τοῦ γνῶναι αὐτόν etc. (Phil. iii. 9 f.).

(b) The mediator of this grace was *Jesus Christ*, in whose face, once unlooked at, the man now saw "the light of the knowledge of the glory of God". The person of Christ, therefore, now fills for him the whole sphere of God and of heavenly truth and evidence. In Him God has stooped to us, therefore in Him alone we rise to God. As all forgiveness, wisdom, and power from God are through the Mediator, so all thanksgiving, confession, and prayer are to be addressed to God "through" Him. Just, then, as St. Paul can say, "Not I, but the grace of God", so he can also say, "*Not I, but Christ liveth in me*" (Gal. ii. 20). In this manner he makes the Mediatorship of Jesus *the condition and foundation of his whole existence*. St. Paul's theology and life alike will, accordingly, start not from any general truths respecting God and man, but from the glory imaged in the face of Christ.

(c) The Christ, who is the Mediator, is the *Crucified*. Here had lain the offence, the "scandal", the insurmountable objection to the Nazarene position in the eyes of the persecutor. That one who had borne the curse of the Law should be the Messiah of God! Impossible! But now the Cross which had been the scandal, becomes the luminous and fascinating centre of all interest for the convert. "Be it never for me to glory," he writes, "except in the Cross of our Lord Jesus Christ" (Gal. vi. 14). "He died for our sins," said the Nazarenes. St. Paul will make the Cross the focal-point of all theological reality, through which will pass all his axes and co-ordinates in making his graph of divine-human relations. "Become a curse (κατάρα) for us" (Gal. iii. 13), "set forth as an 'expiation' (ἱλαστήριον) for us" (Rom. iii. 25, "made to be 'sin', an '*asham* for us" (2 Cor. v. 21), in how many ways St. Paul will seek to fix the theological significance, and to take the theological measure of this paradox in the manifestation of God!

(d) The Christ who was crucified is the *Risen One.* If so, it is the *New Creation* that stands revealed. And all God's gifts in Christ are gifts of the New Creation. Because Christ is risen in the New Creation, then all the things the gospel offers are of the New Creation: Justification (δικαιοσύνη, (νυνὶ δέ)) (Rom. iii. 21) (now for the first time made possible for man with God), the lifting away of the guilt of sin (οὐδὲν κατάκριμα, (νῦν), Rom. viii. 1), sonship to God (υἱοθεσία), freedom, the Spirit, peace with God (εἰρήνη πρὸς τὸν Θεόν) —these gifts which Judaism had not known, because they all belonged to the *Eschaton*, the Age to Come, were now thrown open to mankind with the Resurrection of Jesus. And God is the God of the Resurrection, the gospel is the gospel of the Resurrection, the Church of Jesus is the Church of the Resurrection, and the Christian life is the life of the Resurrection.

In this analysis we have passed beyond the immediate Manifestation of God in Christ which came to St. Paul, and launched upon the substance of the theological conclusions which he drew from it. Once again, let us look at *the primary vision.* It is *the manifestation of God in, and through, His own nature.* There is a most illuminating passage in the treatise of Philo of Alexandria known as *Allegories of the Laws*, Book III, 99 ff., in which the Jewish theologian, after speaking of those who think to derive the knowledge of God from His works in creation, points out that there is "a more perfect and more purified intelligence (νοῦς) which has been initiated in the great mysteries and which does not look for God in nature, but raising the eyes beyond, and above, created substance, seeks the manifestation of God *in Himself*". And citing Moses' prayer to God, "I beseech Thee, show me thy self" (Exod. xxxiii. 13), Philo explains it as meaning: "I would not that thou shouldest manifest Thyself to me through heaven or earth or water or air or any thing of a created kind, nor would I see Thy form reflected (μηδὲ κατοπτρισαίμην) in anything save in Thee, O God!" The verb "see Thee reflected" which is here used is the one St. Paul employs in the great word (2 Cor. iii. 18): "We all, with unveiled face, beholding the glory of the Lord in reflection (κατοπτριζόμενοι), are being changed (μεταμορφούμεθα) into the same likeness." St. Paul means that we see God reflected in Christ, who is His image and therefore of His own nature, and therein lies the transforming power of Christianity. *We see God in Himself.*

(3) We must now pass to the vital practical consequences as regards the form of the *Christian Life,* which spring from St. Paul's primary engagement with the revelation of God in Christ. With the Resurrection of Christ has come the New Creation. Therefore the life of religious response to Christ is the life of the New Creation. He, the first-born from the dead, summons to membership in a new humanity, and is the Head of this renewed humanity, the Church. Hitherto, St. Paul teaches, we have belonged to the old humanity, the world-order of sin and death. We have been *in* Adam (ἐν τῷ 'Αδαμ), *in* the flesh (ἐν σαρκί) and subject to its evil will, *in* or under law (ἐν νόμῳ) and therefore under condemnation. But now through the Resurrection of Christ we are offered life *in* Christ (ἐν Χριστῷ), *in* the Spirit (ἐν πνεύματι), and *in* or under grace (ὑπὸ χάριν). In other words, we are called to the life of the *New Creation.* Yet not in the sense of envisaging a purely future goal, but—and this is of supreme importance for understanding the Pauline expression of Christianity—in the sense that we already possess through Christ the gifts of the World to Come. We already have Christ as our *Righteousness,* we have peace with God and access to *grace,* and we have the *hope* of the *glory* of God (Rom. v. 1–2). But, until the *final* glory of God is revealed, we live by faith in an interim-period, in which the old Adam and the new, the flesh and the Spirit, the law and grace contend and overlap not only in the world but also in the soul of the Christian (Rom. viii. 1–11). In this connection *Romans viii* is perhaps the most moving and colourful picture of life in the Age of Grace which has come down to us. The Apostle describes it as a life of tension (Rom. viii. 1–11), of moral obligation (18–19), of suffering and defeat (18–25), but also as a life in which we have the assistance of the Holy Spirit (26–8) and are supported by assurances of the unalterableness of God's purpose for us and of His inalienable love (29–39). Yet St. Paul will give us the *morphology* of the life "in Christ"—compare Gal. iv. 19 μέχρις οὗ μορφωθῇ Χριστὸς ἐν ὑμῖν—in even more precise terms.

For this man was one who in earlier days, apparently, had insisted on bringing the whole Law of God to the test of his personal experience. Now by an equal compulsion he insists that all the mighty acts of God in redemption shall fulfil and reproduce themselves in the Christian. These mighty acts of God are the Incarnation, Death and Resurrection of the Son of God. In these acts eternity has broken into time. St. Paul sees in these acts the pattern of the New Creation. On this showing, the manifestation of God in Christ is a *mystery* in which the redeemed participate. All the things that happened to Christ have their counterpart in the Christian experience. Did the Son of God take our nature and *live* in the flesh a human life? St. Paul will draw the consequence that in Christianity it is not we who live, but Christ who lives in us (Gal. ii. 20; Phil. i. 21), and in the famous passage (Phil. ii. 5 ff.) which begins: "Let this mind be in you which was also in Christ Jesus," he will give us the ethos of that life. Again, did the Son of God *die* for us upon the Cross? St. Paul will make it plain that this involves our dying in Christ to sin and self. Romans vi is the great exposition of this, but compare also Gal. ii. 20—Χριστῷ συνεσταύρωμαι—also Gal. vi. 14 and Col. iii. 3. In *baptism*, which is the formal reproduction (ὁμοίωμα) of the death of Christ, the Christian is incorporated (σύμφυτος) with the Redeemer (Rom. vi. 5–6). St. Paul can speak of himself as συμμορφιζόμενος τῷ θανάτῳ αὐτοῦ (Phil. iii. 9–10). Again, Is Christ *risen*? Here St. Paul will remind us that the reverse side of the ὁμοίωμα of baptism is the resurrection of the Christian in newness of life. The union effected with Christ by baptism is union with Him in His Resurrection (καὶ τῆς ἀναστάσεως, Rom. vi. 5). He says also in Phil. iii. 10, that the goal of Christian existence, is γνῶναι αὐτὸν καὶ τὴν δύναμιν τῆς ἀναστάσεως αὐτοῦ. Finally, is Christ *ascended*? Then the Christian also must "seek the things that are above, where the Christ is seated at the right hand of God" (Col. iii. 1–2). Cf. also Eph. i. 3; ii. 6. These passages combine to show how very concrete in its structure is the Pauline conception of the life ἐν Χριστῷ. The Christian shares with the Redeemer:

(i) Life,
(ii) Death,
(iii) Resurrection,
(iv) Ascension.

Because here (through the Manifestation of God in Christ) the Christian enters into the experience of the Redeemer, Christianity may be said to be the supreme example of a mystery-religion.

Yet how realistic and how practical this life ἐν Χριστῷ is! Here the most revealing of all documents are the two *Corinthian Epistles*. In these two letters the Apostle has to make it clear to his converts that all Christian qualities and, above all, the qualities of

(i) Knowledge, or Wisdom,
(ii) Righteousness,

(iii) Freedom,
(iv) Spirituality,

have and retain their Christian character and validity only as they are held and exercised *within the sphere of communion with the Crucified.*

The Corinthian Christians, many or most of whom had been drawn from the Greek proletariat, had apparently in a large number of cases received the Gospel as a sort of *philosophy* or "gnosis", and had proceeded like the philosophical schools to divide up into wrangling and self-opinionated groups which threatened the unity of the Church. A similar consequence followed from an insistence on Christian *liberty* in certain quarters which took no account at all of the scruples of weaker brethren who felt their souls endangered by any relaxation of the Christian rules governing association with pagan religious rites. Again, there was a prevailing tendency to interpret *spirituality* only in terms of abnormal and ecstatic phenomena, such as were familiar to the Corinthians in the mystery-cults. In 1 Corinthians we find St. Paul dealing patiently and in succession with these aberrations and in every case applying as the test the principle that the Christian must maintain communion with the Crucified. He it is who had been made "wisdom to us from God" (1 Cor. i. 30). He alone represents to us "the power of God", and He alone brings to us "philosophy from God" (1 Cor. i. 22–3). As regards *gnosis*, "gnosis", he says, "inflates, but love builds up" (1 Cor. viii. 1). While, therefore, he accepts in principle the contention that "all things are lawful" for the Christian (πάντα μοι ἔξεστιν, 1 Cor. vi. 12, etc.), he subordinates its exercise at every point to the higher demand of *love*, which is the sharing of the fortunes of Christ and the gospel (1 Cor. ix. 12, 21–3). Lastly, as regards spirituality, St. Paul leads off from the fact that the one criterion of the Spirit is the confession of Jesus as Lord (1 Cor. xii. 3). Whereas the Corinthians think a man is spiritual "in proportion as he is out of his natural mind," St. Paul makes love the supreme expression of the Spirit, the way superlative (1 Cor. xii. 31; xiii).

(4) Such in outline is the form of the Christian life according to Paul, the life ἐν Χριστῷ. As on the Damascus road grace had stooped to him on his earth-level, and opened to him a new life, so St. Paul takes the ἐν Χριστῷ expression of the Christian's calling, and relates it to the humblest duties and circumstances of common, every-day existence. The day when Christ took him renews itself again in every constitutive moment of his life.

There remain some other aspects of the ἐν Χριστῷ existence on which we have not touched. For example, there is the *ontological* aspect, under which Christ is preached and received as "the first-born of all creation, since in Him all things were created" (Col. i. 15). This ontological aspect, linking the life of the New Creation with the very foundation and structure of cosmic reality may be reserved for discussion when the Johannine literature comes before us. But a closing word should be said about the *sacramental* aspect of all life ἐν Χριστῷ. We have spoken of Baptism as the ὁμοίωμα, that is, the sacramental representation of Christ's Death and Resurrection. As the Christian life begins in a sacrament, so it is sacramentally sustained and developed. "The cup of blessing which we bless, is it not a participation in the blood of Christ? The bread which we break, is it not a participation in the body of Christ?" (1 Cor. x. 16.) The sacraments remind us that, in the present stage of Christian life, in which the New Creation has begun, but is not yet present in all its fullness, the gifts of God in Christ are received only proleptically through sacrament, and that must continue to be so until faith shall pass into sight. But the sacraments also remind us of the *givenness* of the life to which we are called under the present order of grace. Christ is not only the ground of our faith, and the sphere in which it operates, but He is the *substance* on which it feeds.

IV

The Pilgrimage of Faith in 1 *Peter and Hebrews*

The New Testament writings which now fall to be considered sound a common note which, despite the colour-variations of the compositions into which it enters, justifies the taking of these writings together. This common note, the C major of the two expositions, is that the Christian life is essentially the call and the impulsion to seek a divine ultimate event not yet disclosed to our eyes.

Let there be, however, no misunderstanding in this matter. *All* New Testament Christianity is borne or drawn forward to an ultimate End variously described as "the Kingdom come in power" (Mark ix. 1), "the consummation (συντέλεια) of the age" (Matt. xxiv. 3), or "the regeneration" (παλιγγενεσία, Matt. xix. 28). All of these are bound up with the coming of Christ in glory (παρουσία). While the New Creation has made its advent in Jesus, it has not yet revealed the fullness of its nature. That fullness waits over. The entrance into time of God's eternal purpose of redemption has taken place in the Incarnation of the Son of God and has inaugurated the *Age of Grace*, but with the exaltation of the Redeemer to the right hand of God the further course of that purpose has receded beyond our vision, so that we walk by faith and not by sight. Thus the Age of Grace awaits the *Age of Glory*, and Christian life is a *pilgrimage*. The New Creation is here, and yet it is not here. It is now, and yet it is not now. Faith swings between two poles of tension. There arises a dialectic of faith.

Thus in the *Gospels*, while heaven opens over Jesus at His baptism, and it is signified to Him that He is the Messiah—Son of God, the bearer of the Spirit (Mark i. 10–11)—and while in the strength of this revelation He proclaims the immediate advent of God's reign, and summons His followers to the life of the New Creation (Mark ii. 19–22), we find Him nevertheless saying: "I came to cast fire on the earth, and how I would it were already kindled, but I have a *baptism* to be baptized with, and how embarrassed I am until it is accomplished" (τελεσθῇ, Luke xii. 49–50). Evidently the "fire" with which John said the Messiah would baptize (Matt. iii. 11; Luke iii. 16) had not yet been ignited, nor His "baptism" completed. The consummation of the work of Jesus, therefore, is held up to a future date. Further, in many of His *parables* the situation of His followers seems to be this, that, though called already into the Kingdom of God and given talents and gifts to exercise (Age of Grace), they must yet expect a judgement of the returning Son of Man on their works (Age of Glory). This is most important. Christian life in the Gospels is a life in which we expect and go forward to an ultimate decisive crisis, albeit under the present sign and power of the New Creation.

Similarly *St. Paul*, with all his sense of present possession and joy in the Christian life, can say: "It is not that I have already obtained (ἔλαβον) or have already been perfected (τετελείωμαι). . . . Brethren, I do not consider that I have yet attained, but one thing I do, forgetting what lies behind, and stretching forward to what lies in front (τοῖς ἔμπροσθεν ἐπεκτεινόμενος) I keep pressing towards the goal for the prize of the high calling (τῆς ἄνω κλήσεως) of God in Christ Jesus" (Phil. iii. 12–14). Here too is a sense of distance in the Christian perspective. So in a great passage he contrasts the sufferings of the present time (τοῦ νῦν καιροῦ) with the glory (δόξα) yet to be revealed to us, and he links our present sense of deficiency with the passionate longing (ἀποκαραδοκία) of all creation for the final unveiling (ἀποκάλυψις) of "the sons of God" (Rom. viii. 18–25). He can speak of our real commonwealth (τὸ πολίτευμα ἡμῶν) as in heaven, "from which we await a Saviour to transform the body of our humiliation (ταπεινώσεως) into the likeness of the body of His glory" (Phil. iii. 20). The sense that the life of faith is a pilgrimage is thus writ large over the whole New Testament.

If nevertheless we select 1 *Peter* and *Hebrews* for particular consideration under this head, it is because of the high relative prominence of the idea in these two documents. In the *Epistle to the Hebrews* there is nothing of that sense of present repose and of peace and joy in believing, that mystical sense of faith-union with the Redeemer which is the core of the Pauline norm of life. Rather is faith carried past every intermediate stage and condition of life in grace towards a Christ who, *though He was made historically one with us on earth, is now "within the veil"* (Heb. viii. 1 ff.), where He carries on His work on our behalf. And Christians are runners in a race (ἀγών, Heb. xii. 1–2) which lies before them, in which they "look away" or look ahead (ἀφορῶντες) to a Jesus who, as He has been the pioneer or inaugurator of faith (ἀρχηγός), must also be its consummator. Similarly in *1 Peter* the readers are reminded from the beginning that the New Creation is pointed towards the hope of "an inheritance incorruptible and undefiled (1 Pet. i. 3–4), unfading", which is held over for them in heaven, and the writer speaks of the present Christian life as "the time of your exile (τὸν τῆς παροικίας ὑμῶν χρόνον, 1 Pet. i. 17)". It is to be remembered that both in 1 Peter and in Hebrews the communities addressed stood under the near threat of *persecution*, which may account for the prominence given to this particular aspect of the Christian life.

Before we pass to the two Epistles, a word should be said about the conception of the ultimate *End* towards which the faith of the New Testament moves. Attention to this is the more necessary because a great deal is heard in our day about "Realized Eschatology", and in some quarters it is argued that the Christian religion would be the better for the abandonment of all futurist hopes of an *apocalyptic* kind. It is pointed out rightly that the Age of Grace, introduced by Jesus, already fulfils the prophetic and apocalyptic hopes of the Old Testament dispensation. Such was the mind of Jesus and of His Apostles (cf. Matt. xiii. 16–17; Luke x. 23–4, xxiv. 26–7; Acts ii. 16 ff.; 1 Pet. i. 11–12, etc.). But Jesus did not say that *everything* in the apocalyptic hope had already come to pass. He who spoke of Himself and His disciples as already celebrating the Messianic banquet on earth (Mark ii. 19) spoke also of "that day" when He would keep the feast anew in the Kingdom of God (Mark xiv. 25; Luke xxii. 16). He who spoke of the "Son of Man" as having already come on earth spoke also, according to the Synoptic tradition, of the Son of Man as coming after death, at the end of time. In the light of this New Testament tradition it will not do to regard the apocalyptic element in Christianity as a mere hang-over from Judaism. It is true that the coming of Christ on earth fulfils the Old Testament vision of the future. It brings the Reign of God, righteousness, the Spirit, sonship to God and atonement for sin. Nevertheless by the very nature of these gifts it creates the hope of a fuller Glory lying beyond.

In this connection may I take a mathematical illustration? There are certain geometrical curves which we call the parabola and the hyperbola. It belongs to the nature of these curves that they have two *foci*, but that only one of them comes within the plane of our observation. The other *focus*, through the curve's recession, lies at infinity. Yet, given the mathematical understanding of the nature of the curve, the existence of that other *focus* is certain, and its relations are definable. So, if we may pass to the theological realm, we may say that God's action in redemption can be described as eternity *intersecting* our plane of history. The visible *focus* is *the Incarnation of Christ,* who draws round Him a company of believers which becomes the body of Christ, the Church. But by His exaltation Christ passes again beyond our bourne of sight. As the writer to the Hebrews puts it, He has entered "within the Veil". Yet by the very nature of the New Creation which He came to bring, He Himself in the days of His flesh was impelled, and His followers after Him were impelled, to look forward to *a greater glory,* of which He is again the centre. "Christ, offered once for the bearing of the sins of many, will", says the writer to the Hebrews, "appear a second time (ἐκ δευτέρου . . . ὀφθήσεται), not to deal with sin, but for the redemption (εἰς σωτηρίαν) of His waiting people" (Heb. ix. 28). The New Creation, then, is a present fact of faith, but a fact that by its very character implies the Parousia. Consequently it will not do to speak of a "Realized Eschatology" in a sense which excludes that final consummation. What the true relation of present and future in this connection is is very simply, and very wonderfully stated in the words: "Beloved, we are now children of God, and it has not yet been made apparent what we shall be, but we know that when He is revealed, we shall be like Him, for we shall see Him as He is" (1 John iii. 2).

The First Epistle of Peter

It would appear from hints given in the letter that the persons addressed—the scattered Christians in Pontus, Galatia, Cappadocia, Asia and Bithynia—were regarded by the writer as in imminent danger of *persecution* for their faith. "Do not be alienated", he writes, "by the fiery ordeal which comes on you to try you, as though it was some alien thing that was befalling you, but rejoice in so far as you share the sufferings of the Christ, that at the revelation of His glory also (ἐν τῇ ἀποκαλύψει τῆς δόξης αὐτοῦ) you may rejoice and be glad" (1 Pet. iv. 12–13). Whether this necessity of suffering is merely dogmatically asserted by the writer or rests on actual knowledge of contemporary events in these provinces of Asia cannot perhaps be made out from the evidence. The apprehension is present to the writer's mind, however, and it sets the keynote for the Epistle. It finds expression even in those sections which incorporate instructions to neophytes before or after their baptism (cf. ii. 1–2, 9–17; iii. 13–17; iv. 1–5, 14–19).

(1) *The Manifestation of God.* This is through the revelation to Christians of *the Risen Lord*, which gives the resultant Christian life a doxological character (εὐλογητὸς ὁ Θεός, i. 3). By this numinous manifestation the Father has brought us into *the New Creation* (ἀναγεννήσας ἡμᾶς), and therefore the neophytes addressed on the occasion of their baptism are called "newborn children" (ἀρτιγέννητα βρέφη, ii. 1). But it is interesting that from the first words of the letter onwards this New Creation is said to be "to a living *hope*", and this hope lies towards "an inheritance incorruptible and undefiled and unfading" (i. 4), therefore to a state of existence surpassing all that is offered in the present age of Grace. This life towards which the Christians addressed in the letter are to keep their faith directed is at present "kept in heaven" pending "the last time" (i. 4–5), and the assurance is given that in the maintenance of their faith they are under the protection of the power of God, as well they need to be. For this interim-existence is one of joy, but it is also one of pain because of the various "trials" which beset the Christian. These have, indeed, a precious purpose, when life is regarded, as the writer says it should be, as a *probation* for the perfect salvation. This can only come "at

the revelation of Jesus Christ", whom, meantime, the converts love though He is hid from their eyes (i. 6–9). Here we have the note which runs through the whole exposition. Life is a probation. It has acquired that character through the revelation to us in Christ of a greater *life* for which we long, and which by God's grace shall be the inheritance of the faithful at the End. Even in this present provisional era the results of faith are of positive value, representing as they do the New Creation which Christ by His example and His passion has inspired.

Thus through the Resurrection of Jesus Christ God has "called us out of darkness into His marvellous *light*" (ii. 9). The manifestation has produced the *regeneration* of our souls, baptism being the inaugurating sacrament of salvation (iii. 21), and we being "re-created (ἀναγεγεννημένοι), not of mortal but of immortal seed, through the living and abiding word (λόγου) of God" (i. 23). Both time and eternity, therefore, interblend in Christian life, both a human element and a divine. Christians are reminded that in this life of response to the *resurrection* of Christ they are "strangers and sojourners" in the world. They must abstain from the passions of the flesh (ii. 11). At the same time they must by the nature of their calling live an exemplary life in all social and public relations (ii. 11–12, 13–17; iii. 13–17; v. 6–10).

(2) Passing to the *theological* aspects of the Manifestation of God in Christ, we may say that the writer is deeply conscious that the Christian salvation is both the *fulfilment* of the inspired intuitions of the prophetic religion of the Old Testament and the *refutation* of the whole construction which Judaism had placed upon that religion. Thus, to take the former of these points, he writes as follows: "Concerning this salvation, the prophets who prophesied of the grace that was to be yours made very searching inquiry, seeking to discover to what person or to what period of time the Spirit of Christ within them pointed when witnessing in advance to the sufferings of Christ and to the glories which were to follow (τὰς μετὰ ταῦτα δόξας). And it was revealed to them that the service they were rendering was not to themselves but to you. It had to do with those things which have now been declared to you by those who preached the gospel through the Holy Spirit sent from Heaven. These are matters into which angels desire to look" (i. 10–12). It may be assumed that, in speaking of this prophetic concern, the writer was thinking of such Old Testament passages as Isaiah 53. That chapter testifies to problems which have only received their answer now in the Resurrection of Christ. As for

the other point, the reversal of Judaism, the writer, like all the apostolic apologists for Christianity, reminds the readers that Christ, the stone which the temple-builders rejected, has been made by God's grace the "corner-stone" of the Church (ii. 4–10).

It is to be noticed, however, that this writer who looks so consistently to the Resurrection of Christ, and behind the Resurrection sees the *sufferings* which give it its weight of theological significance, never, like St. Paul, thinks of Christ's Death and Resurrection as acts which are to be reproduced in the Christian. There is nothing in him of St. Paul's Christ-mysticism. What he stresses is rather the *objective* impact of Christ's Spirit and example on our lives.

(3) So we come to the "Via Crucis". No writing in the New Testament bears more consistent or eloquent witness than 1 Peter to the character-shaping influence of the love and passion of the Redeemer. This theme stands in relation both to the Christian attitude under persecution and to the duty (the *noblesse oblige*) which the Christian owes to society. Under both aspects his conduct must show that he is only "a stranger and sojourner" in the present world (i. 11–12). Examples are too numerous to be quoted, but we may note the following. Enjoining patience under provocation, the writer says: "It was to this you were called, because Christ also suffered for you, leaving you an *example* (ὑμῖν ὑπολιμπάνων ὑπογραμμόν) that you should follow in His steps (τοῖς ἴχνεσιν αὐτοῦ). He committed no sin. . . . When reviled, He did not revile in return. . . . He Himself bore our sins in His body on the tree . . . by His disfiguration you were healed" (ii. 21–4). "You must in your hearts reverence Christ as the Lord. You must be ready always to give an answer to anyone who calls you to account for the hope within you, yet with gentleness and reverence, maintaining a clear conscience. . . . For Christ has died for sins once for all, the just for the unjust, that He might bring us to God" (iii. 15–18). "As therefore Christ suffered for us in the flesh, arm yourselves with the same thought. . . . The time that is past has been ample enough for doing what the Gentiles like to do" (iv. 1, 3). For the end (τὸ τέλος) of the world has drawn near (iv. 7). "If you are reproached for the name of Christ, blessed are you, for the spirit of glory and of God rests upon you" (iv. 14). In no book of the New Testament does the Christian life as the *Imitatio Christi* come to clearer and more passionate expression.

The Epistle to the Hebrews

Very different in some ways from 1 Peter, though very closely related in other ways, is the anonymous writing which has come down to us as the Epistle to the Hebrews. Here also the Christian life is a journey, a march begun in God. "It is indeed the very summit or culminating point of the writer's argument" (κεφάλαιον ἐπὶ τοῖς λεγομένοις, Heb. viii. 1), "that the Christ who is our High Priest with God has passed through the heavens, and is *within the veil.* He has carried with Him the *anchor* to which our souls and all our hopes are made fast, and has thus transported the gravity-centre of our lives, as Christians, to the supernal world." Christian life is in this Epistle "a tense, all-out concentration of hope" directed to a transcendent and ultra-mundane goal. It is the attainment through Christ of a heavenly country (πατρίς), a city of God which has foundations. Indeed the writer's very definition of *faith* is that it is "a firm persuasion regarding the objects of our hope" (ἐλπιζομένων ὑπόστασις) "a conviction (ἔλεγχος) of the reality of the invisible world" (Heb. xi. 1). But this supra-mundane outlook is not conceived on idealistic lines, though the writer is well acquainted with the Platonic philosophy. He makes great use of Platonic ideas in chapters viii–x of the Epistle to bring out the counterpoint of heavenly substance and earthly shadow. But the real basis of his conception is the Jewish apocalyptic vision of the Age to Come. For the writer of this Epistle the promise of God is bound up with the ultimate event of *the Last Advent* of Christ.

> For yet, in ever, ever so short a time, He who comes will come. He will linger no more (Heb. x. 37).

A word should be said about the purpose and destination of this mysterious Epistle. Many theories have been advanced, but I may be permitted to assume the results of a study of the book which I have published.[1] In my view the Epistle was addressed to a minority group within the Church at Rome which was in danger, if not of falling back to Judaism, at least of calling a halt to its progress in the Christian life. For the writer of the Epistle the very life of Christianity depends upon the reference of everything in it, thought and practice alike, to the *World to Come.* It is possible that the minority group at Rome, under the threat of persecution or social disfavour, was tempted to

[1] W. Manson, *The Epistle to the Hebrews* (London, 1951).

look backwards, to seek cover under the *religio licita* of Judaism, and in subtle ways to be drawn under the spell of its ritual and ceremonial practices. This temptation was the greater because at Rome, more than at other centres, Christianity appears to have grown up within the Synagogue. To the writer of Hebrews this tendency signified a deadly danger to the soul. He speaks of it as a "drifting" from the course, a "falling away", or "crucifying" of the Lord afresh, a resiling into perdition (ὑποστολὴ εἰς ἀπώλειαν). He points out that with Christ has come the revocation of the cultus and law of Judaism, and the replacement of its priesthood by the ministry of Jesus in the heavenly sanctuary. And two words in particular would linger in the readers' minds because of their relevance to the group's situation: (a) Jesus "for the sake of the joy that was set before Him endured the Cross, disregarding its shame" (xii. 2), and (b) "Jesus, in order to consecrate the People through His own blood, suffered outside the gate" (xiii. 12). Hence it is for us, the writer urges, to "go out to Him beyond the camp, bearing the reproach which He bore" (xiii. 13).

The lesson here inculcated is of extreme importance to the Church at the present day. The Church is always under the danger of failing to maintain itself under an adequate sense of God's final purpose for it. There is a tendency to hark back to the past, to insist on historical origins, to build on the foundations and achievements of other days, and to forget the judgement of God on us at this moment. But "the Church stands under the sign not only of the Beginning but of the End". "I am the Alpha and the Omega, says the Lord God, who is and who was and who is to come, the Almighty" (Rev. i. 8). We cannot rest where we are. "We have to turn towards the End, towards the ultimate Fulness of the Church, towards the Return of the Lord." The Church has its pilgrimage.

(1) *The Manifestation of God.* In the Prologue to the Epistle it is stated that the *Son of God*, through whom the God of revelation has spoken to us us "in these last days", "reflects the glory of God and bears the very stamp of his nature" (i. 1–3). Yet, interestingly enough, the primary element in the writer's vision is not the Resurrection or glorified life of Christ, but *His incarnate life* of humiliation and suffering by which He became qualified to be our High Priest with God. With this emphasis on the Incarnate life we may connect the following rather remarkable features of the Epistle: (a) the almost complete absence of reference to the *Resurrection* of Jesus (an exception is xiii. 20, cf. vii. 16); (b) the comparative infrequency of references to the

Holy Spirit (but see ii. 4, vi. 4, and the wonderful statement in ix. 14); and (c) the total omission of anything corresponding to St. Paul's "in Christ" conception of life. All these features are best explained if we consider (1) the very central and impressive significance which the Incarnate life of Jesus has for the writer, forming as it does the presentation-point of the divine revelation of grace; (2) the fact that Jesus, after being qualified by His suffering and death to be our High Priest, passes at once to the presence of God to present His oblation and intercession for us; (3) the persuasion of the writer that Christ, thus exalted, is Lord of the World to Come, and calls us to inheritance in that world, therefore to a life that leaves no place for contentment with present attainments, even in the things of the Spirit.

Certainly the emphasis of the writer on the incarnate life of Jesus, and the radicality of his interpretation of it (see the great passages ii. 5–18 and v. 7–10) are very remarkable, and carry his interpretation of Christianity very close to that which we find in the Synoptic Gospels. In ii. 8–9 we read that "we do not yet see everything in subjection" to Jesus, i.e. the vision from which we *start* is not of the heavenly and triumphant Lord, "but we see Jesus, who for a little while was made lower than the angels, crowned with glory and honour for the suffering (διὰ τὸ πάθημα) of death". The glory, the essential self-evidence of God in Christ, is to be seen first in His earthly humiliation. The writer, here and elsewhere (cf. iii. 1, "Consider Jesus") calls us to the contemplation of Jesus as one whose lowliness and suffering not only qualified Him to be our High Priest with God, but have raised Him above the angels, so that He is Lord of all coming history, *Lord of the World to Come.*

Hence the trans-mundane and supernal character of the Christian calling. "We share in Christ, if only we hold our first confidence firm to the End" (iii. 14). "Let us fear lest, a promise being left us of entering into His rest, any one of you should be judged not to have reached it" (iv. 1). The writer speaks of the duty of going on to "perfection" (ἐπὶ τὴν τελειότητα φερώμεθα), which means here the completion of their pilgrimage (vi. 1). Above all, he pictures Jesus as having, when He passed within the veil, carried the anchor of our hope with Him (vi. 19–20). All this, and more in the same strain, is said to the minority group at Rome, in order to spur them to resume their journey to the city, whose builder and maker is God.

(2) Only a word or two can be added about the *theology* of the Epistle. But it is interesting that the author is found reflecting on the

deep divine meaning of the Christ-manifestation, and is drawn into a number of profound theological observations. One of these is the remarkable statement in ii. 10 where, after speaking of the predestination of the Son of God to suffering, he comments on the divine *appropriateness* of it all: "It was fitting", he says, "that He, for whom and through whom the whole of things exists, should in the act of bringing many sons to glory, perfect by suffering the Pioneer of their salvation." This is the only passage in the New Testament to speak of what was proper for God to do. What was the writer's standard of reference here? Was it antecedent religious revelation, such as the knowledge of God imparted to prophets like Jeremiah or Hosea? More likely the writer is starting from the *self-evidence* of the Incarnation and Passion of Jesus Himself. He had not known, and no one had known, what the character of God in His grace demanded, until the life and sacrifice of Jesus showed it, and now he knows that this manifestation in Jesus is of *the very structure and essence of the world.* A similar statement is the one in ii. 17 that "*obligation* was upon Him" —it is Jesus who is referred to—"to become in every way assimilated to His brethren". Again in vii. 26 we read that "it was fitting that we should have a High Priest such as this", fitting, that is, in respect of our guilt and weakness. In the same strain the writer says in ix. 14 that Christ "through the Eternal Spirit offered Himself to God". The expression διὰ πνεύματος αἰωνίου means that the death of Jesus "was no mere historical accident, but expressed the very nature of the eternal Mind and World". *Eternity* was in the act, and therefore "time cannot impair or devaluate its significance".

The supreme contribution of the Epistle in a theological viewpoint is its development, starting from Psalm cx. 4, of the priestly aspect of the atoning sacrifice of Christ. It results from this that the heart of the Christian religion lies in this eternally mediated access of the sinner to God (iv. 14–16). The *priesthood of the Redeemer* is set out from many angles. He is Priest by predestination and Priest by incarnate qualification. He is Priest of the Resurrection "in virtue of an indissoluble life" (κατὰ δύναμιν ζωῆς ἀκαταλύτου, vii. 16). He is Priest in the Heavenly Sanctuary and Mediator of the New Covenant; He is Priest through the Eternal Spirit. And the character of the pilgrimage-life is reflected in, and sustained by, the thus continually mediated approach of the Christian soul to God.

(3) The Christian *way of life*, which the Epistle inculcates, has been already sufficiently indicated. It is governed by *the call to "Go out!"*,

the call which was at the heart of God's election of Israel, and which is now renewed in Christ who "Suffered without the gate" (xiii. 12). Therefore the word to these halting Christians at Rome is to "go forth to Jesus outside the camp", leaving behind all the advantages of the ancient, buttressed, privileged and legally protected religion of Judaism, and accepting whatever earthly loss and suffering that course may involve. Go out! Go on! Eyes forward! Yet not without mark and sign to show the way. "Hath He marks to lead me to Him, if He be my guide?" Yes. That is all! But that is everything. The past must give way to the future, the Church of the past to the Church of the future, the beginning to the ending, time to eternity, history to God.

V

Johannine Fellowship with the Father and the Son

It will be helpful to begin our study of the Johannine writings with two observations.

(1) It is characteristic of these writings, both the First Epistle and the Gospel, that the relation established by faith between the Christian and the Son of God is taken back to a ground within the life of God Himself. In other words, that *sharing* of life with Jesus Christ which forms the essence of Christianity both in its individual and in its communal expression is a sharing in the *eternal life* which the Son had with the Father before the world was. It accords with this conception that both Epistle and Gospel open with theological prefaces in which the content of revelation is carried back to a date at, or preceding Creation (ἦν ἀπ' ἀρχῆς, 1 John i. 1; ἐν ἀρχῇ ἦν, John i. 1).

In the Epistle the manifested divine reality is defined as the eternal life which was with the Father (πρὸς τὸν πατέρα, 1 John i. 2), and the resulting gift to the Church on earth is *fellowship* (κοινωνία, 1 John i. 3) with the Father (μετὰ τοῦ πατρός) and with His Son Jesus Christ. The same high ridge of thought runs through and through the pages of the Johannine Gospel. To take only one example: Jesus says to His disciples, "If a man loves me, he will keep my word, and my Father will love him, and *we* will come to him (πρὸς αὐτόν) and make our home with him (μονὴν παρ'αὐτῷ ποιησόμεθα, John xiv. 23). This amazing *sublimation* of Christian existence to a share in the *koinonia* subsisting between the Father and the Son in the unity of the Godhead helps in turn to explain another characteristic of the Johannine books.

(2) In the Johannine books, though less in the Epistle than in the

Gospel, the tension or polarity which exists elsewhere in the New Testament between the ideas of the Christ with or within us and the Christ on high, between the present age of Grace and the future age of Glory, is transcended, or at any rate greatly reduced, so that apocalyptic language practically disappears. From the Johannine standpoint the world-darkness is passing (παράγεται) and the true light is now shining (ἤδη φαίνει, 1 John ii. 8). The Christian walks in the light, and in keeping himself there, and in knowing, loving and obeying Christ, he is conscious of eternal life being granted to him. Now, while it will not do to say that this *attenuation of the apocalyptic element* in the Johannine version of Christianity has not its roots in other causes also, it is impossible not to connect it closely with the anchoring of Christian life within the eternal being of God. As in God the present and the future, time and eternity, co-exist and are held in one, so in Christian experience the sharp distinctions which make themselves felt on the horizontal plane between the Now and the Then, between the Age of Grace and the Age of Glory, lose their edge when Christian life is lifted into participation in the eternal communion of the Father and the Son.

Certainly in Gospel and Epistle alike the *verticality* of the soul's relation to God is emphasized above its horizontal bearings. The Christian life, for instance, is birth "from above" (ἄνωθεν, John iii. 3–4), an expression which only the myopia of Nicodemus leads him to construe in horizontal terms. Again, the Son of Man comes "from heaven" and is "in heaven": "No-one", we read, "has seen God at any time; the Only-begotten, who is God, who is on the Father's breast, has interpreted him" (John i, 18). Again, "You (the Jews) are from below, I am from above" (ἐκ τῶν ἄνω, John viii. 23). Or take the words in which the saving work of Christ is made to depend upon His being *lifted up* (ὑψωθῆναι), as for example this: "When you lift up the Son of Man, then you will know that I am" (ὅτι ἐγώ εἰμι, John viii. 28), or this: "I, if I am lifted up from the earth, will draw all men to myself" (John xii. 32). Here the very heart of the divine revelation in Christ (ὅτι ἐγώ εἰμι), lies in the Saviour's being lifted up, and the same is true of the moral power of Christianity to attract and subdue (πάντας ἑλκύσω πρὸς ἐμαυτόν).

While, then, the horizontal aspects of faith are not altogether displaced or ignored in the Johannine scheme of thought, they tend to be absorbed into the vertical.

We come now to the first of our books.

The First Epistle of St. John

The theological *preface* (i. 1–3) is difficult, and calls for a word or two of comment. As the opening relative pronoun is a neuter ("that which was from the beginning"), and as the writer presently injects the explanatory qualification "(I speak) concerning the Word of life" (περὶ τοῦ λόγου τῆς ζωῆς, 1 John i. 1, 3), it would appear that the start is made, not as in the Gospel, from the *person* of the Living Word, but from the *reality* or truth of which He is the expression. We may then paraphrase the preface as follows: "That primordial reality (or thing, or fact) which (being revealed in the flesh of Jesus Christ)—for I speak of the Word of Life—we have heard, have seen with our eyes, have looked upon, and touched with our hands (that reality), we, the witnesses and auditors of it, now proclaim also to you, that you also may have fellowship with us, a fellowship which, in its full true sense, is with the Father and with his Son, Jesus Christ."

We are now in a position to subject the Epistle to religious analysis.

(1) *The Manifestation of God*, which is the basis of all religious reality, is presented in the form: "The Life was manifested (ἐφανερώθη). . . . We have seen, and testify to, and proclaim to you the *Eternal Life* which was with the Father and was made manifest to us" (1 John i. 2). The incarnate life of Jesus Christ in its own character and by its own effects (cf. John i. 14 ff.), without the aid of any adventitious circumstances or concomitants whatsoever, is the thing that has subdued the soul and holds it and is the source and power of the Christian doctrine of God and the Christian ethic.

(2) *Theology*. This is stated in the propositions that the manifested life of Jesus reveals and communicates to us the nature of the Godhead, and that God's nature is *Light* (1 John i. 2; i. 5). The consequences of this will be developed, but we need only note at present these points, that in God is no darkness at all, that Jesus "was manifested to take away sins" (iii. 5) and "to destroy the works of the devil" (iii. 8), that God is love and that "he who abides in love abides in God, and God abides in him" (iv. 16). The application of these truths will appear presently.

(3) *The Way of Life*. This is given succinctly in the principle that the Christian "walks in the light" (1 John i. 6). "If we say that we have fellowship with Him while we walk in the darkness, we are false and act against the truth." We might say that we have here the exact

Christian counterpart to Israel's law of *holiness*. Under that law strict conformity to ritual regulations of Purity was the condition of Israel being preserved in communion with God, and therefore of the divine blessing, virtue, energy and grace of God being made available for the people. This is now replaced by the principle. "If we walk in the light, as He is in the light, we have communion with one another, *and the blood of Jesus His Son cleanses us from all sin*" (1 John i. 7). The working out of this theme fills the pages of the Epistle.

For, unfortunately, the *koinonia* of the Church to which the apostle writes, has been disrupted. We hear of certain persons who have "gone out" of the fellowship of the Church because, says the writer, they "were not of us" (1 John ii. 19). It is generally considered that these were persons who under the influence of trends of thought prevalent in the Hellenistic religious world, had laid hold of Christianity as a species of *gnosis* or divine enlightenment, and had insisted on conforming Jesus to the type of the Gnostic Redeemer or divine Revealer, whose function is to awaken men to a sense of the primal light which is latent in themselves, and who thus creates in them a superior consciousness. Certain it is that the sectaries at Ephesus repudiated the idea that the heavenly Redeemer had come in the flesh. It was just from the flesh or matter that these brethren felt they needed to be redeemed, and therefore they rejected the idea of a real Incarnation. Certain it is also that they refused the requirement of humble service to the community and the subordination of themselves to the ordinances of grace in the Church. The writer assails them in no measured terms. He calls them "*Antichrists*" (1 John ii. 18; iv. 3); who deny the Son of God deny also the Father. For him the Christian life means the acceptance of the *Incarnation* in all its reality, for it is only in the Son made flesh that we see and know God. And in its practical expression it means confession, humility, love, service, unity, the keeping of the commandments of Christ.

The physiognomy of the Gnosticizing group can be made out more fully from an analysis of the Epistle. (i) The statement "if we say we have no sin, we deceive ourselves" (1 John i. 8) is probably aimed at persons who professed perfectionism in virtue of a superior consciousness based on enlightenment, and on the supposed possession of a new nature raised above good and evil. The writer rejoins that *sinlessness* in the Christian sense can only come by confession, forgiveness, and cleansing through the blood of Christ, i.e. by remaining in the *koinonia* (1 John i. 9). If Gnostic perfectionism signifies any indifference to moral evil, he makes it known that there can be no such indifference under application of the blood of Christ. (ii) Certain allusions in the Epistle suggest that the claim to "*know*" *God* (1 John ii. 4), or to be in the "light" (ii. 9), or to be of the "truth" (iii. 17–19), was made by the party. It is replied that such claims have no justification where there is disobedience to Christ's "commandments", or where there is hatred of "brethren" or failure to help our needy neighbours by sharing the "world's goods" with them (1 John ii. 6). (iii) Similarly the claim *to* "*abide*" *in Christ*, which the Gnostic would support by reference to the conjunction of his personal light-nature with the heavenly light-revealer, is self-deception, for only he abides in Christ who conducts himself as Jesus did (1 John iv. 12, 13, 20), and does not live in sin, but keeps Christ's commandments, and receives the Holy Spirit, not any "false Spirit" that is going the rounds. (iv) It would appear from the writer's saying to the readers, "You have an anointing (χρῖσμα ἔχετε) from the Holy One, and all have knowledge" and again, "The anointing (τὸ χρῖσμα) which you received from Him abides in you . . . and teaches you about everything" (1 John ii. 20, 27), that the separatists prided themselves on a special *unction* conferring special "knowledge". The writer retorts: "Yes. An unction indeed, but not from Christ." It is not strange, he writes, if in this last critical hour of history Antichrist is active, and is putting his seal on his own. The "unction" which the separatists have received is the χρῖσμα of the latter, for who is the *Antichrist* but he who, like these Gnostics, separates the Christ from Jesus, and thus gets rid of both the Father and the Son (1 John ii. 22, 23)? (v) The same persons profess to be "born of God" (γεγεννημένοι ἐκ τοῦ Θεοῦ) or to be "children of God" (τέκνα Θεοῦ, 1 John ii. 29; iii. 1; iv. 7; v. 1; v. 4–5; v. 18). The writer replies that to be children of God means to be like Christ, and involves a purification of oneself, it means the practice of righteousness and love to one's brethren, it means that there can be no disjointing of Jesus and the Christ, it means the overcoming of the world by faith. (vi) A special form of the Gnostic pretensions is the claim, apparently, to have the "seed of God" (σπέρμα αὐτοῦ, 1 John iii. 9) as an inward possession, making the claimants incapable of sin. The rejoinder is: "We know that any one born of God does not sin; nay, He who was born of God (ἀλλὰ ὁ γεννηθεὶς ἐκ τοῦ Θεοῦ) keeps him, and the evil one does not touch him" (1 John v. 18). This passage is of capital importance. Apparently the Gnostics think that a new nature, a divine "seed", has been implanted in them, and forms a constituent element in their existence. The Apostle denies that there is any such implanted or inherent new nature in the Christian which of itself is able to save him. What the Christian has is *Christ, nothing less and nothing more, Christ alone is the Son* and "Seed" of God, Christ alone keeps the Christian and redeems him from evil.

Over against a group, then, who, on the strength of a supposed divine grace communicated to them and inhering in them as a new nature, profess to be morally impeccable, to know God and to abide in Him, to have an "unction" from above, to be born of God or to have a divine "seed" of life within them, the Apostle asserts that Christ and Christ alone is the measure of Christianity. *Sinlessness, knowledge of God, heavenly unction, birth from above, divine life have no meaning apart from the incarnate Son of God and fellowship with Him.* Christian life is unthinkable except in terms of the holy obedience, humility, charity, and oneness with men which Jesus exemplified and which He commands. The Gnostic group may think they are "prophets" and moved by the Holy Spirit. But the Apostle's criterion of the Spirit cuts counter to such notions. Only he has the Spirit who believes in the Incarnation of the Son of God. "By this you know the Spirit of God," he writes (1 John iv. 2–3). "Every spirit which confesses that Jesus Christ has come in the flesh is of God, and every spirit which does not confess Jesus is not of God. This is the spirit of Antichrist" (cf. 1 Cor. xii. 3).

The Gospel according to St. John

The Fourth Gospel carries forward and confirms the tenets of the Epistle, but as addressed not to a particular community with aberrant members but to the whole Church in the World, its teaching has a more general quality and range.

(1) As regards the *koinonia*, the Gospel dwells much on the parallelism in unity which exists between the Saviour's work on earth and the eternal work of the Father in heaven. There are, for example, the matters of resurrection and judgement. "As the Father raises the dead and gives them life, so also the Son gives life to whom he will. . . . He has granted the Son to have life in himself, and has given him authority to execute judgement, because He is the Son of Man" (John v. 21–7). So also the teaching of Jesus is not His own, but its divine origin is self-evidencing for all who will do God's will (John viii. 16–17). And Jesus is the visible representation of the Father, so

that he who has seen Jesus has seen God (John xiv. 8–10). "Do you not believe", Jesus says to Philip, "that I am in the Father and the Father in me?" But the Gospel is equally emphatic on the oneness of the Christian community with the Father and the Son. We have the Saviour's prayer for His disciples "that they may all be one, even as thou, Father, art in me, and I in thee, that they also may be in us" (John xvii. 21), and there are many similar passages.

(2) In the matter of present and future there is even a greater *avoidance of apocalyptic imagery* than in the Epistle. Yet the Last Things are present in shadow: there is a resurrection and judgement at the End as well as in the Christian present, and there is a coming of the Lord at a time future to His earthly ministry (John v. 28–9; xi. 23–4). "Father," we read in our Lord's intercessory prayer, "those whom thou hast given me, I will that where I am, there they too may be with me, to behold my glory which thou hast given me in thy love for me before the foundation of the world" (John xvii. 24). A very interesting feature of the Gospel in this connection is the recurrence over and over again of the formula "*An hour comes and now is*" (John iv. 23; v. 25; v. 28). It is applied to the ending of legal religion and the worshipping of the Father in spirit and in truth, to the dead hearing the voice of the Son of God, and to the resurrection. Nothing could better illustrate that holding together in unity of present and future, time and eternity, which goes with the vertical dimension of Christian life in the Johannine estimation.

We come to the *Prologue* to the Gospel (i. 1–18). As in the Epistle, the writer goes back behind the Christian manifestation proper to the eternal presence of the *Logos* with God and to His function in creation and religious history. The opening verses of the Prologue thus become a Christian transcript of Genesis i. In this Christian interpretation the personal Logos (like Wisdom in Prov. viii. 22–31) appears by the side of God as the instrument or organ of divine creation. It is said of him both that He was *with* God (ἦν πρὸς τὸν Θεόν) and that He *was* God (Θεὸς ἦν, John i. 1). We have then to adjust our thought of God to the fact that one who was with God was God. If we seek a point in the Genesis-narrative at which theology might find room for the Wisdom or personal Word of God, it might be possible to find such a place in Gen. i. 3: "God said, Let there be light, and there was light." This was before any of the other works of creation, before even the separation of the light and the darkness. But such engagements are speculative. Certain it is that the activity of the personal divine Wisdom or Logos is to be seen in the creative *words* of God by which in succession all things were fashioned. "All things were made through him, and apart from him was not a single thing made" (John i. 3). But while all these other things "became" (ἐγένετο) through the Logos, He Himself "was" (ἦν) at the beginning. He belonged, therefore, not to creation but to God.

The deep importance of all this is that, when the Logos is identified with Jesus Christ, the Son of God, this means that the Christ of the evangelist's faith is given an *ontological* relation to cosmic reality (John i. 14). The stamp of His mind and the touch of His hand have gone to the making of all things in their original design and character. That is why creation, the cosmos, is a living thing. As the evangelist says, according to the most ancient understanding of i. 3–4, "Everything that came to be in (or by) him was life" (John i. 4). Because it was *life*, it has meaning for man: "the life was the light of men". Ultimately, of course, this means that the Logos is the one true light of men, apart from whom the world is meaningless, does not make sense. But sin had come in, and "the light shines in the darkness" (John i. 5). Such is the background, then, of the salvation-history which culminates in the Incarnation.

Reserving for the moment the question how Christianity came to speak this great language by which in effect, all provinces of reality, and all departments of thought, all science and all philosophy, are ultimately claimed for the Christ of faith, let us look briefly at the heart of the revelation as the evangelist presents it.

(1) *The Manifestation of God.* This is declared shortly but movingly in the words: "And (or indeed) the Logos became flesh (σάρξ ἐγένετο) and made his dwelling among us—and we looked upon his glory (τὴν δόξαν αὐτοῦ), glory as of the only Son from the Father—full of grace and truth" (John i. 14). God was in Christ, in *the humanity, the flesh of Jesus,* in the completeness and perfection of that humanity, not in something else that was merely draped around it, or in something different from His humanity of which His humanity was but the transparent. Christ's humanity was no phantasma, but *the unique glory of the Son of God* was revealed in it; the fullness of grace and truth was there, and man has never seen it except there. And it is to the manifestation of this completeness, this plenitude of grace and truth, that the Christian Church has owed all the grace that is in it. For grace in the Church corresponds to grace in the Redeemer. Manifestation, then, and answering life—that is the starting-point. "No one has ever

seen God: the Only-begotten, who is God, who is at the Father's heart, has disclosed the mystery" (John i. 18).

(2) *Theology*. The Logos, who was with God, *was and is God*. How one who was πρὸς τὸν πατέρα was at the same time God now sets a problem for theology, the magnitude of which was not appreciated so long as the Church was content to think of the Revealer by aid of the term "Son of God" with its Biblical background (Adoptionist) and its Hellenistic affinities (Euhemeristic). But now the conception of God must open up to take in the person of One who, being with God, was God, and was also "in the beginning". Such a statement as John i. 1 rules out in advance any notion of there being "a time when the Logos was not", and prescribes the working out, sooner or later, of a reasoned doctrine of the nature of God. But the Fourth Evangelist's interests are not in ontology but in revelation and in redemption, and so in the main body of the Gospel the title Logos disappears in favour of "Son of God", "Son of Man", and "Life" and "Light" of men. Let us remember that in the New Testament all these conceptions belong to what theologians call the "*Last Things*", that is, they belong not to our present world-order and our time, but to the promised age of God, the New Creation, and *its* time. Particularly is this true of the conceptions of *Life* and *Light*. In the present sinful and fallen world there is no life and no light. If Jesus, the incarnate Word, has brought life and light into history, it is because, until He became flesh, the world was in darkness and death. While the Logos was eternally, though behind the scenes, and was the centre of life and light to the world—for "In Him was life, and the life was the light of men"—this did not become palpable until in Jesus the Word became incarnate, and "we beheld his glory" (John i. 14). Then the work of the Logos became not only visible but effectual.

In other words, Jesus is "the Life" because what He reveals to us about ourselves is that, apart from Him, we are *dead*, and He is "the Light" because He shows that, apart from Him, we are in the *dark*. It will suffice to instance the case of Nicodemus. The Word of the Son of God to Nicodemus: "Unless a man is born from above, he cannot see the Kingdom of God" (John iii. 3) means that he, Nicodemus, and all the rest of us who are like him, are in our state of nature dead, and unable to do anything about it. "That which is born of the flesh is flesh": there is no getting further along that road (John iii. 6). "But that which is born of the Spirit is spirit"—what is driven home to Nicodemus by the word about the birth "from above" is that with men this thing is impossible, but not with God, and we must leave it at that. Jesus is the Life; we do not have life as something that is, or can be created, in us by *ourselves*, or that, being given to us by God, becomes a part or quality of *us*, a nature of *our own*. Our new life is *Christ*. Here a word should be said about the difficult passage: "For every one who does evil hates the light, and does not come to the light, lest his deeds should be reproved. But he who does what is true comes to the light, that it may be clearly seen that his deeds have been wrought in God" (John iii. 20–1). According to a common interpretation of these words we are to suppose that whether or not a man comes to Christ depends on what his past life has been, and on that interpretation we should have to say that the good man at least is not dark or dead, but has enough light and goodness in *himself* to bring him to Christ. But is that the correct interpretation? I do not think it is. The passage rather means: "the man who does evil does so in every case by hating, and not coming to the light in Christ, etc.," whereas "the man who does what is true does it by coming to that light, that it may be clearly seen that his deeds are wrought (*not in himself*) but in God". *Christ, in other words, marks in every case the beginning of the decisive personal life in men, whether that life be good or evil.* This understanding may not explain why some men come to Christ and some do not, but it gets over the difficulty of supposing that none but the good are called by Christ and none but the good come to Him.

(3) *The Way of Life.* This is, above all, the keeping of the commandments of Christ, "abiding" in Him, that is, preserving the *koinonia* into which we have been brought. Remember the fifteenth chapter, the allegory of *the Vine and the Branches*. It is sometimes thought and said that the monotone of the ethical teaching of John leaves much to be desired. It is all about love and keeping the commandments of Christ, and it lacks the rich illustrativeness of the applications given to love and the other commandments in the Synoptic teaching. That is, in fact, true, and we should be much the poorer if, with all the theological sublimity of the Fourth Gospel, we had to depend on it alone for the knowledge of Him who as Son of God walked this earth. Fortunately we are not in the position of having to do without our incomparable Synoptic Gospels. We have all these, and John too. But in justice to the Johannine writer be it said that in chapters like xiii, xiv and xv of the Gospel we have very concrete presentations of what Christian love is and requires. Moreover, it must not be forgotten that, along with the Fourth Gospel, we have the

First Johannine Epistle with its amazingly practical presentment of Christian love in the context, the social context, of human relations. Above all, let us not forget what is implied, as regards Johannine Christianity, in one of the greatest passages of the Gospel. It is where the disciple Thomas says to Jesus: "Lord, we do not know where you are going; how can we know the way?" And the Lord's answer is to say: "I am the Way, and the Truth, and the Life" (John xiv. 4–6). That is to say, Jesus Himself, in His person, character, and work, is alone the measure of Christianity—to the very end! He is the *Way*, in that He comes from God to us, and leads back from us to God. He in His incarnate life and vicarious death and resurrection, establishes the contact, the traffic, and the communion of our souls with God. And because He is thus the Way, He is also our Theology, the *Truth*, and our Ethic, the *Way*. The foundation of our theology is not St. Paul, or Augustine, or Thomas Aquinas, or Luther, or Calvin, or Karl Barth, but *Jesus*. And in the difficult and vexed field of the moral debate of the world it is equally so. "Lord, to whom shall we go (if we leave Thee)? Thou hast the words of eternal life" (John vi. 68–9). Jesus has the final word, the ultimatum, the word that will still ring, when the world's debate is done.

CHAPTER 2

The Argument of the Epistles to the Romans (Chapters 1–8)

Introduction

Questions numerous as bees about a hive beset the critical approach to the Epistle to the Romans, but in the main the interest settles down around two primary concerns. One relates to the character of the Roman Christian community: Was it Jewish-Christian or Gentile-Christian in its composition, and is any evidence on the point to be extracted from the Epistle? The problem here lies in the circumstance that while the writer names his readers as Gentiles or assumes their Gentilic character, he everywhere argues with them as if their religious background was Jewish. The other question starts from the Epistle itself: Does its matter stand in substantive and apposite relation to the character of the Roman community, or is it possible that a general statement of Pauline evangelistic teaching was incorporated with covering matter in the Apostle's letter to the as yet unvisited Church at Rome? The latter view has been advanced to account for the existence of variant recensions of the Epistle in the early centuries. Less doubtfully it may help to explain the dislocation between the Gentile-Christian address of the letter and the predominantly Jewish-Christian orientation of the subject-matter.

(1) The question regarding the origin and religious history of the Roman Christian community has an interest going beyond any precise conclusions to be drawn from the Epistle. We have to distinguish the Church-history issue from the literary problem posed by the letter. A tradition handed down by the patristic commentator "Ambrosiaster" (*c.* 370) states that the Roman Christians were originally Gentiles, but received the Gospel from believing Jews who *tradiderunt Romanis ut Christum profitentes legem servarent.* Without having seen any miracles or been visited by any apostle they had taken up the Christian faith *ritu licet Judaico* (see Sanday and Headlam, *Commentary on Romans*, p. xxv; and T. Zahn (ii. p. 420). This interesting tradition was taken

by F. C. Baur, together with what appeared to be the supporting evidence of St. Paul's Epistle, to establish the Judaic character of Roman Christianity. With the waning of the influence of Baur's theoretical construction of Church history, there came a reaction away from this position. The Gentile character of the Church has been affirmed by a majority of modern scholars, a notable exception being the historian Eduard Meyer (*Ursprung u. Anfänge des Christentums*, 1923, III, pp. 465–7), who reasserted its Judaic complexion, and certainly if St. Paul's letter was composed with an eye on the Roman community, it is difficult to see that any other conclusion than Meyer's is satisfactory. The present writer has elsewhere set down what seem to him irresistible material arguments in favour of the Judaic view (*The Epistle to the Hebrews*, 1951, pp. 172–84). Two considerations are of quite paramount importance. (a) There is the circumstance already noted that, while the Apostle names or classifies his readers as among the "Gentiles" (i. 5, 6; i. 13; xi. 13; xv. 16, etc.), he argues with them everywhere as if their religious training was Jewish (e.g. iv. 1; vii. 1; vii. 6, 9, 10, etc.). (b) There is the striking absence in the Epistle of allusion to those characteristic aberrations of a speculative-gnostic type which in other letters, such as Galatians, 1 Corinthians, and Colossians, are associated with Gentile Churches. All these considerations would, however, lose their force if there was reason to think that the didactic substance of the Epistle was not originally framed with specific reference to Rome.

(2) The textual phenomena presented by the Epistle constitute, in Lietzmann's words, *ein eigenes und höchst kompliziertes Problem* (HNT, *An die Römer*, p. 130). There is, first, the well-known textual disturbance manifest in the variant positions of the doxology which our best uncial authorities exhibit at xvi. 25–7. There is, secondly, the omission in G of ἐν Ῥώμῃ at i. 7 and of τοῖς ἐν Ῥώμῃ at i. 15. Dr. Kirsopp Lake has submitted these phenomena to patient examination (*Earlier Epistles of St. Paul*, 1914, pp. 335–70), and decides on the strength of evidence drawn from the chapter-division of Codex Amiatinus of the Vulgate, from Cyprian's *Testimonia*, and from Tertullian, that in the second and succeeding centuries a recension of Romans was current which omitted chapters 15 and 16 and ended with the doxology at xiv. 23. This recension also lacked the references to Rome in i. 7 and i. 15, and was only gradually abandoned, Lake thinks, in favour of the long recension. Nevertheless Lake has to admit the genuinely Pauline authorship of chapter 15. It is organically

connected with chapter 14, and cannot be considered a later addition to the short recension by another hand. "We have to face the existence of the long recension as genuinely Pauline." Lake offers in explanation of the two recensions the alternative hypotheses: either (1) St. Paul's letter was the long recension, and the short recension was made by someone else (Marcion), or (2) St. Paul wrote both recensions, "issuing the letter in two forms, either simultaneously or successively" (op. cit., pp. 349–50). Lake personally inclines to the latter view.

The case for this hypothesis, however, according to which the Apostle emitted, simultaneously or successively, two different versions of his letter, creates difficulties. It leaves unsolved the question, what then did Marcion do? According to the statement in Rufinus' translation of Origen's *Commentary on Romans xvi. 25–7*, Marcion removed the Doxology from the Epistle (*penitus abstulit*) and also cut away everything from xiv. 23 to the end (*usque ad finem cuncta dissecuit*). If this means anything, it means that Marcion's basis of operations was the longer recension which extended beyond xiv. 23. Marcion had this longer text, and if what he did was not to *produce* the short recension, what was it? To assume the currency of a short recension in the West in order to avoid the conclusion that Cyprian, Tertullian, and the chapter-divisions of Codex Amiatinus were somehow all indebted to Marcion for their text of Romans is to save the face of these authorities at the expense of putting Marcion out of business. The case, then, is against a short text of Romans having existed in the West before, and independently of Marcion. What was first there was a longer text including at least Chapter 15.

A more helpful approach to a solution of the problem had been offered by Dr. T. W. Manson ("St. Paul's Letter to the Romans—and Others", *Bulletin of John Rylands Library*, vol. 31, 1948, pp. 224–40), and is discussed by Dr. Johannes Munck (*Paulus u. die Heilsgeschichte*, 1954, pp. 191–4). Basing his position on Chester-Beatty Papyrus Codex P^{46} which was not available when Lake wrote his *Earlier Epistles,* but which contains the doxology at the end of Romans xv, Manson contends that this third-century codex incorporates the original form of the letter which St. Paul sent to Rome, and which was the basis on which Marcion got to work. As St. Paul wrote the letter, it was without the doxology and Chapter 16, but the argument is that a copy was simultaneously sent to Ephesus, occasion being taken by the Apostle to add Chapter 16 with its personal greetings to Ephesian friends. This composite copy came later via Ephesus to

Egypt, and there the Roman and the Ephesian texts were worked together into the final form now represented by Papyrus Codex p^{46}.

The reason why St. Paul sent a copy to Ephesus as well as to Rome was that the letter epitomized the main theological positions reached by himself in the course of his long controversy over the relations of Law and Gospel in the Churches. The didactic substance of the letter was not originally framed with a view to the Roman Church. Perhaps in this way we account for the dislocation between the Gentile address of Romans and the intimate Jewish colour and background of its theology.

Analysis of the Epistle

I. Apostolic Salutation and Address to the Roman Church (i. 1–17)

This touches on three main topics.

(1) The subject of the Apostle's Gospel is the Son of God, Jesus Christ, whose revelational significance the Apostle defines by reference to the two successive stages of His manifestation: (a) the earthly life (κατὰ σάρκα) in which Jesus appeared as Davidic Messiah, (b) the post-resurrection existence (κατὰ πνεῦμα ἁγιωσύνης) in which He is definitively presented through the Holy Spirit as Son of God "in power" (i. 3–4). It is the same Son of God who is demonstrated in both stadia. The antithetic terms "flesh", "spirit" do not divide His substance but unfold the economy of His manifestation. The sublimation of the first phase in the second, by which the second becomes definitive for the understanding of the whole presentation, makes this passage the key to the enigmatic word (2 Cor. v. 16) about our no longer knowing Christ after the flesh. The Jesus of Jewish history is also supra-historical.

(2) The Apostle's interest in the Roman Christians (i. 10, cf. xv. 23) rests on his commission to preach the gospel "among the Gentiles" (i. 5; i. 14): compare xv. 16, "that I should be a priest (λειτουργός) of Christ Jesus to the Gentiles, exercising the sacral office in the sphere of the gospel of God." The Gentile-Christian character of the Church addressed seems clearly indicated unless the term "Gentiles" is given a merely geographical connotation. The special purpose of St. Paul's projected visit to Rome is the communication of a "spiritual gift" (χάρισμα), but the Apostle with the delicacy natural to one approach-

ing a Church not founded by, or known to himself, amends this into: "that I may share with you the encouragement which our common faith inspires, yours and mine" (i. 11–12). So explained the "spiritual gift" is not necessarily an imparting of apostolic order or foundation to an *ex hypothesi* as yet incohate religious community, but rather a contribution to the common faith.

(3) Faced by daunting circumstances, the multiplicity of salvation-cults offered to mankind in the contemporary world, the antipathy of Jews and Judaizing Christians to his teaching, and the aversion of those who dislike him and fancy he will not show his face among them (cf. 1 Cor. iv. 18 f.), the Apostle comes to Rome and relies on the Gospel as God's instrument for effecting men's "salvation". In a world that yearns for redemption, he has found it to be God's δύναμις, God's way of getting that redemption accomplished (i. 16; cf. 1 Cor. i. 21–4), and this because it opens up a "righteousness of God" for men, a way of salvation which does justice to the moral reality of God's relations with men, while at the same time enabling men's restoration to right relations with God. At the supreme crisis in history marked by the coming of Jesus Christ, God's righteousness, while declaring His condemnation of the world's sin (ὀργή, κρίμα, δικαιοκρισία) offers absolution (δικαιοσύνη Θεοῦ) through the work of Christ.

II. The Righteousness of God

A. *This Righteousness of God is on its negative side His Judgement upon a world that is apostate from Himself* (i. 18–iii. 20). The indictment is directed against (a) the ethnic world (i. 18–32), (b) the Jewish people (ii. 1–29), (c) the guilt of all humanity before God (iii. 1–20).

The verb ἀποκαλύπτεται (i. 18) indicates, when taken with the same term in i. 17, that the "Wrath" of God here introduced belongs to the same disclosure as His "Righteousness". It is organic to the Gospel as a sign of the eschatological crisis, the κρίσις τοῦ κόσμου τούτου (John xii. 31), which has come with Christ. While the indictment of the ethnic and the Jewish worlds in these chapters is grounded formally on the moral facts of the human situation, the real starting-point is Christ and His cross. This has given the Apostle the luminous centre from which he looks at the sin of the world, the holiness of God, and the grace and wonder of forgiveness. The latency of the Gospel under the indictment appears clearly when the edge of the argument happens to be turned up as it is in ii. 16.

(a) The gravamen of the charge against the pagan world is that it has rejected the divine revelation given to it in creation. God has made His eternal power and divinity known, not indeed to the eye, but to the mind or νοῦς of man (i. 19–20). The indictment follows the lines of the traditional Jewish-Hellenistic theology developed at Alexandria (cf. Wisdom xiii), but has a vigour and force which are Paul's own. The nations have turned from revelation to embrace the "lie" of idolatry, and God has handed them over to the moral consequences of their apostasy. "Because (despite the evidence offered) they refused to acknowledge God as real, God has given them over to a mind now void of all sense of the real" (i. 28). Nothing is said about eschatological promises being given to the world.

(b) In ii. 1–29 the argument graduates from the Gentiles to the Jews, whose guilt lies in the pride which has led them, as the privileged recipients of an eschatological revelation, to overlook the moral realities of their existing situation. If in the preceding section the Apostle had Wisdom xiii in mind, here he is thinking of Wisdom xv where the Jewish writer turns from the heathen with the comforting reflection: "But Thou, our God, art gracious, true, long-suffering.... Even if we sin, we are Thine, etc." This delusion of the Jew lies behind the Apostle's taunt in ii. 3–4. While acknowledging the magnificent privilege of the Diaspora Jew (ii. 17–20), he presses the rigour of God's ethical demand. The Jew has in the Law "the very embodiment of religious knowledge and divine truth", but the Gentile also has an inward law, the sanctions of which he recognizes in conscience, philosophy, and life. Thus Jew and Gentile stand alike before the one tribunal of God's inexorable holiness, and this, according to the Apostle's Gospel, is the judgement-seat of Christ (ii. 16).

(c) In iii. 1–21 the Apostle sums up. The tests of law and truth have as applied to men revealed their total bankruptcy in a moral point of view. No righteousness but that of God remains. If man's relation to God is to be rectified, it must be by the operation of that divine righteousness, not man's own. Διὰ γὰρ νόμου comes only ἐπίγνωσις ἁμαρτίας (iii. 20).

B. *The Righteousness of God is in its positive aspect the Atonement effected for us by God in Jesus Christ, who is the* Ἱλαστήριον, *the Agent or Ground set forward by God for the Expiation of sin* (iii. 21–v. 21).

The Apostle here presents the Righteousness of God as (a) manifested (πεφανέρωται) in Jesus Christ (iii. 21–30), (b) underlying the Old

Testament and establishing the Law (iii. 31–iv. 25), (c) verified by its results in Christian experience (v. 1–11), and (d) marking the Great Divide between the past world-age of Sin and Death and a new world-age of Righteousness and Life (v. 12–21).

(a) This righteousness is χωρὶς νόμου, but being prefigured in the law and the prophets it signifies no dismissal of law as an eternal factor in the determination of divine-human relations. Rather it means the transcending of law by the gracious act of God in Christ. If law is marked off from this transaction, it is, as Denney says, in the sense in which a Jew laid stress on his fulfilment of the Mosaic commandments or a Gentile on his life according to natural law as constituting a claim upon God. All such claim is excluded by the moral failure of the recipients (iii. 23) and by the nature of the "redemption" (ἀπολύτρωσις) effected for men in the "forthsetting" of the Christ as our ἱλαστήριον. He is the manifestation (ἔνδειξις) of God's will so to present His righteousness as effectually to cover us with regard both to past guilt and to the establishment of a totally new relation between God and our souls (iii. 25–6). Faith, the condition of acceptance, is essentially the abandonment of all self-rightousness, it is the casting of ourselves on God (iii. 27–8). The language employed—the "forth-setting" of Christ and the "exhibition" of divine righteousness—is to be understood in a dynamic and activist, not in a merely demonstrative sense, God has acted not merely to vindicate His integrity (iii. 25) but to make His righteousness *operative* henceforth in us (iii. 26). The result is the supersession of legal religion (iii. 27).

In this exposition the expiatory sacrifice of Christ is the pivotal conception on which the relations of God and man are finally seen to turn. While elsewhere (Gal. iii. 13; 2 Cor. v. 21; Rom. viii. 3–4) other metaphors are employed to describe the redemptive work of Christ, the expressions all converge on His being an *'asham* for the guilt of men. The righteousness of God is thus no mere overflowing of His goodness and mercy, but is conditioned by the atoning act of Jesus, in whom alone the reality of sin is grappled with and disposed of, and the righteousness of God made *transitive* to us as the only righteousness we can ever have. In this representation:

(i) "Righteousness' retains its Biblical sense, in which it has been defined as "the triumphant assertion or action of God's sovereign will, whether in requiring obedience, or in achieving victory over man's rebellion, or in victoriously accomplishing man's salvation". It is used here in this third or eschatological sense.

(ii) The righteousness of God is a concept primordial to Christianity, for it is implied in our Lord's requirement "Repent", for "the Kingdom of God is at hand" (Mark i. 15), also in His word "seek first the Kingdom and the righteousness of God" (Matt. vi. 33). In response to this demand men may turn, and their lives take a new direction towards God, but can they give themselves a new mentality, a new nature, a new heart? And faced by the Sermon on the Mount, men may acknowledge the perfection of God's commandment, but can they achieve full obedience to it by their own power or righteousness? Inevitably what God here requires He must Himself put in our way. Christianity sees this truth flashing in the vicarious obedience and sacrifice of Jesus Christ.

(b) St. Paul's particular description of this communicated righteousness as justification by "faith" is due to his doctrine being hammered out on the anvil of his anti-Jewish conflict in which his Gospel of grace was opposed by determined insistence on "works". Over against the latter position the Apostle contends that the Gospel is the true vindication of the law (νόμον ἱστάνομεν, iii. 31), since the law itself preaches faith. In proof he cites God's acceptance of Abraham (Gen. xv. 6) and the blessedness of the forgiven whose sins are "covered" (Ps. xxxii. 1–2). Law, prophecy, and the hagiographa attest a righteousness conferred upon and covering man which is not man's own but God's. While the appeal to Abraham leaves much in the Abraham story out of account, at one point it brings the patriarch's faith very close to the substance of the Christian religion, and that is where Abraham's faith in God's promise is interpreted as essentially "faith in the God who gives life to the dead" (iv. 17), thus being an anticipation of Christian trust in the resurrection of Jesus (iv. 24–5).

(c) In Romans v. 1–11 the doctrine of divine Righteousness is taken to the test of Christian experience. As "justified" by faith, that is, as covered by the saving action of God in Christ, we are taken out of the condemnation of the sinful consciousness into a status of grace and peace, and are given a new hope through God (v. 1–2). St. Paul analyses the nature of the Christian's assurance that the tide in divine-human relations has turned (v. 3–4), finding its ground in the palpable fact that "the love of God has been poured into our hearts through the Holy Spirit imparted to us" (v. 5). When the persecutor of the Church capitulated to Christ, he had identified the upsurge of love in his own soul with the experience which the Nazarenes described as the descent of the Holy Spirit. Now, in stammering words that necessitate more than one effort at successful expression, he sets over against all limited human ideas of justice the ineffable proof of divine love given in the fact—he is thinking of himself—that "while we were still sinners, Christ died for us" (v. 6–8). This release of love in Christian hearts is for the Apostle the sign that the eschatological order of grace has broken into time. The "much more" argument significantly makes its entrance at this point (v. 9–10). "If, being enemies, we were reconciled to God by the death of His Son, much more, being now reconciled, we shall attain salvation by His life." This statement is important as asserting the Christological basis of the whole Christian life: cf. Chapters vi–viii.

(d) The note of "triumph" (v. 11) suitably introduces a section in which the Apostle, conscious of having attained a climax in his argument, is conscious also of having reached the high watershed of *Heilsgeschichte* (v. 12–21). From the altitude at which he can say, "We have received the Reconciliation (τὴν καταλλαγήν)", the entire past history of the race appears as a domination of life by death through the separation of man from God by sin. "As through one man sin entered the cosmos, and death through sin, and thus death passed to all men because all men sinned" (v. 12)—the sentence which has started off with words derived from Wisdom ii. 24, here breaks off, because the writer is diverted at this moment by the necessity (v. 13–14) of explaining some of his terms, leaving his further meaning to be supplied from the sequel. But certain things are clear. *Heilsgeschichte* divides into two aeons. At the head of the first stands Adam in corporate relation with the race. At the head of the other stands Jesus Christ, head of the new humanity through His representative action on our behalf. Over against the "fall" or "trespass" of Adam (παράπτωμα, παρακοή) stands Christ's "act of righteousness" or "obedience" (δικαίωμα, ὑπακοή), over against "condemnation" (κατάκριμα) stands "acquittal" or "justification" (δικαίωσις ζωῆς, δικαιοσύνη), over against the reign of death through sin stands the reign of life through "righteousness". But, as St. Paul insists, this is no mere balancing of accounts. "It is not a case of the gift of grace (χάρισμα) merely corresponding to the transgression" (παράπτωμα, v. 15). The old order is overwhelmingly reversed: "Where sin (multiplied by law) has come to its full measure, grace has flowed beyond all measure" (v. 20).

One or two comments may here be made:

(i) Grace has come when, through the operation of law, sin had attained its full quantum (v. 20).

(ii) The two orders, the new and the old, now exist in the world together.

(iii) The order of sin dates from Adam, whose express act of disobedience introduced it, but the organic connection between Adam's sin and ours is not made clear. If indeed the statement ἐφ' ᾧ πάντες ἥμαρτον should refer to men's individual sins, we have here an overlag from the Jewish position that every man is the Adam of his own soul, but this would have no counterpart on the Christian side of the account. It is therefore better to take the ἐφ' ᾧ (Old Latin *in quo*) as bringing out the corporate solidarity of human guilt—"all men sinned in Adam".

(iv) Death is conceived not merely biologically but theologically or, if the expression may be allowed, sacramentally: that is, biological death is the sign or symbol of the extinction of man's spiritual life in God. That loss is now made good in the "eternal life", also sacramental, which the righteous act of Christ has procured (v. 21).

C. *The Righteousness of God in its concrete effects is the incorporation of our lives into Christ through the Spirit. Here is the radical meaning of Justification by Grace and the finality of Christian Faith* (vi. 1–viii. 39).

The argument takes account (a) of what is effected in Christian baptism (vi. 3–14), (b) of the new service into which Christians have entered (vi. 15–vii. 6), (d) of the dethronement of sin and the victory of life in the new Christian order (viii. 1–39). Into this scheme is intercalated (c) a dialectical analysis of the nature of life under law (vii. 7–25).

(a) The Apostle, concerned to establish that Christians reconciled to God by the death of His Son will be saved by His life (v. 10) dismisses first the captious charge that to emphasize abounding grace is to put a premium on sin: "Are we to continue in sin that grace may abound?" (cf. iii. 7–8). His answer is that this charge forgets the nature of what takes place in Christian baptism. Lietzmann suggests that St. Paul here is merely giving an ethical direction to the sacramentalist tendencies of Hellenistic Christians. The truth rather is—cf. vi. 3: "Do you not know, etc.?"—that he is *injecting* a profounder and more radical sacramentalism into their ordinary thinking. He is not so much qualifying the sacramental as raising it to its full significance for faith. The ordinary Christian interpreted baptism as a cleansing from sin, or as an initiation into the eschatological community of salvation. St. Paul insists that it means the incorporation of the Christian into

Christ, so that sacramentally he is dead in Christ to sin, and alive in Him to righteousness. "Do you not know that all of us who were baptized into Christ (i.e. to belong to Him) were baptized into His death (i.e. to share His death and resurrection)?" The Apostle illustrates this truth by reference to the symbolism of the rite (vi. 4). Baptism is the ὁμοίωμα, the concrete representation, or effectual sign, of Christ's death and life in its application to the Christian. "Our former personality has been crucified with Him that the sinful body might be rendered inactive. . . . He who is dead has been pronounced free from sin" (vi. 6–7). But though this status in Christ is sacramentally complete, it has to be ethically actualized by faith (vi. 8), knowledge (vi. 9), and obedience (vi. 12–14). Clearly St. Paul is here not abandoning justification by faith for a new ground of life in "Christ-mysticism" but showing Christ-mysticism to be the conclusion to which by inner logic justification leads.

(b) Against antinomian dangers St. Paul also places the fact that the transition from law to grace leaves no middle ground of autonomous Christian freedom (i. 14–23). He hesitates to apply the word δουλεία to the life of grace, but does not reject it altogether. The Biblical term *'ebed* primarily connotes personal obligation to a master and, as such, St. Paul retains it. Changing the metaphor, he compares the transition from law to Christ to the release of a woman from marriage by the death of her husband (vii. 1–6). The illustration is not happy, for the law does not die. The Apostle's point, however, is that the Christian is freed from law through the death of Christ (διὰ τοῦ σώματος τοῦ Χριστοῦ) in order to transfer to the risen Lord his total devotion.

(c) The sinister part ascribed to law as inciting sinful παθήματα in the soul wedded to it (vii. 5–6) and generally the intimate conjunction in which it stands with the sin-flesh-death complex of ideas leads the Apostle at this point to clear up certain ambiguities in his teaching. Apart altogether from his indicting of Jewish legalism in its opposition to the Gospel as enmity towards God, certain expressions of his seemed to suggest that he made the law responsible for sin (vii. 7). This idea Paul repels. As that which exposes sin, the law stands off from sin, flesh, and death as "spiritual", as "holy and just and good" (vii. 12–14). On the other hand, and bearing in mind the question (vi. 15): "Are we ever to sin because we are not ὑπὸ νόμον but ὑπὸ χάριν?", St. Paul has to dispel the opposite assumption that the practice of law *per se* has saving value. There were in his Churches those who, like the persons indicted in Gal. iii. 2–5, had started the Christian life in dependence on the Spirit but later proposed to supplement faith by legal observances. St. Paul's answer in Galatians is well known, but possibly the existence elsewhere of the same tendencies explains why at this point, when defending the principle that the Christian is not under law but under grace, he throws the weight of his argument into what is really a psycho-analytic exposure of the state of the soul ὑπὸ νόμον. In the whole delineation (vii. 7–25), accordingly no account is taken of the element of grace either in Judaism or in Christianity. The Apostle affirms:

(i) That while law exposes sin, it has also the psychological effect of exciting it (vii. 7–8). Rebellious instincts, latent or moribund in the soul, are aroused by the No of the commandment, and St. Paul says he has not been a stranger to the experience (vii. 9–11). But was there ever an actual time when Paul lived χωρὶς νόμου? The difficulty of locating such a time in his historical experience, coupled with the hyperbolical nature of his expressions—"I died" (ἀπέθανον) and "Sin deceived me" (ἐξηπάτησεν, recalling the language used of the serpent by Eve in Gen. iii. 13, LXX)—suggests that here the Apostle is not speaking historically of himself, but theologically. He is seeing all human life, his own included, against the background of Gen. iii.

(ii) Man's weakness ὑπὸ νόμον is grounded in the circumstance that, though the commandment is beneficent, sin has invaded and usurped control over his σάρξ. It is the essence of demonic evil that it takes the holy law of God and makes it an instrument of ruin to our corrupted nature (vii. 13–15). Paul, like every son of Adam, recognizes himself as in this matter "sold" (πεπραμένος) under sin. The law, though exposing sin, cannot extricate us from its demonic sway.

(iii) What follows in vii. 15–25 is a dialectical analysis of the slave-relation so described. The Greek Fathers, founding on the hopelessness of the condition depicted, have seen in the chapter a transparent of the Apostle's pre-baptismal experience. The Western Fathers, notably St. Augustine, and the Reformers, especially Calvin, founding on the goodness of the will or νοῦς engaged in the conflict, have given the analysis a post-baptismal reference. But if the Apostle was writing of his unregenerate experience in Judaism, why have the glory and grace of God vanished from the Torah? And if he was writing of his Christian experience, why is no mention of grace made until the end (vii. 24)? If we take the representation as autobiographical in any strict or real sense, we are in the curious position of having to say that *either it reflects a Judaism in which the glory has passed from the law, or a Christianity in which the glory has not yet arisen on the Gospel.* For this reason the chapter should be taken rather as a dialectical analysis of the state of the naturally sin-enslaved soul ὑπὸ νόμον. This is made definitely certain by the conclusion of the argument in vii. 25, where the subject of the representation is described as αὐτὸς ἐγώ.

(d) With Chapter viii we pass out again into the sunshine of the life of grace. The κατάκριμα inseparable from life under the law (cf. iii. 20) has been lifted not only by the acts of divine grace asserted in iii. 21–6 and v. 12–21, but by the supplementary proofs established in vi. 1–vii. 6, that the Christian life is no more a life in sin. A new principle, "the law of the Spirit of life in Christ Jesus", has become operative in it, ending the bondage under sin and death to which the former life was subject (viii. 2). For—and here St. Paul's conception expands to take in the full cosmic and apocalyptic dimensions of the Christian redemption—God's act in sending His Son to be incorporated in humanity and to become a sin-offering for us has dethroned sin from its absolute empire in our nature, and has introduced the Age of the Spirit (viii. 3–4). Christian life is life on this renewed level, i.e. the eschatological order of God has intersected our life in time, and we, though still in the flesh, are sustained by the Spirit or, as St. Paul alternatively puts it, by the indwelling of Christ. St. Paul analyses the nature of this life in grace.

(i) It is a life in which tension still exists between flesh and spirit, between the old nature and the new (viii. 4–11). Though dethroned by Christ's victory, sin has not been finally disarmed, because the existing world-order has not yet come to its end: "the body indeed is dead on account of the sin (for which Christ suffered), and the spirit is alive on account of the righteousness (which He has achieved)" (viii. 10). But what has thus been sacramentally certified in baptism (vi. 3–14) has to be completed by the hallowing of personal life.

(ii) It is a life in which, through the new orientation of our spirits to the Spirit of God, man's sonship to God is recovered (viii. 12–17). St. Paul may well be thinking here of the position of simple Christians who, unable to rise to the height of his great argument—"no condemnation", "peace with God", life risen with Christ—plead that all they can do is to fall on their knees and cry "Our Father!" The Apostle accepts this protestation as itself the veriest proof of the Spirit's presence with believers (viii. 15–16; cf. Gal. iv. 6–7), but points out that God, having restored us to sonship, is not yet done with us. He has a future for His children: which is to make them "inheritors of God and co-inheritors with Christ", if they accept present suffering with Christ as the condition of sharing His glory (viii. 17).

(iii) The suffering and frustration of present existence must be seen against the bright counterfoil of the glory towards which, both in the cosmos and in the individual life, God's purpose of redemption is working (viii. 18–30). A *cosmic* redemption is proposed, of which man's spiritual redemption is a present first instalment. While man possesses the first-fruit of the Spirit, nature has to wait for its deliverance until man's reinstatement in the image of God is completed by the redemption of his "body", which awaits the Resurrection (viii. 22–3). It is plain here that St. Paul thinks of man's present redemption as limited to his spirit. Meantime the Holy Spirit assists our weakness; a striking instance is the spiritual power of prayer (viii. 26–8).

(iv) In the end the Christian's assurance lies in the inalienable love of God, signified to us in His foreknowledge and predestination of us, in our calling, in our justification, and in God's final purpose to glorify us (viii. 29–30). The Christian argument is unanswerable when we think of what is involved in the Incarnation and in the Death of the Redeemer (viii. 31–2), and on this note St. Paul ends. The Christian in his good fight of faith has overwhelming powers working on his side; for over against the physical forces of life and death, the arbitrary tyranny of demonic spirits, the unknown contingencies of present and future history, and the malign influences of the stellar powers, the Christian trusts that the Love of God in Christ will never forsake him (viii. 33–9).

It has not been possible within the limits of this survey to include chapters ix–xi, dealing with "The Righteousness of God in History", nor to bring to a fuller conclusion the question raised at the beginning concerning the relation of the matter of the Epistle to the specific community addressed. On this question, however, it seems probable that, even if the subject-matter was not originally thought out with an eye on the Roman Church, which is not certain, but represents the mature product of years of earlier debate with Jews and Gentiles throughout the world, the first occasion of its commitment to writing may well have been the Apostle's desire to open communications with the unvisited Church at Rome. Personal touches pervade the writing, and the design to give literary embodiment to the matter may have shaped itself in the writer's mind as the conveying of a truly apostolic charisma. In this matter the critical hypothesis of Dr. T. W. Manson is distinctly helpful.

CHAPTER 3

A Reading of Romans vii[1]

The Biblical exegete who has occasion to go back on to former trains of thought and finds much that is a-wanting and much that stands in need of repair in his earlier pronouncements, may take heart of comfort from some words which Mr. W. B. Yeats wrote in the preface to the 1901 edition of his Poems. Alluding to additions and alterations he had effected in the form of some of his earlier pieces, the Irish poet says with relation to his muse: "The goddess has never come to me with her hands so full that I have not found many waste places after I had planted all that she had brought me." The spirit of truth does not on any occasion impart its gifts in fullness to the theological student any more than to the poet. Defects of judgement have to be remedied. Assumptions once confidently made need to be revised. Thus in an earlier statement on Romans vii the present writer was led to argue that the substance of that famous chapter might be regarded as historical, was indeed autobiographical. On going back upon the subject now he is not so sure of that position.

Assuming that Romans vii was the transcript of *some* historical stage in St. Paul's religious life, I contended on the former occasion that it could only reflect a time when the claim of the Mosaic Law to be the final word of God to man and the sufficient instrument of human salvation was no longer in undisputed possession of St. Paul's spirit. *Ergo* we had to relate the chapter to a situation lying already within the circle of St. Paul's conversion experience, when for the first time an alternative to the Law, indeed a higher means of grace than the Law, had demonstrably lifted itself above his horizon. Only so was it possible to imagine a Jew brought historically to the point of abstracting the Law from the grace of Israel's God and willing to contemplate it purely in itself. Obviously the situation was one in which the glory of God had moved from the Law into a neutral, if not an opposed position. So I suggested that Romans vii belonged to a particular crisis in the Apostle's life and might be taken as the *De*

[1] A paper read to the Durham Colleges Lightfoot Society, 15 May 1953.

Profundis Clamavi of his stricken soul at the moment of his capitulation to Christ. Now for a number of reasons I am no longer able to hold to that hypothesis.

For one thing, the seventh chapter of Romans can hardly be regarded as a confessional utterance of St. Paul's spirit either at this or at any other time. It belongs to the nature of a truly confessional utterance that at every point—witness the penitential Psalms—the soul is thrown in its every word on *God*: "Against Thee, Thee only, have I sinned, and done this that is evil in Thy sight." Psalm li depicts an existential situation. In Romans vii, on the other hand, we have not an existential situation expressing itself in the cry, "Have mercy upon me!" "Wash me!" "Cleanse me!" "Purge me!" "Hide Thy face from my sins!", but the *objectification* of an existential situation, the rational analysis or dissection of a particular self-consciousness by the mind looking at it. This reveals the presence in the delineation of another interest than the purely penitential one, which—witness again the cry of Psalm li, "Against Thee, *Thee only*, have I sinned!"—is always by its nature supra-rational. Romans vii is not, therefore, to be properly described as the *De Profundis Clamavi* of a penitent.

For another thing, if Romans vii really reflected the crisis of St. Paul's conversion-experience, we should surely have expected that one factor in the analysis would be Christ, Christ seen in His grace, over against the law of sin and death. In actual fact, however, Christ does not enter into the delineation until the end, and then He appears not as the creator of the tension described as existing in the soul, but only as the resolver of it. It will not do, therefore, to place the experience, assuming it to be historical, at the actual centre of the crisis marked by St. Paul's conversion. On the other hand, it will not do to push it back behind the conversion to some historical point in St. Paul's *Jewish* experience, for there is no period in the latter at which we can assume, what *ex hypothesi* would need to be assumed, that the glory of God for Paul had passed away from the Law and that an alternative means of grace had lifted on his view.

In fact, if Romans vii had to be regarded as the description of an actual stage in St. Paul's religious history, we should have to say that it represents neither full-orbed Judaism, seeing that the law has lost its glory, nor yet full-orbed Christianity, seeing that Christ does not appear in His glory, nor yet an intermediate conversion-crisis, seeing again that Christ is not present. What kind of reality, then, belongs to the delineation?

Before we proceed to investigate that question a word or two should be said about the structure of the chapter. It falls into two clearly distinguishable parts, (i) verses 7 to 13, dealing with the genesis of the sinful consciousness in man and the part which the ethical imperative of the law of God plays in the consciousness; (ii) verses 14 to 24, analysing the nature of the moral impotence which belongs to his sinful state of existence, and which culminates in the cry ταλαίπωρος ἐγὼ ἄνθρωπος· τίς με ῥύσεται ἐκ τοῦ σώματος τοῦ θανάτου τούτου; (vii. 24). In the first of these divisions, along with the statement (ἐγὼ δὲ ἔζων χωρὶς νόμου ποτέ, vii. 9) "There was a time in my life when the law was not there," which is of doubtful historical application (since when in his life was St. Paul χωρὶς νόμου, not touched by the law?), there are the expressions "Sin deceived me" (ἐξηπάτησέν με) through the commandment" (vii. 11), which is reminiscent of the language of the solicitation addressed by the serpent to Eve in Genesis iii, and "I died" (vii. 10), which can scarcely be called historical. If St. Paul had been referring to an actual event in his spiritual history, he would have said, "I became conscious of being under sentence of death", not "I died". All this is theological, not natural language. He is, as a matter of fact, identifying himself in these expressions with the original man of Genesis iii. In other words, we have to recognize a *theological* interest as affecting the form of the delineation, not a purely psychological interest, and still less a merely historical one. In the second part, which deals with the internal nature of the sinful situation, while psychology undoubtedly to some extent underlies the analysis, a logical or dialectical interest is present in the statement that the ἐγώ he analyses is πεπραμένος ὑπὸ τὴν ἁμαρτίαν (vii, 14). The man has passed under the yoke of sin, he is the slave of the demonic power which has entered into and usurped control of his 'flesh', that is, his Satan-dominated human nature. The verses which then follow, beginning with "The work I do I do not recognize (i.e. as mine). For it is not what I will that I practise, but what I hate I do" (vii, 15), explicate the dialectic of the slave-situation. The slave is not in a position to prefer his own will or his own business to that of the tyrannous master whose errands he is bound to execute. We have to recognize, therefore, that the interest of working out a theological idea is a component in the complex, whatever element of personal religious experience may incidentally be considered to underlie its substance. If thus the possibility that an ideal or dialectical element enters into the construction is conceded, we are provided with an approach to the solution of the problem which is no longer purely dependent on the historical objectivity of the consciousness described.

The history of the interpretation of the passage is of not a little interest. It confines itself largely to the question whether the state of mind described is pre- or post-baptismal. The Greek Fathers from Origen onwards apparently held without exception that the condition described in Romans vii is that of the *unregenerate* man. Emphasis is laid on the prevailing pessimism of the delineation, on the soul's bondage to sin, on its incapacity to perform the good which is willed, and on its despairing cry: "O wretched man that I am! Who shall deliver me from this body of death?" The absence of divine grace from the situation is not, in the eyes of the Greek Fathers, contradicted by the presence within the man of a "mind" (νοῦς) or inward principle which consents to the spiritual law of God, and a will which is set on performing it. For, it is argued, similar complexes appear in the language of the Greek philosophers and even of the poets of Rome. The Greek Fathers, therefore, regard the analysis as falling entirely within the shadow of the pre-baptismal life, and they explain Paul's tenses—"I will", "I assent", "I hate", "I do", "I find"—as dramatic repristinations of a now transcended experience. On the other hand, the Latin Fathers with St. Augustine, and the Reformed Theologians with Calvin are firm that the exposition holds good only of the *regenerate* man. Stress is laid on the will to good which is so marked a feature of the delineation, on the unequivocalness of the testimony of the man's mind or νοῦς, on the present tenses in the passage, on the supporting evidence of other Pauline passages which describe a conflict of spirit and flesh as existing within the life of the faithful, and on the fact, emphasized by Calvin, that pagan statements such as Ovid's "*Video meliora proboque; deteriora sequor*" do not afford any real parallel. It may be remarked that the characteristic difference of Eastern and Western thought in their respective approaches to the ambiguous words of St. Paul reflect a modal divergence in the initial points of view. The Greek Fathers, stressing the element of Logos, knowledge, or illumination as the essential thing in the Christian revelation, are optimistic in their thoughts of the regenerate life. The Latins with their more radical conceptions of sin and redemption are not prepared to exclude the pessimism of St. Paul's narration from the realities of the Christian experience.

There enters now the *modern mind* with its romantic inclinations, its interest in psychology and in personality, and its optimistic outlook.

This has revived the point of view of the Greek Fathers, but with the characteristic addition that what Romans vii depicts is the story of Paul's own pre-Christian development, or at least of the inward process which led up to, and conditioned his conversion. What the limitations of this point of view are we have had occasion already to consider. But with a view to further analysis and by way of focusing the problem we may select an instance of the modern approach to the subject, followed by an instance of the older reformed approach, and see whether either does justice to the character of the chapter.

I take first the genial handling of the problem in Dr. C. H. Dodd's *Commentary on Romans.*

Professor Dodd holds that, though St. Paul's use of the first personal pronoun "I" does not always imply personal experience, yet "when he is describing religious experience, his 'I' passages bear the unmistakable note of autobiography". He appeals in this connection to Gal. ii. 19–21 and Phil. iii. 7–14 (p. 107). He also observes that, though the influence of theological ideas like that of the Fall is clearly stamped on Paul's analysis, it does not follow that Romans vii is an ideal construction, for "when a man sets out to allegorize the Old Testament, he finds there what he puts in" (p. 106). Dodd therefore finds no reason for resisting the *prima facie* impression that in Romans vii we have autobiography (p. 104), and pre-baptismal autobiography at that. For though the writer uses present tenses when he speaks of himself as "sold under sin", as incapable of performing the good which he wills, and as wretched to the point of despair, the condition which he describes cannot possibly have held good of him at the time of writing. It would stultify his argument, and utterly conflict with his statements elsewhere, if, "with all his sense of struggle and insecurity, he ever had such an experience as this after his conversion" (p. 108). So Dodd accepts the chapter as pre-Christian in its reference, and as an authentic transcript of Paul's experience during the crisis which came to a head in his vision on the Damascus road (p. 108).

This view Dodd then proceeds to work out in detail. The statement that the Law not only brought to Paul the knowledge of sin, but gave an impulse to the principle of sin, is illustrated by a story which St. Augustine tells about his own boyhood in the second book of his *Confessions* (p. 109). The assertion "I was alive apart from the Law once" is taken to describe "a happy childhood—happier and freer in retrospect, no doubt, than it ever really was", an age when authority was not yet felt as restrictive, and when troublesome conscience had not yet awaked (p. 110). But soon "in a Puritan home like Paul's, 'Shades of the prison-house begin to close upon the growing boy.' He became aware of the precepts and prohibitions of the Law. His desires were thwarted and repressed. The instincts asserted themselves in rebellion, and imperious desires for forbidden things forced themselves into his mind" (p. 111). "When the commandment came, sin revived, and I died." In this experience the old story of the Fall of man has come true in Paul's own life, and offers material for his psycho-analysis. And so on. The second stage in the delineation, which starts with verse 14 and employs present tenses, is understood as follows. Side by side with the bias towards the lower desires of which the growing boy is conscious, there is something in him which wants to be good. "Only, wrong desires have already been provoked. False sentiments have been formed. He cannot act as he would wish" (p. 113). Dodd compares the condition of mind described by Ovid, and identifies Paul's state with that ἀκρασία which Aristotle recognizes as the second of the four stages in the individual's ethical history. It is "a very intense experience of divided personality. . . . So complete is the separation between the will to do and the deed, that the man feels that some alien power in him is actually performing his actions" (p. 114). Such a condition is particularly distressing to a religious man, such as Paul was before his conversion, and characterizes his mind, Dodd thinks, at the time when he set out for Damascus. The closing words of the chapter (verse 25b), which in their present position impart a stamp of finality to the spiritual conflict, are removed wilfully with Moffatt to a situation before verse 24, and thus a pre-baptismal significance is secured for the whole delineation.

Is it possible to accept this typical modern interpretation of the meaning of Romans vii? I pass over the fact that the genial description of the growing boy smacks more of Rousseau, Wordsworth, and modern psychology than of the mental attitudes of the ancient world. St. Paul sometimes finds it in his heart to speak of childhood, as when he says, "When I was a child, I spoke as a child, I felt as a child, I thought as a child," but the purpose for which he recalls his youth in that famous passage does not encourage the belief that he attached much significance to youth's sensibilities and feelings. There are some weightier objections to which reference must be made.

(1) No other allusions of St. Paul to his Jewish upbringing breathe the idea that conflict or despair characterized his religious self-consciousness. In Gal. i. 13–14, which refers to the time before his

conversion, he speaks of himself as one who was making progress in Judaism beyond the mass of his contemporaries among his own nation, and who had an immeasurable enthusiasm for the traditions of the fathers. This does not suggest that any shake had been administered to the man's internal balance. A still more important consideration is that in Phil. iii. 5 ff., after dwelling on his proud privileges as a Jew, he describes himself as having been "in point of the righteousness which is of the law, blameless", and then adds, "But what things were gain to me, these I have counted loss for Christ." If St. Paul's inner experience as a Jew had taken the sinister turn supposed to be revealed in Romans vii, could he have claimed that his Judaism was all "gains" (κέρδη), and omitted to set anything down on the debit side of the account, or would he have described himself as κατὰ δικαιοσύνην τὴν ἐν νόμῳ γενόμενος ἄμεμπτος?

(2) Was it possible for anyone brought up in the religion of Judaism, while still a Jew, to look at the Law so detachedly, and in such terrible abstraction from God, as St. Paul does in Romans vii? If a religious Jew felt that his actions or thought came short of the Law's demands, if he felt the malignity of the *Yetzer-ha-Ra* within him, he would not indeed excuse himself, but he would not abandon hope. What he would have felt was that his case called for more prayer, more fasting, more study of Torah, more hope in God. It is inconceivable that he would despair of the *Law*. He would have cried to God with the writer of Psalm lxxiii:

> Nevertheless, I am continually with Thee . . .
> My flesh and my heart faileth;
> But God is the strength of my heart, and my
> portion for ever.

Indeed, the kind of Law and the kind of legal experience depicted in Romans vii never existed for any pure Jew, either St. Paul in his Jewish prime or anyone else. (It is a bloodless category, the dead ghost of a Law from which the glory of God has departed, a mere conceptual thing.)

(3) It must always be doubtful whether *the present tenses* in the section are adequately explained as dramatic representations of older experiences of St. Paul.

We turn now to a very different approach to the problem of Romans vii, this time to Calvin's treatment of the subject in his *Commentary on Romans*. Here it is a main concern of Calvin to insist on the regenerate character of the type of life portrayed by the apostle. It will be sufficient to cite a number of the main points in his exposition.

With reference to verse 9, "I was alive apart from the Law once," Calvin writes: "The question is, what time that was, wherein, by the ignorance of the law, or (as he saith) by the absence of the law, he did confidently claim life unto himself." Calvin considers it as certain that St. Paul "was brought up as a child in the doctrine of the law." But he adds that this was "a theology of the letter, which doth not humble its disciples; for, as he saith in another place, the veil was interposed, that the Jews could not see the light of life in the law". At once the more radical character of Calvin's exposition, as contrasted with the modern, appears, for, he continues: "So he also, so long as he, being void of the Spirit of Christ, had his eyes covered, did please himself in the external show of righteousness. He, therefore, counteth the law absent, which though it were present before his eyes, yet did not unite him with a perfect sense of the judgement of the Lord" (C.T.S. edit., pp. 177–8). Therefore over against the modern idea of a period of blissful innocence preceding Paul's knowledge of the Law, Calvin sets the less sentimental idea of a condition of spiritual darkness continuing with him all the time he was under the doctrine of the Law. While Dodd's idea is that of an immature thoughtlessness terminated by the onset of adolescence in Paul, Calvin's is that of an inveterate blindness to the real character of the Law terminated only by the opening of Paul's eyes by Christ. Not only the point of view, therefore, but the substance of the delineation is, in Calvin's eyes, Christian.

In the second section of the chapter (verses 14–25) the apostle propounds, says Calvin, "an example of a regenerate man, in whom the relics of the flesh do so dissent from the law of the Lord, that yet the spirit doth willingly obey the same law. But, first of all, he setteth down a bare comparison of man's nature and the law" (p. 181). These last words are worth noting, for they signify a qualification of Calvin's main contention. "The integrity of the doctrine of the law is set against the corruption of man's nature," for—"the law requireth a certain celestial and angelical righteousness, wherein there should appear no blot, to whose cleanness nothing ought to be wanting; but I, carnal man, can do nothing but strive against it" (p. 182). "Verily", he goes on, "whilst the will of a faithful man is led unto good by the Spirit of God, thereby appeareth plain the corruption of nature, which obstinately resisteth and striveth to the contrary. Therefore, thou hast in a regenerate man a very fit example, whereby thou mayest know how contrary the righteousness of the law is to our nature" (p. 183). On the same page of his Commentary Calvin says, apropos of the conflict, that "this conflict of the which the apostle speaketh, is not in any man before he be sanctified by the Spirit of God. For man, being left to his own nature, is wholly carried without assistance unto concupiscences" (p. 183). He means that Ovid and others of his kind ended up by throwing in their hand, and so would Paul but for the grace of God. The conflict of flesh and spirit, the Christian warfare proper, cannot be eliminated from the life of faith. "For regeneration is only begun in this life; the remnant of the flesh which remaineth doth always follow its corrupt affections and so moveth war against the Spirit" (p. 184). Calvin cites St. Augustine as one who at first thought that Romans vii revealed the unregenerate or "base" nature of man, but afterwards retracted this view (p. 185). And he considers that the confession that he did not the good that he would refers not to a few faults in the godly, "but in general noteth the whole course of their life" (p. 188).

So the cry "O wretched man!" means that "Paul, bewailing his state, did fervently covet death: yet he confesseth himself to rest in the grace of God. For it is not meet that the saints, whilst they examine their own imperfections, should forget what they have received of God" (p. 192). On this showing, verse 25b is in place at the end of the chapter, for it means that "the faithful never come unto the mark of righteousness so long as they dwell in their flesh" (p. 193). Perfectionism is excluded.

It is impossible not to feel the strength, fascination and even consistency of the Western and Reformed exposition as contrasted with the other. It takes the "celestial and angelical righteousness" required by the holy law of God seriously and radically in its relation to Christian life. But the question remains whether Calvin's radical interpretation of the spiritual life corresponds with the data of the representation in Romans vii. To my mind it does not. If for the reasons I have already stated it will not do to regard the chapter as mirroring a stage in St. Paul's experience as a *Jew*, neither can it be taken to reflect St. Paul's normal or fully developed consciousness as a *Christian*, and for this reason. The apostle makes no mention in the chapter of the Spirit or of grace, nor does he, as we have observed, bring in the name of Jesus until the close, when the cry "I thank God through Jesus Christ our Lord" marks the resolution of the discords.

In Calvin's words he allows himself to set down "a bare comparison of man's nature and the law".

In fact, we are in the curious position of having to say that, if Romans vii portrays a phase of Judaism, it is a Judaism in which no aura of grace or redeeming love attaches to the Law: and if it portrays a phase of Christianity, it is a Christianity in which no aura of help from Christ or the Spirit attaches to the Gospel. These considerations are sufficient to raise the question whether in Romans vii we are dealing with a real and not rather an hypothetical situation. The latter represents the conclusion to which I have come. The seventh chapter of Romans represents a religious situation which never really existed under this particular form except for argument's sake. It has been developed dialectically out of experiences which, though derived from religious life, never figured just in the formal setting in which Romans vii has placed them. In support of this thesis, I suggest that we turn back to Romans vi and examine the purpose of the whole section of the Epistle in which this analysis of the state of a soul under the Law is embedded.

In Romans vi St. Paul, having already established that God alone is the source of righteousness to man, and that this gift of righteousness in Christ is (a) revealed on the Cross, (b) confirmed at the deepest levels of the Old Testament religion, and (c) verified by the facts of the Christian experience, proceeds to show how this righteousness becomes actualized in Christian holiness. He starts from the question, which takes up a contemporary jibe against his teaching, "Are we to continue in sin, that grace may abound?" The "we", of course, refers to Christians. In vi. 15, the question emerges again in the sharper and more definite form, "Are we ever to sin (ἁμαρτήσωμεν, aorist), because we are not under law but under grace?" The challenge to Christianity, which is implied under the form of this question, turns on the idea that to give up the Law is to give up ethic, whereas St. Paul's position is that sin consists in falling not from the Law, but from Christ. The same idea is implied also in the Jewish criticism that St. Paul in casting off the Law is classifying it with sin and other "old things" belonging to the life of the flesh. St. Paul, therefore, has to deal with the charge that he makes out the Law to be Sin. At the same time he has to counter the Jewish claim that the Law is the indispensable basis of Ethic. In this way we get the right line of approach to Romans vii. Paul is simultaneously repelling the idea that he makes out the Law to be Sin, and answering the question, "Are we, i.e. we

Christians, to sin because we are not under Law?" His way of doing this is (i) to show what the Law means to the Christian whose eyes Christ has opened, and for whom religious ethic possesses a far more radical and inward significance than the Jew, untaught by the Sermon on the Mount, was ever able to perceive; and (ii) to ask what would become of the Christian, what would be the fate of the Christian if he were left alone with the Law. *What is life under the Law?* It is implied by the conditions of this argument that grace should be excluded from consideration. On the other hand, the Law is envisaged in the sharpened form, which its imperative has received from the teaching of Jesus Christ.

It is in this way, I think, that we grasp the actual character of Romans vii. It is an unreal, in the sense of a non-historical, a hypothetical situation which is called up before us. It corresponds to no actual phase either of Jewish-Christian or of Pauline-Christian existence, for in neither of these situations can we suppose the soul's darkness to have been unrelieved by some ray of heavenly grace. St. Paul has set the stage for an enquiry dictated by a purely argumentative necessity. *What is life under the law according to the logic of its nature?* St. Paul presents the case from the standpoint of Christianity, but a Christianity not present in all its terms. We are contemplating an abstraction developed by dialectic, not the actual situation either of the regenerate or of the unregenerate man, but only the hypothetical condition of a Christian under Law, a *Contradictio in Adjecto*.

It is not necessary to develop the point in detail, but only to submit my thesis to your consideration. I have admitted that St. Paul has made use of genuine religious material for the purposes of his dialectic. So it is in the first section of the argument, where he speaks of the intensified realization of sin which resulted when the Law "came". I agree with Calvin that he is thinking here not of an adolescent awakening to moral reality but of the final removal of the veil from his eyes by Christ. In the second section, where he speaks of the consciousness of slavery and impotence which is experienced *vis-à-vis* the Law, he may be drawing to some extent on actualities of the crisis preceding his conversion. But the encounter of Christian with Law is, for the rest, an ideal construction. I would only add that we ought to give up the idea of writing a pre-baptismal biography of the great apostle. If we still attempt it, we should be sparing in our use of the supposed evidence supplied by Romans vii.

PART III

Eschatology and Mission

CHAPTER I

Early Christian Eschatology

I

Early Christian Eschatology—it may seem that I have chosen, if not a meagre and worn-out theme, one which is a little out of season. A score of years ago the subject was very much alive, it formed indeed the battle-ground of a critical controversy, and a Cambridge professor, introducing Schweitzer's *Quest of the Historical Jesus* to English readers, could speak of his age as on the brink of a new theological vision. "We are beginning to see", wrote Dr. Burkitt, "that the apocalyptic vision, the New Age which God is to bring in, is no mere embroidery of Christianity, but the heart of its enthusiasm." But that controversy has passed, the armies have withdrawn from the field, the fruits of victory have been solidly secured, and he who now visits those scenes does so in a spirit of detachment like a quiet wayfarer who takes the air. Be it so! There are some things that are best observed with a quiet eye in the off-seasons. I notice that both parties in the late conflict were concerned with the place and significance in the Christian system of what were really *Jewish* ideas. The Liberals argued that the apocalyptic elements in early Christianity, the ideas of the future Kingdom of God and of the coming of the Son of Man, were Jewish ideas and therefore not of Jesus. The Eschatologists replied that they were Jewish, and therefore of the very essence of Jesus' teaching. What neither side sufficiently considered was whether these Jewish ideas, from the moment that Christianity touched them, were not *transformed* and turned into sources of a spiritual energy such as Judaism had never known.

I

What we have actually to consider now is the *religious* aspect presented by early Christian eschatology, that is to say by those vivid ideas of the World and Life to Come which exercised so potent an influence on the early Christian mind. Here two separate questions may be distinguished. (1) We may inquire into the *origin* of these ideas, which for us here will mean the determining not out of what Judaic elements the substance and form of the ideas shaped themselves, but what religious necessity compelled the use of these ideas and the whole tone of enthusiastic other-worldliness which is so marked a feature of early Christian thought. It will not do to dismiss this question with a mere wave of the hand in the direction of the Hebrew prophets and apocalyptists, for neat explanations leave untouched the thing which above all others needs to be explained, viz. the immensely increased vitality and attraction which the ideas of the Kingdom of God, of the World and Life to Come, and of Resurrection, exercise in the Christian system.[1] (2) We have at the same time to enquire into the nature of the forces in Early Christianity by which these same ideas, the ideas of the Life and World Beyond, etc., were held in *control*. There were instincts in Christianity which opposed themselves to the making of too great a separation between the life of the spirit here and hereafter, and these instincts to resist in the name of the Spirit a too complete absorption of religion in ideas of the Other World must have had their root in the Christian experience, and must, like the ideas which they held in check, have some organic relation to the message of Jesus. Why did the ideas of the Other World, so bright, so vivid, so filled with a new personal significance through their association with Jesus, not oust altogether the Church's interest in the present life? Here we have a very remarkable feature of Early Christianity, which ought not to be overlooked, but which has hardly received the attention which is due to it. The two schools of critical interpretation, for instance, which divided the field between them a generation ago, nowhere showed themselves more unsatisfactory than in their failure to do justice to this fact.

On the one hand, Liberal theology proceeded by ignoring almost entirely the apocalyptic ideas embodied in the Gospel. It regarded these ideas as merely the old rags and trappings of Judaism. Its mode of approach to Jesus was constituted by nineteenth-century ideas of what it became the Founder of a World-Religion to be. Whatever did not fit together with these presuppositions was ruthlessly extruded. Thereby Liberalism not only failed to observe how *modernizing* a method it pursued, but proved helpless to explain why with Chris-

[1] There is a release of new religious potentiality in connection with these ideas which resembles the release of atomic energy when atoms disintegrate.

tianity the ideas of the Other World took so new and so immensely strong a hold upon the minds of men. But if the Liberals went astray by ignoring one important element in the situation, the school of radical Eschatologists which followed showed itself even more blind on another side. If the Liberals modernized, how can the Eschatologists be acquitted of *archaizing* when they insisted that traditional ideas and beliefs must bear for Jesus the same significance which they bore for the preceding or the contemporary generation? The Eschatologists assumed this. They would not concede to Jesus the resolution of a single Other-Worldly idea, state, or thing into a form of present spiritual experience. If anywhere such ideas as the Kingdom, or the Resurrection, or the Coming of Christ, or the New World or the Life to Come appear in the New Testament as invested with a present spiritual reality, such an interpretation is declared not to be of Jesus. Thus a number of passages in the gospels are given up, while, as for St. Paul, the origin of most of his distinctive ideas is sought outside of Jesus.

In this situation one may be pardoned for asking whether there is not need for a fresh return to the mind and teaching of Jesus. Is it not possible to find in Him a better synthesis of the disparate elements appearing in Christianity, a reconciliation at once of the vividness with which the World and the Life to Come are apprehended by His Christian imagination and of the calmness with which these same supernal realities are felt to be embodied or reflected in interior experiences? Can we unite a little more fully the outward and the inward aspects of the New Testament revelation? Such a task seems at least in need of being attempted.

2

Jesus began His work with the affirmation that the Kingdom, the Supernatural Reign of God for which Judaism had been waiting, was at hand. Not Mark alone gives His primary pronouncement in this apocalyptic form. Q also with its "Blessed are ye poor, for yours is the Kingdom of God," and L with the Sermon of Jesus at Nazareth and the word "Today this scripture is fulfilled in your hearing," testify that the initial direction of Jesus' mind lay towards the realization of a Divine Idea or state of existence which hitherto had been a matter only of religious vision. With this initial character of Jesus' message agree numbers of vivid sayings, chiefly characteristic of Jesus' later ministry, such as "There are some standing here who shall not taste death till they see the Kingdom of God come with power," "The Son of Man comes in the glory of His Father with the holy angels," "I shall not eat this passover, until it is fulfilled in the Kingdom of God," "It is my dying will for you that, even as my Father appointed a Kingdom for me, you should sit and drink at my table in My Kingdom, and you shall sit on thrones judging the twelve tribes of Israel," "You shall see the Son of Man sitting at the right hand of Power, and coming with the clouds of heaven." But side by side with such sayings which retain for the Kingdom of God its familiar transcendent or Other-Worldly cast, we have in the same authorities other sayings which ascribe to this same supernatural Kingdom a present existence and reality. And it does not seem to me satisfactory to take some of these sayings such as "Neither shall they say, Look here! or there! for the Kingdom of God is in your midst," or again parables like the Leaven and the Mustard Seed, and to bend and twist them about till they come into line with the idea of the Eschatologists. This is to force on them a sense contrary to their face value, and one which it would never enter the mind of any unsophisticated person to suggest. Rather ought we to enquire whether, when Jesus spoke of the Kingdom, apocalyptic conception though it was, He did not do so in a way that, without ceasing to make it supernatural, gave the Kingdom an actual and immediate relation to the present life. This would have the effect of retaining for Jesus many of these sayings in the Gospels which the Eschatologists reject, while at the same time it would throw out a link between Him and St. Paul, with whom ideas such as the Kingdom, the New Creation, and the Resurrection have, without losing their supernatural character, definitely taken root on this side of the grave. For this reason it is worth while to examine more closely what Jesus meant when He said that the Kingdom of God had come near.

The full pronouncement was, as you remember—and I quote Mark's words as indicating at least the sense in which early Christianity grasped the matter—that "The time is fulfilled, and the Reign of God has come near." The Kingdom of God for Jesus, as for Judaism, was not an idea existing outside of time but an event or consummation to be realized in the time-process. From the earliest period Israel had grasped salvation as coming through an Act of God in the future which would have consequences for the whole nation. Even when some four or five centuries before Christ the conception of a future life of blessedness for the individual disengaged itself from the wider conception of the nation's destiny, it was only for a moment. The final perfection of Israel's fortunes reasserted itself, and the future of the individual fell again into line with that of the nation, save that now it took the form of a resurrection of the righteous to share in the consummated blessedness of the community. From this time forth the perfected destiny of the nation attracts to itself a supernatural form. In the second century B.C., when the Maccabean star was in the ascendant, it shaped itself as a kingdom upon the earth. In the first century, with the waning of the same dynastic fortunes, it here and there abandoned hope of the present world and located itself in a new heaven and a new earth. But it was always a future event, a thing in time, a vision which moved onwards before the mind of the nation.

The characteristics of Hebrew thought were uniformly (i) the conception of God as revealing Himself to man by acts of power, (ii) the conception of a Divine plan to which these acts were subordinated, and which must one day stand complete for the world to see, (iii) the vesting of this Plan in the fortunes of the chosen people, and the completion of history in a divine Reign upon earth. To some extent the Jewish statement of these ideas presented the features of a protest against world-civilization. This was accidental. It was due to the peculiar circumstances of Israel's political destiny. To some extent also the Jewish idea corresponded with the demand for a final explication of the dark problems of life, of sin, of unmerited suffering, of sorrow and death. Judaism no longer sought a solution for these ills within the existing world. It postponed its hopes to the New Age, for when this New Age moved into position alongside of the present world it would be so adjusted to the facts that the world would have no ragged edges left. "The crooked places would be made straight, and the rough places plain, and all flesh should see the salvation of God."

Now the essential ideas of the Hebrew scheme all, as Professor Bevan points out, reappear in Christianity. Jesus too speaks of an appointed "time" or season. He speaks also of the Kingdom coming with "power", i.e. by God's Mighty Act in the world-process. He says that the Son of Man will come in the "glory" of his Father with the holy angels. For Jesus therefore the Kingdom of God marks an event in time, the emergence of a supernatural order discontinuous with past history, which brings upon the stage the Eternal or Wholly Other. Never in Jesus' teaching has the Kingdom of God a non-supernatural character. But what is meant by its *nearness*? When Jesus said, "The time is fulfilled, and the Kingdom of God has drawn nigh," can we possibly think that He differed from His contemporaries only in that He assigned to the Kingdom an earlier, they a later date? Did He see the Kingdom merely as part of the unwinding scroll of time? It was in this way upon the whole that His nation looked at the Kingdom. It projected its visions upon the map of the future. By *postponing* the consummation it salved its conscience from the sense of any immediate *moral* urgency in God's plan for the world. Judaism was profoundly interested in signs of the future Kingdom. It exhausted its ingenuity in calculations of weeks and years. It looked for the Kingdom to come, as Jesus said, μετὰ παρατηρησεως. *Waiting* for the event came the normal attitude, a second nature to Judaism. There were always such and such "times" to be fulfilled. There were always such and such "signs" to be given. So the Kingdom went on being a vision, which receded like the rainbow before the traveller's advance. God would one day make an end of sin, but not yet! God would one day establish communion with His people, but not now! But is there anything of this kind in Jesus? Does He calculate by signs, or speak of times yet needing to elapse? Does He know by means of what is happening in external history? Is He found asking whether the times have yet reached their lowest point of darkness? Or does He say that there will be the end of sin, but not yet! Or that there will be reconciliation to God, but not now! It is here, I think, that we must recognize that when Jesus says "Thy Kingdom is at hand," He cannot be thinking merely of *temporal* nearness. His contemporaries thought of the Kingdom merely as in time, and therefore for them it ceased to enter really into time. He thought of it in intensely moral, religious terms. Its urgency was moral urgency. Its instancy lay in the very nature of the redeeming will of God. Can one think of *God* as needing to wait for the accomplishment of His purpose. No, it is now that sin is to be ended, and the power of God to be put forth. He who had looked into the faces of Israel's crowds at the Jordan had seen with compelling insight what the nation lacked. Alone in Israel's history He recognized that God's Kingdom needed not to be waited for, but to be *received* by faith.

3

We suggest then that when Jesus said "the Kingdom of God has come near," He was speaking of moral urgency. He meant that the supernatural Reign of God was now to express itself in terms of supernatural present experience. God was waiting to bring about for man the things which "prophets and righteous men had yearned to see, but which they had not beheld". In other words, God waits for man's consent, for man's surrender of himself to His purpose: better still, for man's faith, since faith alone not only assents to, but *anticipates* the will of God. And it is only because Jesus not merely preached this immediate will of God to redeem men from present moral, physical and temporal evil, but succeeded in imparting to some a share of His faith, that the New Testament explains itself at all. The New Testament throbs and rings with the sense that the line between expectation and fulfilment has been crossed. All eschatological conceptions have drawn nearer and have increased immeasurably in force, because, through the one door opened for God's power to set up His Kingdom, all these other concepts, righteousness, peace, power, resurrection, have entered with it. Only as we interpret the matter in this sense, can we speak of the teaching of Christ as rooted in apocalyptic.

Here then, as I believe, we have the real beginnings of Christian Eschatology. Not in Jewish concepts as such does it start, but in Jewish concepts as filled with immediate moral regenerative significance. The will of God, just because it is so holy and good, is instant for accomplishment. The Kingdom of God, just because it is *God's* cannot from His side require to be delayed. The victory over sin, which the Kingdom carries with it, cannot be retarded except by man's resistance. There must have been hours when Jesus pointed out to His disciples in intimate converse with them just what it was that was coming between their souls and the full power of God. Sin, the barrier between man and God, had to be surrendered to His omnipotent will to deal with it as with every other thing that disputes His government of men. Faith in God's *power* is demanded, the unquestioning assurance that what God wills to be He will accomplish if there is consent. "Amen I say to you, whosoever shall say to this mountain, Be lifted up and cast into the sea, and is not doubtful in his heart that what he says comes to pass, it shall be to him. For this reason I say to you, all things that you pray and ask for, believe that you have got them, and they shall be yours." Jesus when He spoke these words was according to Mark standing on the Mount of Olives, where the prophet Zechariah had said that God would set His feet in the last days, and where the mountain would part in twain. Jesus is implying that if His disciples had faith to take God's will with sufficient seriousness, they would see the Messianic age realized. So again when the disciples, alluding to the Rich Man who went backward, said, "Then who can be saved?" Jesus answered, "With men it is impossible, but not with God, for with God all things are possible." All that Jesus offers to men, and all that He asks of them is in the context of God's immediate will to set up His Kingdom now.

Jesus' doctrine is, therefore, that the supernatural Kingdom of God, so long expected, is now to express itself in terms of supernatural life in the Here and Now. What are the proofs of this position?

(i) There is the absence, as already noted, of all indications that Jesus' initial message rested on any calculation of external signs or dates or events, or that He ever even hinted at a merely *temporal* nearness of the Kingdom.

(ii) There is the emphasis which He puts on *faith* or surrender as the primary constituent of man's response to God. Jesus does not inculcate an attitude of waiting but an active appropriation of the *power* of God now to make an end of evil. The faith in question is not only faith in God's power but faith in God's *way* of accomplishing His ends, for how else are we to interpret such words as those about not resisting evil, about loving enemies, about forgiving seventy times seven, about denying self, etc.? Such teaching signifies a *revolution* in human nature, but it is the divine revolution which God wills and which is equivalent to the Reign of God in life. So Jesus also inculcates faith in God's *love* and care to an extent that goes beyond everything that seems *humanly* possible. But that is because God's will to set up His Kingdom is assumed as the starting-point. In fact it is only by making this assumption that we get a proper *rationale* of the ethics of Jesus. It is commonly acknowledged that His teaching is no mere interim-ethic. Actually it is final because it expresses the consummation of man's life in *God*.

(iii) There are words that definitely give the Kingdom a place in present existence. Jesus, claiming men for God, says, "If I by the Spirit of God cast out demons, the Kingdom of God has come upon you." To the Pharisee He says, "The Kingdom of God is in your midst," meaning that it was already represented in Himself and His disciples. Of John He says, "He who is least in the Kingdom of God is greater than he." There are moreover the parables of the Mustard-seed and Leaven which may well mean that though the disciples of Jesus, those who have believed in and experienced the redeeming power of God are a small handful, they shall yet be a very great number. The regenerating power of the *Euangelion* will spread from soul to soul till all the ransomed are gathered. Such evidence is not to be distorted to suit the stringency of any preconceived apocalyptic theory.

(iv) There is the place which Jesus Himself takes in the faith of His disciples. To them He is not the herald or harbinger but the *bringer* of the Kingdom. The secret of it belongs to Him, and through Him it is shared with others. Faith in the power of God therefore shapes itself into identification of life with Jesus.

(v) Finally there is the evidence of the apostolic church. Ought any man to disconnect from Jesus' own historical work the kind of experience which fills the pages of St. Paul or of the Fourth Evangelist? Take words like these: "If any man is in Christ, (there is) a new creation; old things have passed away; behold, they have become new," "God was in Christ reconciling the world unto Himself," "If you are risen with Christ, seek the things that are above," "I am the resurrection and the life." Such words shift the emphasis from the future to the present, from an apocalyptic programme to an already realized experience. They make the Mighty Acts of God centre no longer exclusively in the World to Come but already in the Here and Now. If, as Professor F. C. Porter has told us, St. Paul held and taught no doctrine about Christ which did not verify itself both in the Jesus of History and in the Christ of living experience, have we not here a confirmation of our view that what Jesus set Himself to do was to translate the supernatural Reign of God, else only a vision, into terms of present supernatural regenerated life?

This I believe He did, and it was because His disciples rightly took Him up here that the Christian movement went forward. The Christian Church advanced by a kind of cellular reproduction of its units as one soul communicated to another the regenerated life which it had received. But there is another side to this matter. Jesus, while bringing the Kingdom of God into present relation with the life of men did not abandon the conception of its final glory. It was the supernatural Kingdom which had struck root here, but the same supernatural Kingdom had still its final climax. As time went on, and the opposition of His foes drew the limits of His earthly activity closer around Him, He came to throw increasing emphasis upon that ultimate aspect. But this side of the matter must be reserved for the next lecture.

II

The opposition which Jesus encountered, and the clearness with which He saw that His time on earth was short, had effects upon His work. His way had become restricted to a single narrow path with rejection and a Cross at the end of it. He does not during this period in any way abandon the primary position that the Kingdom of God is to be received now in terms of supernaturally regenerated life and that men are to enter now into this life at whatever cost, but He brings to His aid more frequently the language in which prophecy or apocalypse had spoken of the Kingdom. As He faces the prospect of rejection and death, there burns and shines more constantly before Him the apocalyptic word of Daniel about the Son of Man who should receive from the Most High an everlasting dominion and kingdom and power. The symbolism of Daniel enables Him to sum up the finality of the passion which possessed Him. It helps us, I think, to group round this great crisis in His earthly mission most of the formal apocalyptic utterances which we find scattered over the gospels, as well as most of the teaching which turns on the supreme renunciations which His disciples are to make. We have the support of Mark for this ordering of the material, and also, I think, the authority of the Q source. The Kingdom which is thus envisaged in its final completeness and in association with Resurrection, the Final Judgement, and the Life Beyond is not different from the Kingdom to which Jesus had already given an immediate ethical spiritual interpretation. That supernatural Kingdom has already projected its arc into time, and enfolded the present life in its embrace, and it is but of the further reaches of the same Kingdom, between which and Himself now stand the folding-doors of death, that Jesus now speaks. But this final realization of the vision is not distinct from the present experience otherwise than as the final sum of a series is distinct from the terms of the series. I need not here speak of this teaching further than to recall some of the significant words belonging to this period: "There are some standing here who shall not taste death till they see the Kingdom of God come with power," "The Son of Man will come in the glory of His Father with the holy angels," "I shall not eat of this Passover until it is fulfilled in the Kingdom of God," "It is my dying will for you that, even as my Father appointed a kingdom for me, you should eat and drink at My table in My Kingdom, and you shall sit on thrones." Finally the answer to the High Priest's question, "You shall see the Son of Man sitting at the right hand of Power, and coming with the clouds of heaven."

Now as it was on this note that the earthly teaching of Jesus ended, it is not surprising that the more apocalyptic or future aspect of the Kingdom was the one which chiefly dominated the mind of the Christian community in the succeeding generation. While the work begun by Jesus went on, and the experience of regenerated life propagated itself from soul to soul, there was a danger in some quarters of pure apocalypticism reasserting itself, and of significance being drawn away from the present experience and present task of the Christian community. There was a danger of interest being wholly absorbed in the Return of Christ, particularly under conditions of persecution, and here we come to the second of the questions with which we started out. We have to take account of the *control* which we now find being imposed upon a too one-sided emphasis upon apocalyptic ideas, particularly upon the expectation of an ideal age upon earth to be inaugurated by the Parousia of the Son of Man. "Lord, wilt thou at this time restore the kingdom of Israel?" In the condensed and symbolistic narrative of Early Acts we find this question asked, and answered by the fact that Christ forbade inquiry regarding "times and seasons", and turned the eyes of His Church to its present world-mission of testimony, for which it was to receive the Holy Spirit. This implies a return to Jesus' teaching that the Kingdom of God is primarily to be interpreted as divine regeneration of life. Only if this is realized will the Kingdom of God upon earth be ever anything else than a vision.

In dealing with the question which emerges here, I propose to take up a certain word in the apocalyptic discourse which, a generation or more after the death of Christ, the evangelist Mark puts into His lips.

CHAPTER 2

The Ego Eimi of the Messianic Presence in the New Testament[1]

The investigator of the Old Testament, approaching his subject from the standpoint of worship, cannot but, sooner or later, come face to face with the question whether the history, the theology, and the ethics of Israel do not, in the last analysis, represent the surface-aspect and indeed, in a very real way, the rationalization of a deeper underlying mysticism of spiritual life. The theology and the ethics of the Old Testament, are not these the refraction on the historical plane of the engagement of the Hebrew mind with God? In the Old Testament I found the remarkable stories of Jacob at Bethel, Jacob again at Peniel, Moses in the desert of Midian, the child Samuel at Shiloh, Elijah in the cave at Horeb, Isaiah in the temple at Jerusalem, and the like. Such stories would not have acquired or retained so great a place in the Old Testament records if an underlying element of the numinous or supernatural had not been a constant and normative factor of Israel's religious existence. Here, then, was something by which one was taken, so to speak, behind the chancel-rails of the Biblical history, theology and ethics, and given entrance into an inner shrine where God and the human spirit met. And here God was revealed as the Holy, the Existential, who names Himself to Moses as the אֶהְיֶה, the Ἐγώ εἰμι ὁ Ὤν of the LXX. I found that it was the God thus revealed who sent Moses and the prophets to the children of Israel, and who, when Moses and the prophets faltered and said, "Who are we that we should go?", answered, "I will be with you," and gave them a mouth and wisdom. Primary impulses set up by what were believed to be direct interpositions of the Divine thus translated themselves into the history, the wisdom, and the law of the Hebrews. They integrated and vitalized traditions and ideas, some of

[1] A paper read at the first General Meeting of the Studiorum Novi Testamenti Societas, held at Oxford in March 1947. Reprinted from *The Journal of Theological Studies*, July–October 1947 (Vol. XLVIII, No. 191–2), pp. 137–45.

them of Babylonian or Canaanite origin, by which the experience was rationalized.

This being so, it was natural to ask whether in the New Testament also the same relation of primary reality and secondary presentation was not clearly to be recognized. Here the Divine manifestation is essentially centralized and localized in Jesus, but here also the primary experience is, in time, rationalized historically, theologically, and morally. For example, in the Synoptic record the revelation of the living God in Jesus finds expression ultimately in terms of the Messianic beliefs of Judaism. Jesus the Revealer of God is confessed to be the Christ of whom the prophets spoke. Here historical Messianic ideas are, in the last analysis, the reagent bringing out the significance which Jesus has, in Jewish Palestine, for the religious nature of man. Later in the Pauline and Johannine writings a further rationalization takes place. Philosophical-mystical ideas of Hellenistic provenance are in this case the reagent, and Jesus is declared to be the Lord, the Incarnate Logos, whose message is Wisdom from God. Behind both presentations can be recognized the intuitive religious apprehensions which support the theological and historical thought-forms and language. They come to expression, for example, in the 'Εγώ εἰμι with which the disciples hear Jesus speaking to them on the stormy lake and indirectly in the cry "Depart from me, for I am a sinful man," with which Peter falls on his knees before Him. The disciples "worship" Jesus before they can put into words the mystery of His person. In the Pauline religion it is not the Jesus "after the flesh" but the risen and glorified Christ who is the centre of numinous reality and before whom every knee is to bow and every tongue confess that He is Lord. While there is rationalization both in St. Paul's theology of the Atonement and in the mysticism of his death-and-resurrection idea of the new life in Christ—since in the one case he uses Jewish, in the other Hellenistic, religious categories to bring out his thought—there is no mistaking the existential character of the primary experiences lying behind his use of words.

From these high generalities we may pass to observations of a more particular character. There are passages in the New Testament in which the process of rationalization can be seen taking place.

One of these passages I desire now to submit to more exact analysis. It is the opening utterance in the Synoptic apocalypse in Mark xiii, a passage which has received very indifferent treatment at the hands of commentators. In reply to His disciples' query, "When shall these things [i.e. the destruction of the temple] be?", Jesus is reported as saying: "See to it that no one misleads you. Many will come in My name (ἐπὶ τῷ ὀνόματί μου), saying 'Εγώ εἰμι, and they will mislead many" (Mark xiii. 6). Luke xxi. 8 reproduces the terms of this dictum exactly except that he adds to the false rumour of the misleaders the words "and the time has come near" (ὁ καιρὸς ἤγγικεν). In Matt. xxiv. 5, on the other hand, an alteration occurs. Mark's 'Εγώ εἰμι is expanded into 'Εγώ εἰμι ὁ Χριστός, which is presumed to give the meaning. This, however, is a matter which needs looking into.

Expositors from the time of the *Catena Patrum* have universally assumed that St. Matthew's gloss is right and that his words "I am the Christ" give the sense of the original 'Εγώ εἰμι of Mark. One and all, they have taken the "many" of the passage to refer to false claimants to Messiahship, impostors or pretenders, such as, according to the *Catena*, were Theudas and Judas the Galilean. But this exegesis involves the incredible assumption that such persons could be described as coming "in the name of Jesus", that is, as persons making the Christian profession. This being so, and the association of the two things being unthinkable, the commentators have supposed that ἐπὶ τῷ ὀνόματί μου was meant to bear the sense of usurping the name of Jesus, arrogating to themselves His title and privilege. But this is to put a very strained and unnatural sense on the phrase ἐπὶ τῷ ὀνόματί μου, which elsewhere appears ordinarily as convertible with the more usual ἐν τῷ ὀνόματί μου. If there is a distinction of meaning between the phrases, it is that, where ἐν is used, it is instrumental, and the phrase is equivalent to "using or taking on one's lips the name of Jesus", while, where ἐπί is employed, the meaning leans rather to "taking one's stand on the title of Jesus, appealing to Him as one's authority". It is by no means clear, therefore, that the usurpation idea is admissible, nor does it appear that the commentators who have resorted to this interpretation have been very happy about it. It has not everywhere given the green light to those who have proposed to take this road.

In this connection the record of Wellhausen's heart-searchings on the point is illuminating. Commenting on Mark xiii. 6 he says: "Christian false prophets there have been, but scarcely Christian false Messiahs. 'They come in My name' (which means they are Christians) contradicts their saying that they are themselves the Messiah. The offensive ἐπὶ τῷ ὀνόματί μου is attested by Matthew and Luke." On Matt. xxiv. 5 he says that the χριστός predicate, wanting in Mark, is correctly supplied. "In My name" must mean "as though it were I (als wäre ich es)" that spoke. On Luke xxi. 8, however, he says that ἐπὶ τῷ ὀνόματί μου, though the primitive reading, is "vielleicht unecht", for the idea can scarcely be entertained that Christians arrogate the title of Christ. It will be felt that this is not a very encouraging ending to the exegetical course which Wellhausen has travelled.

Is it not time to try another road? Does 'Εγώ εἰμι in the Markan passage really mean, as the author of Matthew took it to mean, 'Εγώ εἰμι ὁ Χριστός? I cannot think so.

The thesis of this paper is that the many who come "in the name" of Christ, asserting His authority for what they say, are, as the language of the passage indicates, Christians, and the 'Εγώ εἰμι does not mean "I am the Christ", but "the Christ is come, the *Parousia* has arrived!" The 'Εγώ, in other words, is not the ἐγώ of the individual speaker, but the ἐγώ of Jesus Christ. The 'Εγώ εἰμι is that of the Messianic Presence.

The many who come and mislead the Church are excited, apocalyptically minded Christians who, from the "wars and rumours of wars", the persecutions, and other strange and portentous happenings which have begun to fill the world, have incontinently concluded that the end of the world has come, or, as they say, "It is Jesus!" Against this premature mixing-up of the *Parousia* with present world-events and against the distraction of the Church from its proper business which is to preach the gospel to all the nations, the Synoptic apocalypse sounds its siren-note of warning.

The interesting thing about the Markan passage on this interpretation is that in its 'Εγώ εἰμι there comes to the surface the Christian thought of "the presence", here meaning the supernatural manifestation of God in Christ, which is the reality lying behind the veil of earthly history.

When the writer of Matthew turns the 'Εγώ εἰμι of Mark into 'Εγώ εἰμι ὁ Χριστός he is scaling down a supra-historical reality to the point at which it becomes the mere statement of one Messianic claim among others in a world of competing and opposed Messianic sects.

What then is the evidence in favour of the view that 'Εγώ εἰμι in the Markan passage means not "I am the Messiah" but "the Messiah is come, His reign is on, it is the *Parousia*"?

In the first place, this conclusion is supported by a close comparison of the Pauline apocalypse in 2 Thess. ii and the Synoptic apocalypse in Mark xiii. The Pauline apocalypse begins by appealing to Christians not to be agitated by the idea which had got about, whether through spirit or through word or through letter purporting to be from the apostle himself, that "the Day of the Lord has set in" (ὡς ὅτι ἐνέστηκεν ἡ ἡμέρα τοῦ Κυρίου). This is a delusion against which the Thessalonians must protect themselves. The analogy between the apostle's appeal and the opening warning in the Synoptic apocalypse is obvious. The Pauline apocalypse goes on to point out that many things must happen before the Lord's advent; above all, there must be the revelation of the Man of Sin. The Synoptic apocalypse teaches similarly that present and coming world-events of a terrifying kind are but the "beginning" of the birth-pangs introducing the Messianic age, and it makes this warning extend to cover the profanation of the Temple by some human act of sacrilege; the participle ἑστηκότα in Mark xiii. 14 is, it will be observed, masculine. Here the parallelism of the two documents at essential points is close. Once more, in the Pauline apocalypse the *Parousia* lies beyond the profanation wrought by the Man of Sin, and it comes with its own special evidence. So is it in the Synoptic drama. Finally, in their general purpose, the two documents agree together. That purpose is to save the Church from paralysis of its energies by an excessive apocalypticism based on current events and to keep it oriented to its supreme task of missionary enterprise. So complete an analogy suggests that in the opening verses of the two discourses the expressions 'Εγώ εἰμι and "the Day of the Lord has set in" can be regarded as identical. 'Εγώ εἰμι in Mark means "the Christ has come, it is the *Parousia*!"

In the second place, the same interpretation of 'Εγώ εἰμι is suggested by the use of the expression in St. John iv. 25–6, where Jesus is speaking to the Samaritan woman. The Samaritan woman has been trying to evade the challenge of Jesus by a series of stratagems. (1) She pretends that she does not know what is meant by the "living water" of which Jesus speaks. (2) She argues that on matters like the worship of God Samaritans and Jews have incompatible ideas. Then, when the affectation of not understanding theological language and the appeal to denominational differences break down before the personal issue raised by Jesus, she makes her last throw. She appeals from the present moment to the time when the Messiah comes, and we can leave these matters over, she says in effect, until that time. Jesus answers: 'Εγώ εἰμι, ὁ λαλῶν σοι. In this context, where the Messiah has been named, these words can, of course, mean: "I am the Messiah, I who speak to you." But they can also mean, "The Messiah is here, He is present in Him who speaks to you." So interpreted, the expression 'Ἐγώ εἰμι indicates an existential situation, not merely an historical claim, and this may well be its meaning elsewhere in the Gospels when it occurs, as it sometimes does, without explicit reference to the Messiah in the context.

For example, in Mark vi. 50 Jesus, drawing near to His awe-struck disciples on the water, is represented as saying: 'Ἐγώ εἰμι· μὴ φοβεῖσθε. A language is used which echoes and recalls the language ascribed to God himself in Deutero-Isaiah. The words suggest a clear experience of the numinous in the self-disclosures of Jesus, which may or may not be expressed in Messianic terminology, but which nevertheless is the real ground of the Christian Messianic confession.

Even clearer is the use of 'Ἐγώ εἰμι in an absolute sense in the Fourth Gospel. For example, "If you do not believe that 'I am', you will die in your sins" (viii. 24), "When you lift up the Son of Man, then you will know that ' I am' " (viii. 28), "I tell you this before it happens (γενέσθαι) that, when it does happen, you may believe that 'I am' " (xiii. 19), "Before Abraham came to be (γενέσθαι), 'I am' " (viii. 58). These expressions mean that "God has come" to men in Jesus, the Incarnate Word. There is an intentional contraposition of "existence" and "becoming" in the last two examples which shows that 'Ἐγώ εἰμι is the claim to an existence above history and time, an existence πρὸς τὸν Θεόν, which, though it acquires a Messianic determination in the human life of the Incarnate Word, is not confined in its range of reality to that specific form. The Jesus of the Fourth Gospel is the Eternal Logos who, as such, shares and manifests to men the life of God.

It is from this point of view that we understand also the incident at the arrest of Jesus in the Garden, where Jesus, informed that the soldiers were seeking Him, answered 'Ἐγώ εἰμι, a word at which His captors "went backwards and fell to the ground" (John xviii. 4 f.). Here it is Jesus of Nazareth, not Jesus the Christ, who is the manifestation of the supernatural Presence of God.

Thirdly, there is the close analogy of the use of 'Ἐγώ εἰμι in the Old Testament as when God appears to Moses in Exod. iii and reveals Himself as אֶהְיֶה אֲשֶׁר אֶהְיֶה, a formula which a preacher once described as "doubling back" upon itself as though waiting for some mysterious incarnation. But 'Ἐγώ εἰμι is also specially characteristic of the style of Deutero-Isaiah where it expresses the self-manifestation of the God of Israel in the redemption of His people from Babylon. It is not necessary to dwell on the many aspects of the Divine activity so made known—its uniqueness, constancy, holiness, righteousness, and loving-kindness. Israel's eyes are summoned by the prophet to behold the direct and never-ceasing agency of the Eternal God on her behalf.

Such evidence may be regarded as establishing that in religious contexts in the Bible the Greek expression, corresponding to the Hebrew אֲנִי or אֲנִי הוּא or אָנֹכִי, is specially associated with the Divine Presence or self-disclosure of God in religious history. And if this is admitted as the meaning in Mark xiii. 6, it is seen that the formula served in early Christianity, not only in Johannine but in Synoptic language, to cover the whole Divine approach to men in Jesus Christ and was extended to include the final coming of Christ to reign. With this established, we return to the special passage in Mark from which we set out. What now are its general bearings?

It is laid down in the passage that the final manifestation of God in the coming of Christ to reign is not to be confused or identified with events in the external world, at least not with the events of that particular age. What light does this throw on the Christian religion of the Synoptic period, particularly in the sphere of the world-mission Church?

It is plain that Christianity in its first historical phase was rooted in Jewish apocalyptic eschatology. The apparatus of ideas provided by the latter gave Christianity the means of the first rationalization of its religious experience. This holds true both of the mind of Jesus and of the minds of His followers. Christianity here took over from apocalyptic Judaism the thought of the Kingdom of God as a transcendent state of existence projected on the historical plane and destined to supersede the secular world-powers in the near future. On the popular level of early Christian thought the whole traditional programme of the apocalyptic world-perspective was carried forward with certain Christian modifications, nor can one exaggerate the value of the resultant religious vision for an age exhausted by political frustration and drained of secular hope. Yet side by side with this determination of the early-Christian mind there goes the evidence that the manifestation of God in Christ did not lend itself to easy accommodation within the limits of this particular historical perspective. It does not appear, indeed, that the general question of the rightness or wrongness of the whole apocalyptic movement in religious thought, which was so remarkable a feature of late Judaism, and which had furnished the Christian Church with the first frame of reference for its idea of world-salvation, was raised in principle in Christianity even when Judaism turned its back on the movement. In point of fact, however, Christianity is obliged, almost from the start, to treat its derived apocalyptic element as an entirely plastic substance, plastic, that is, to the touch of its more primary spiritual component.

It would appear, at least, that no events of an external kind, however critical in world-history, were accounted in early Christianity of sufficient importance to be regarded as the fulfilment of the Christian expectation of the *Parousia.* Again and again the date of the *Parousia* is prorogued, and this not because events proved disappointing to the hopes built upon them, but because there was something in Christianity itself which was not satisfied with an external semeiology. The events alleged on popular levels to be the signs of the End were one by one rejected by the minds directing the Church, and this took place on what are clearly seen to be *a priori* principles. The evidence lies in the two early-Christian apocalypses which we have passed under review. The morphological resemblances of the two documents, despite their differences in date and detail, point to a steady determination of the Christian mind away from immediate events and towards an as yet unforeseeable future. The persecutions which had swept down like a storm on the Thessalonian Church in A.D. 49 or 50 are not allowed, even though their full effect could not yet be known, to mark the end of the age or the onset of the Day of the Lord. St. Paul's rejection of the idea circulating among his converts is obviously *a priori* with respect to the facts of their situation, nor is it possible not to sense the feeling of relief which it gives him to be able to declare his mind on the question. In the Synoptic apocalypse the postponement of the End is definitely related to the Christian conviction that the Gospel has first to be preached to all nations. The fact is that neither at Thessalonica nor at Rome could the Church afford to think that the end of the age was near or the Advent of the Lord due. There was the Church's task to be thought of, its mission to the world. This sense of destiny had come to control and to subdue to itself the early naïve conceptions of the future course of history and to repel an apocalypticism which was for ever seeing itself on the last brink of things.

But this is just another way of saying that the supernatural Presence of God in Christ, the creative manifestation at the heart of Christian life, was not of a kind to be really brought to the test of historical events in the outward world. These latter were not *in eodem genere* with the spiritual certitudes forming the basis of the Church's faith. Christianity here required a larger rationalization of its content, a rationalization made possible by Greek philosophical and mystical conceptions of time and eternity, God and man. In the Fourth Gospel, and in St. Paul to a large extent, we find judgement, resurrection, and eternal life interpreted in a present sense and no longer bound up with an entirely eschatological programme. The 'Εγώ εἰμι of God in Christ affects all history, including the future range of history; it is not dependent on this or that particular crisis in history. So St. Paul can say that Christ lives in him, though he is still ἐν σαρκί. "The life I now live in the flesh I live by faith directed to the Son of God, who loved me and gave Himself for me" (Gal. ii. 20). It is from the 'Εγώ εἰμι of God in Christ that St. Paul derives, though still in the flesh and still in history, his ζῶ δὲ οὐκέτι ἐγώ, ζῇ δὲ ἐν ἐμοὶ Χριστός. It is the overflowing measure of the present *dynamis* of the Messianic Presence, a reality not finally conditioned by historical events in the outward world or by "the flesh" in the inward, that enables the apostle to speak mystically, and in present tenses, of salvation and of life "in Christ". And it is the identical sense of an eternal Presence, the same yesterday, today, and for ever, that gives a real ground in Christianity to the Logos Christology. St. Paul lived by and did his thinking from the standpoint of the numinous reality of the ever-renewed Christ-presentation of God to his soul. In Acts ix. 5 the revelation of the Risen Lord to him is in the form: 'Εγώ εἰμι 'Ιησοῦς ὃν σὺ διώκεις. We might insert a comma or a dash after 'Εγώ εἰμι. The same form of the Divine allocution is repeated in the other references to his Damascus experience. It would appear either that St. Paul was accustomed to describe his experience in these terms, or that the writer of Acts considered the form to be normal.

Lastly, this intensity of the numinous realization of the Manifestation of God in Christ, which keeps it from being too closely measured by external events, and so lifts the Presence above history, is itself the source of a larger Christian hope for history. Christianity finds itself unable, with all its certainty regarding the ultimate outcome of events, to foreclose the course of history. Whatever happens in the external world, and whatever Divine judgement on men and events thereby comes to light, no occurrence, however critical in the human historical sense, not even the Fall of Jerusalem, not even later the collapse of Rome and the Empire, could be regarded as writing "Finis" to the historical process. And the reason comes from within the Christian experience itself. There is the Christian mission to the world to be gone on with; and this, as it succeeds, expands the horizon of Christian hope. The "Not yet the End!" of early Christian prophecy, which cannot regard any foreseeable event as putting a term to the course of the mission, opens ever new possibilities for the life of the world. So Christianity retains the passion and the ultimate hope of apocalypticism, but transcends its impatience and its pessimism, and its consistent principle, "Go on with your work, whatever happens", is not without significance for us today when, sometimes in despair of history, we are tempted to relapse into apocalyptic moods. There is a transcendent constant in Christianity to which hope should hold even in dark days. "Lo, I am with you all the days"—the numinous 'Εγώ εἶμι of God in Christ has become the numinous 'Εγὼ μεθ' ὑμῶν εἶμι of Christ in His Church. It is not denied that there is "a consummation of the age" to be awaited, but we are encouraged not to anticipate unduly the relation in which it stands to the historical process.

CHAPTER 3

Eschatology in the New Testament[1]

I

The Preparation

It is suggested to us as a reason for adopting Eschatology as the theme of this conference that the question of eschatology stands at present on the agenda of the Faith and Order Commission. As the Commission is considering the nature of the Christian hope for the world, this will mean that we shall concern ourselves in these discussions, not with the Christian eschatology as a whole, but with the bearings of that eschatology on the life of the world, on the character of the Church's mission and message, and on the meaning and ultimate issues of history. Accepting this very serviceable delimitation of the province of our inquiry, I shall leave aside, as of merely secondary interest, what may be called the antiquarian part of the Biblical eschatology, that is to say, the body of external imagery, form and symbol by aid of which the Bible expresses the nature of certain "Last Things" which are really ineffable, and I shall concentrate on what, after all, is the essence of the subject, namely, the religious determination of mind by which in the Bible men are impelled to think of all history and all life by reference to an ultimate transcendent Event, an End towards which, under the judgement and the mercy of God, the world is hastening.

It was under the influence of such a religious determination of thought that the older eschatology of Israel, in the age of the prophets, assumed the form under which it was transmitted to later times and became the basis of the New Testament kerygma. And here we see an illustration of the process by which the formal element in a tradition is made plastic to the uses of any higher religion into which it is taken up. The spirits of the prophets are subject to the prophets. Within the history of the Hebrew-Jewish-Christian development of

[1] Reprinted from *Scottish Journal of Theology Occasional Papers*, No. 2, pp. 1–16.

religion this principle is seen to have a general, if not an invariable, operation. I shall here allow myself three observations.

(1) The principle holds good of the classical prophetic age of the Old Testament religion. Traditional eschatological concepts, such as "the day of Jahweh", are here given a vastly greater weight of existential significance by relation to the new insights of the prophets, and the same applies to such other traditional concepts as those of Jahweh's covenant with Israel, the sacral king and kingdom in Israel, the Divine *ruaḥ* and righteousness in Israel, and so forth.

(2) The principle holds true to an even greater extent in the case of Jesus and Christianity. The Jewish conceptions of the "Kingdom" of God, of the "Messiah" and the "Son of Man", of the resurrection and the last judgement, are sublimated as the effect of the revelation of God in Christ. Jesus is the subject of the New Testament religion. Eschatology is the predicate. The subject is not subordinated to the predicate but the predicate to the subject. Eschatology is made plastic to Jesus Christ.

(3) The principle does *not* hold of the intermediate or apocalyptic period of Jewish religious history. It is impossible to think that traditional apocalyptic ideas are here made plastic to the needs of a genuinely higher religious experience. Rather, as the introduction into the picture of cosmology, astrology, angelology, and demonology shows, the development which takes place in apocalyptic thought is speculative and gnostic rather than religious in its inspiration. I intend, therefore, to leave this period to one side as not bearing very materially on the essence of the Christian eschatology, or on the specific question before us. For if, as Dr. R. H. Charles considered, Jewish apocalyptic thinking about the last things, from the year 100 B.C. onwards, took a direction definitely away from this world towards a transcendent heavenly order of existence,[1] it ceases to be helpful for the consideration of our problem which is concerned with an eschatological hope for *history*. Jewish phantasy about a purely heavenly world, like certain forms of Christian millenarianism, represents essentially an evasion of the historical question.

Reverting, then, to our original concern, we can see that it was a primarily religious interest which gave rise to the eschatology of Israel and determined its form. But this form was possibly only because of the unique association of religion with history in Israel, as

[1] R. H. Charles, *Religious Development between the Old and the New Testaments,* pp. 70 ff.

expressed in the idea of Israel's *covenant with God*, an idea which appears to have characterized Jahwism from the earliest time to which we can trace it back. How do we explain this elsewhere unparalleled preoccupation of thought with the revelational value of history, this extraordinary movement of Israel's instinct "in regard", as Dr. Wheeler Robinson has put it, "to the nature and meaning . . . of history"? Dr. Robinson assumes that "a prior belief" was here applied to events: "God is known by what He does for Israel, and history is charged with the fullest meaning that can be ascribed to it. Particular events become sacramental, charged with the whole doctrine of God[1]". Now events were not sacramental to the Greeks, nor did the Greek historians or philosophers see anything of Divine significance in temporality. Possibly if Thucydides had handled events as the Greek tragedians handled their myths, we might have had some kind of approximation to the Hebrew interpretation of history, but, as Dr. G. B. Grundy says, in the educated circles of Thucydides' time the influence of the drama was on the wane.[2] From where, then, came the singular and sustained vitality of Israel's reading of her own history? The answer is that it came from the nature of Israel's religion, and a verse in Psalm ciii suggests that tradition carried it back to Moses or to the earliest circles of his interpreters. God "made known His ways unto Moses, His acts upon the children of Israel".

Certain it is that already in the Jahwist document history and eschatology are linked together in the revelations made to Moses. In Exodus iii, for example, the vision of the Burning Bush which came to Moses is interpreted to mean that He who was the God of Abraham, Isaac and Jacob, has not ceased to act in history. He is the living God who sees, knows, and has come down to deliver His people in Egypt. God does not destroy history. He is incessantly active in it.[3] So when Moses asks to know the name of God, the answer which he receives, "I am that I am"—it should properly be rendered "I will be that I will be" (*'Ehyeh 'asher 'Ehyeh*)—refers not to the ontological mystery of God's person, but rather to the inscrutability of God's future purposes from man's present standpoint. *God reserves His action.*[4] Similarly in Exod. xxxiii. 12–23 Moses in the Tent asks to see God's "ways", and receives answer that he shall have God's "presence",

[1] H. W. Robinson, *History of Israel,* p. 224 f.
[2] G. B. Grundy, *Thucydides,* p. 50.
[3] Exod. iii. 6 f.
[4] Exod. iii. 13–15.

and shall know His "goodness", but shall not behold His "glory". Moses will stand in his cleft of rock, and he will see God's "back", but he cannot run before God and see His "face".[1] Here again the togetherness of Divine history and eschatology! God has His reserved purposes, and it is to be understood that these will later be revealed. The things which God intends will be, but not yet.

Having thus taken the eschatology of Israel back to a root in Moses or in Jahwism, we may go on to observe that intense religious experience in the prophetic period begins to throw the reserved purposes of God into an ever higher prominence. The awareness of God in the prophets, the sense of His holiness and purity signified for example by such events as the call of Isaiah in the temple, casts a deep shadow of guilt and impending doom over the life of Israel and affixes an interrogation mark to all its institutions. Nothing escapes this prophetic sentence of doom, neither holy people nor secular empires, neither sacral anointed king nor priest nor prophet. "My God will cast them away." There remains, however, the covenant, so passionately proclaimed by Hosea. If prophetic religion in Israel is saved from nihilism or despair, if it decries a door of escape from cataclysm, it is because of the past mercies of the covenant God. The *ḥesed* of God, His covenant loyalty and goodness, have stamped themselves upon the history and institutions of Israel, upon kingdom, prince and people. They are reflected in Israel's knowledge of the law and will of God. They have entered into the substance of the nation's life, so that not all of these things can be thought of as destined to be finally cast away. *Righteousness* indeed, national and individual—justification in God's eyes—is wanting. It has been withdrawn from the existing order of life, and if there is any escape from catastrophe, it can only be by the judgement and mercy of God preserving to the chosen people a remnant or residuary stock. "Except the Lord had left us a very small remnant, we should have been as Sodom."[2] So Isaiah, who indeed dubs the nation Sodom. But through the recognition of a reserved righteousness of God and of a salvable stock in the nation —even where, in God's eyes, no man living is justified—prophecy has begun to break with cataclysm.[3] The remnant has become the symbol of an eschatological salvation.

What happens is that the blessings offered to Israel under the

[1] Exod. xxxiii. 21–33.
[2] Isa. i. 9.
[3] A. C. Welch, *Kings and Prophets of Israel*, p. 256.

covenant, but with a greater weight of glory, are projected into the *future*. The prophets could have put their names to all that St. Paul says about the promises of God in Rom. ix. 11. Into the future they project holy nation, righteous prince, holy Spirit of God, but all within the framework of a *New Covenant*. The king of Israel, the anointed of Jahweh, is there, endowed with the Spirit of God, and having the government upon his shoulder. He is a branch from the resected stump of the root of Jesse, but for prophecy this Davidic prince is sacramental, essential, the pledge of God's presence, the symbol of His grace. The Spirit too is there. He is destined to be poured out on all flesh. The knowledge of God is there, waiting to be imparted as inward source of light. And life in the fullest sense is there, justice, peace, the reconciliation of God with man and of man with nature. Theodicy relegates its problems there, for these problems are not soluble under the present order. On the hither side of the consummation, however, stands the Judgement of God, which is the narrow gate to final mercy.

In this manner arose the classical eschatology of Israel which, with some variations wrought upon its pattern by the Exile and later history, and with the more cosmical stamp imparted to it by apocalyptic imagination, Iranian dualism, and other influences, is passed on to Christianity. It is not necessary to pursue the Old Testament development any further, except to remark that even under the conditions of the semi-realization of eschatology in Deutero-Isaiah the same forward-striving impulsion is still creatively active. For example, Professor H. H. Rowley in his illuminating recent study of "The Servant of the Lord" inquires whether in Deutero-Isaiah's thought there was not a development in the conception of the *'Ebed Jahweh*, and "whether what began as a personification did not become a person". He answers that this was so. In the fourth of the Servant Songs (Isa. liii) the Servant, who is elsewhere Israel, has become not only an individual but an eschatological figure, *one who is yet to be*. Also the evolution of ideas within the conception of the Servant corresponds with the development of events in the Incarnate life of Jesus.[1]

[1] H. H. Rowley, *The Servant of the Lord* (1952), pp. 51–2, 54–7.

II

The Fulfilment

When we turn to the New Testament, we pass from the climate of prediction to that of fulfilment. The things which God had foreshowed by the lips of His holy prophets He has now, in part at least, brought to accomplishment. The *Eschaton*, described from afar—*ripae ulterioris amore*—has in Jesus registered its advent. "Blessed", Jesus had said, "are the eyes which see the things that you see; for I tell you, many prophets and kings desired to see the things that you see, and did not see them."[1] The supreme sign of the *Eschaton* is the Resurrection of Jesus and the descent of the Holy Spirit on the Church. The Resurrection of Jesus is not simply a sign which God has granted in favour of His Son, but is the inauguration, the entrance into history, of *the times of the End*.

Christians, therefore, have entered through the Christ into the New Age. Church, Spirit, life in Christ are eschatological magnitudes. Those who gather in Jerusalem in the numinous first days of the Church know that it is so; they are already conscious of tasting the powers of the World to Come. What had been predicted in Holy Scripture as to happen to Israel or to man in the *Eschaton* has happened to and in Jesus. The foundation-stone of the New Creation has come into position.[2] As time goes on, as things fall into better perspective, it is seen that the Righteousness of God, the visible salvation of the Lord, which the prophets had declared not to belong to the present order, has taken shape in Christ, and in Him is offered to men in Word and Sacrament.

All the more remarkable in view of this present impartation of the promised gifts of the age of salvation is *the reassertion in Christianity of the eschatological impulsion*, the same impulsion which in the older days raised men's eyes from sin to grace but now operates in Christianity to raise their eyes from grace to glory. For not all the predictions of the prophets have yet been actualized in Christ. Not all the words believed to have been spoken by Jesus have been fulfilled. For had not the prophets predicted that God would in the last days visibly come to judge the world and to make an end of death, and had not

[1] Luke x. 23–4.
[2] Acts iv. 11–12; 1 Cor. iii. 11.

Jesus spoken of the Son of Man coming with the clouds in great power and glory? The experience of the brotherhood, with all their sense of being redeemed to God and raised to a new existence in conjunction with Christ, stands in strange and painful tension with the facts of continuing earthly conflict, and thus faith shapes itself around an eschatology of the *Parousia*.

Inevitably so. There is a realized eschatology. There is also an eschatology of the unrealized. There can be no such thing under any imaginable conditions as a fully realized eschatology in the strict sense. The eschatological impulse awakes and asserts itself again in Christianity, for eschatology, like love, is of God. In the words of Dr. Bultmann, God Himself is the Christian future, and Christian life is absolute *Offenheit* towards God. Until that which is perfect is come, that which is in part is present only in sacramental, proleptic, provisional form, though St. Paul excepts one thing which belongs to the full realization of the final order of things and which, therefore, does not pass. What *is* realized in Christ in the present era is the character of the *Eschaton*, not its complete substance. But that the present age has not received the substance, the fullness of life, does not mean that that fullness will not yet come to manifestation.

Christianity, therefore, from the beginning exhibits an essential bi-polarity. The End has come! The End has not come! And neither grace nor glory, neither present proleptic fruition nor future perfection of life in God can be omitted from the picture without the reality being destroyed. The consummation of life in God is not here, but if it exists *in part* here—this is the particular point of the Biblical presentation, the point at which it differs most sharply from the Greek point of view—will it not yet also come in its fullness?

Let us look at a passage like 1 Peter i. 3–5 where the writer blesses God:

> Who according to his great mercy has begotten us again unto a living hope by the resurrection of Jesus Christ from the dead, unto an inheritance incorruptible, and undefiled, and that fadeth not away, reserved in heaven for you who by the power of God are guarded through faith unto a salvation ready to be revealed in the last time.

The passage is fully eschatological in the Christian sense. The new birth of the Spirit is real, but has created the hope of a further and larger inheritance. That inheritance—incorruptible and undefiled—has not yet been entered upon, but is said to be "reserved in heaven".

But does this mean that the inheritance is always to be located "in heaven", and that Christians must finally be translated into that higher realm for its fruition? Not necessarily from the New Testament standpoint! In Acts iii. 20–1, for instance, while we hear of heaven "receiving" Christ until the appointed time of the final restoration of all things, we find the expectation also expressed that the Christ will be "sent" again from God. And this draws attention to a point of special interest.

How do we explain the extraordinary fact that the early Christian anticipation of the final glory of Christ takes the form of the Son of Man appearing again on *earth*? The basic passage in Daniel vii, on which the text of the New Testament tradition of the hope is mainly formed, says nothing about the celestial figure there likened to a son of man as coming back to earth. He goes to the Ancient of Days, and is given an everlasting kingdom, but he does not return. Nor does the Son of Man of the Similitudes of Enoch descend to, or make any contact with terrestrial history. The Christian hope of the New Testament has at this point clearly by-passed the Jewish apocalyptic teaching, and has completed the circuit of the Messiah to the earth, and we must explain the Parousia expectation, either by supposing with Dr. Glasson that the Christian mind was influenced by the Old Testament prophetic passages which spoke of Jahweh of Hosts coming down to judge the world in righteousness,[1] or by accepting the fact that Jesus Himself thought of the scene of His earthly humiliation, the stage of His love and suffering, as also the scene and stage of His glory and final reign.

In either case eschatology and history, history and eschatology go together. In no great religious experience (Hebrew-prophetic or Christian-apostolic) can history exist without some final hope in God nor can any final hope in God exist which does not take account of history. To taste, here on earth, the powers of the World to Come, to realize, now in time, the eternal significance of Christ, is to make an end in principle of all ultimate and eternal separation between the Kingdom of God and the world of temporality.

Let us look again at the New Testament in Gospels and Epistles. We shall consider in turn the following aspects of the presentation.

(1) The *Baptism of Jesus*, the initial act of our salvation. Mark how clearly the mission of John and its sequel, the ministry of Jesus, reflect the eschatology of the fortieth chapter of Isaiah. The voice

[1] T. F. Glasson, *The Second Advent*, pp. 161 ff.

heard by the prophet, "Prepare the way of the Lord,"[1] is fulfilled in John's baptism. The following voice, "Behold, the Lord God will come as a mighty one, and His arm shall rule for Him,"[2] is fulfilled in Jesus' proclamation that "The fullness of the time has arrived, and the reign of God has come near." Here eschatology is fulfilled, and yet it is not fulfilled. For though, when Jesus was baptized, the Spirit descended upon Him and thus, as Dr. G. W. H. Lampe has shown,[3] began the baptism of water and the Spirit which is the sacramental sign of our salvation, Jesus is heard later saying: "I came to cast fire on the earth" (John has said that his Successor would baptize with fire) "and how I would it were already kindled!" (evidently it was not yet kindled), "but I have a baptism to be baptized with" (Jesus' baptism was not yet completed) "and how constrained I am until it is accomplished!"[4] So the Christian fulfilment of earlier eschatology in Jesus points to the necessity of a *further* accomplishment, an eschatology of Cross, Resurrection, and Parousia, and our baptism into Christ, which is the extension of His baptism to us, involves for us a baptism into His death, as St. Paul expresses it, a baptism which is only sacramentally enacted in the present. Yet the word "on earth" —"I came to cast fire on earth"—plainly suggests the earth to be the scene of the final redemption to be wrought by Christ as well as of the interim sacrament.

(2) The *Temptation of Jesus* and His Conflict with the Powers of Darkness. In the wilderness experience Jesus, called as eschatological Son of God in baptism, resists the solicitations of Satan, and in Galilee He proclaims the fullness of the times and the advent of the Reign of God. We must not forget that, as often as Old Testament prophets and psalmists say that God "reigns", there is reference in the context to "enemies" whom God overthrows. So Jesus, having announced the Reign of God, engages at once, in the synagogues of Galilee and elsewhere, with the powers of darkness, the demons who have invaded and occupied the bodies and souls of men. That the Reign of God and the exorcizing of the demons go together is shown by the word: "If I, by the Spirit (or finger) of God cast out the demons, then the Kingdom of God has lighted (ἔφθασεν) upon you" (Matt. xii. 28). Jesus by driving back the forces of the enemy is clear-

[1] Isa. xl. 3.
[2] Isa. xl. 10.
[3] G. W. H. Lampe, *The Seal of the Spirit*, pp. 33 ff.
[4] Luke xii. 49–50.

ing a space for the Reign of God. Yet here too the coming of the *Eschaton* is only partial and encounters opposition. The enmity of the powers of darkness is part of that frustration at which Jesus darkly hints in His word about the "fire", not yet ignited, which He came to bring, and the "baptism", not yet accomplished, which He still has to undergo. At the end, when Satan enters into Judas (Luke xxii. 3) and Jesus is face to face with His captors, we hear Him say: "This is your hour, and the power of darkness."[1] Here again, with all the realism of our Lord's sense of the actualization of the salvation of God in the living present, there is an appeal to further and still outstanding reaches of the Divine purpose in an eschatology of the Cross, Resurrection and Parousia. Nevertheless, as Jesus had joined issue with the powers of hell here on earth, are we to think of that further eschatology in terms of the ultimate abandonment of any hope for history?

(3) The proclamation by Jesus of *God's Will to Righteousness*. We cannot consider in detail the nature of the ethical-spiritual encounter of Jesus with our souls in which, as in the Sermon on the Mount, He confronts us with the immediate actuality of God's will to reign in life. The realism of this encounter meets us in the moral absolutes of Jesus, but not a word is said about any of these existential demands having relation to another world than this. Not one word of Jesus transports us into the conditions of a purely heavenly order of existence, not even the saying that "when the dead rise, they neither marry nor are given in marriage, but are as the angels in heaven" (Mark xii. 25), for the *palingenesia*, the reconstitution of life which is there alluded to, does not *per se* demand another sphere of life than this. Love, the highest of the absolutes of Jesus, is organic to the structure and needs of human existence as we know it, while the other demands, purity, sincerity, and non-resistance to evil, have no kind of relevance to any order of society not constituted like ours.

And yet these demands, embodying the law of the Kingdom, and so indisputable in their relevance to human life in the present order, remain beyond our imaginable power to fulfil. The nature of the eternal, the Divine, the *Eschaton*, is in them; they speak the last word of truth to us, they are "the words of eternal life". But because the Reign of God is present only in part, not yet "in power", under the existing order, the re-creation of life which these words of Jesus require points to a further stage in the unfolding of the *Eschaton*.[2] The present stage corresponds to St. Paul's "justification by faith". The

[1] Luke xxii. 53. [2] Cf. Mark ix. 1.

perfect righteousness which God wills is exhibited and embodied in Christ alone, but sacramentally it covers and applies to all who acknowledge His existential claim.

(4) *Jesus the Son of Man.* In the Son of Man sayings in the Gospels, so oracular in style and content, we have a body of material which, if any part of the tradition can claim to stand in special closeness to the heart of the Christ-mystery, may be considered to do so. The sayings fall into two groups, one group integrating the fortunes of the Son of Man with the condition of man in history, man's sin, sorrow and want, the other group sublimating and transporting these fortunes into the realm of glory. According to the New Testament tradition it is one and the same Son of Man who figures in both sets of relations, and the collocation of the two sets of sayings makes clear that this eschatology of the *sublimation* of the Son of Man rests not on Old Testament and Jewish teaching but on the incarnation and passion of Jesus. The Christian eschatology of glory cannot, therefore, be dismissed as a lag-over or residuum from Judaism. It arises from the very nature of the revelation made in Jesus, and His asseveration before the high priest: "You shall see the Son of Man seated at the right hand of power, and coming with the clouds of heaven" (Mark xiv. 62), indicates, as I have written elsewhere, that "the recession towards eternity of the movement which begins in the Incarnation does not cut out the earth, or by-pass its process, but takes the world and history up into itself".[1]

(5) The same inseparable connection of Christian present and Christian future appears finally, and most explicitly, in the institution of the *Last Supper*, which by its very substance points to a future consummation in the Kingdom of God. Like Baptism the Eucharist is an eschatological sacrament. It reminds the Church for ever that it lives not only by what has been accomplished for it in Christ but by what is yet to be effected for it in Him. The Church is consecrated to the Lord for a destiny which, as its present fragmentation, among other signs, shows, is not yet realized but, as Dr. T. F. Torrance has impressively demonstrated, is eschatologically borne in upon us as often as the rite is celebrated.[2]

(6) Passing to *St. Paul*, I shall confine myself to a few observations.

[1] "The Son of Man and History," *S.J.T.*, Vol. 5, No. 2 (1952), p. 116; *vide supra*, p. 67.

[2] T. F. Torrance in *Intercommunion* (1952), pp. 303–50, "Eschatology and the Eucharist" (*Conflict and Agreement in the Church*, Vol. II, pp. 154–202).

The new life in Christ includes for St. Paul all the spiritual blessings, foreshadowed in the Old Testament as appertaining to the age of salvation. But a glance at any page in his letters will show that this realization goes with the eager expectation (ἀποκαραδοκία) of a further End towards which redemption moves. In 1 Cor. i. 4–9 we have a typical picture of Church life in the apostolic age. The Corinthians have been "enriched in everything" by the grace of God, so that they "lack no spiritual gift". Yet this happens only as they await "the revelation of our Lord Jesus Christ". The blessing predicted by the prophets as symptomatic of the *Eschaton* have been granted, but by their intrinsic nature they point to a climax not yet in sight.

For example, *Wisdom, the Knowledge of God.* In 1 Cor. i–ii St. Paul brings out the extreme paradox of the relation in which the new knowledge of God imparted through the Spirit stands to "the wisdom of this world", a paradox only equalled by the relation between the now existing Christian knowledge and the knowledge to be revealed in the future, when we shall see "face to face". The present Christian knowledge is itself knowledge of things which, as yet, "eye has not seen, and ear has not heard". Such knowledge is held only in Christ who by God's act is made "wisdom to us from God, righteousness, sanctification, and redemption". But because the day of our Lord is still ahead, all these gifts are proleptic. They half-reveal, but half-conceal the consummation.

Righteousness or Justification. This status before God, which the Old Testament prophets had denied to their times, and which they had projected into the eschatological future, is embodied in the Christian Redeemer, and is offered to us in Him (Rom. iii. 21–6). The new status is not formal but substantive, since it is equivalent to being "in Christ", and being in Christ means having Christ not merely as the ground, or as the sphere of our new Christian life, but as its substance. Yet the day of God's righteous judgement (δικαιοκρισία) is still future, and therefore the full fruition of the new relation to God is carried forward. While our baptism commits us to a present death to sin and a resurrection to newness of life (Rom. vi), the apostle himself confesses (Phil. iii. 9–12): "I have not attained the end" (τετελείωμαι.) He prays still to be found in Christ, and to know the power of His resurrection, and the fellowship of His sufferings, in the hope that he may eventually attain to the resurrection from the dead.

The Spirit and the Flesh. Very impressively in Romans viii St. Paul analyses the nature of the tension between the new life in the Spirit and the old, not yet extirpated instincts of the sin-dominated human nature which he calls "the flesh". This tension still conditions Christian existence, revealed as it is in conflict (verses 5–11), in the necessity of moral effort (verses 12–17), and in the experience of suffering and deficiency (verses 18–25). But the Spirit and the grace of God cooperate with the Christian in his conflict (verses 26–30), and there is the assurance of final victory through God's inalienable love in Christ (verses 31–9). That consummation still outstands, for creation awaits a *cosmic deliverance* which includes the resurrection of the dead, and that is not yet. Christians who have the first-fruit of the Spirit are said still to await the redemption of the body (verses 20–3). Salvation, therefore, is still conditioned by hope. While the Reign of Christ has begun, not all the Messiah's enemies are yet under His feet, not yet is the End (τὸ τέλος) (1 Cor. xv. 24–7). It is to be remarked, in this connection, that all individual eschatology is made strictly subordinate to this cosmic End.

As regards this *individual eschatology* St. Paul makes it clear to his converts that death may come to them before the Consummation arrives, in which case they are to consider that they will enter on some blessed intermediate state of life in which they will be "with Christ" (Phil. i. 23). At this point the Jewish conception of Paradise or *Gan Eden* is taken over by the Christian eschatology, but made subordinate to the thought of all life as "Christ" (Phil. i. 21). It is probable that physical death, what we call the debt to nature, was construed as incidental to, and part of that "dying with Christ" to which the believer was committed in baptism. It must be noticed, however, that the apostle did not find it easy to adjust his mind to the idea of an intermediate state (2 Cor. v. 1–8). As a Christian of the first generation he looked for everything that is mortal to be at the earliest date "swallowed up in life". With the Parousia the resurrection-body would in some way be superinduced on our existing mortal nature. In any case, whether with or without death and the intermediate state, there will come at the Second Advent a *change* which in the case of those who "sleep" will be a rising from the dead, and in the case of the living a complete transformation of our mortal nature into an immortal state of being. The Eschatology of Glory presupposes this miracle. St. Paul regards its nature as a secret directly revealed to himself. "Behold, I declare to you a mystery: we shall not all of us sleep, but all of us shall be changed, in a moment, in the flick of an eye, at the last trumpet" (1 Cor. xv. 51).

It is not necessary to pursue further the New Testament teaching on the life "hid with Christ in God". Sometimes, as in the Epistle to the Hebrews, there is extreme emphasis on the final End of the course; sometimes, as in the Fourth Gospel, there is a restful acceptance of eternal life as present possession. But everywhere there is the recognition of Christian life being a bridge life between two aeons, and everywhere this life is conditioned by what Dr. Rudolph Bultmann has called *Offenheit* towards God.[1] The Christian life is not bounded on its Godward side, because it never, as experience, takes us out of time. Faith by its nature can never close the circle of events to come, because the future to which it looks is nothing less than God Himself.

III

Conclusions—The Eschatology of Glory

Two or three things fall to be said by way of general comment on the New Testament Eschatology.

(1) The Christianity of the New Testament, while it is pervaded throughout by the sense of fulfilling the law and the prophets and thus of representing the Era of Redemption, creates its own *Eschatology of Glory* centring in the Parousia of Christ. This eschatology is not to be explained as a hangover or relic of Judaism, though certain formal elements of the language in which it is clothed have come to it from the past. It stands on its own proper ground, which is the religious revelation made in the Incarnation, in the love and suffering of Jesus, and in the new life begun in Him. Christianity is determined by its own nature to reach forward to the consummation of the life in Christ.

> The invisible world with thee hath sympathised,
> Be thy affections raised and solemnised.

The curve of the *Eschaton* has intersected the orbit of our historical life. One focus has taken position in the Incarnation of Christ; the other, the Second Advent, lies beyond our horizon and power to conceive.

(2) The scene of the *Eschaton*, the Age of Glory, is, it would seem, the world in which man's life is lived and in which Christ died and rose. New Heavens and a New Earth signify not the final destruction

[1] R. Bultmann, *Das Urchristentum* (1949), pp. 83, 98 f., 203 ff., 218, 232 f., etc.

or displacement of the cosmos, but its *renovation* (παλινγενεσία, καινὴ κτίσις, ἀποκατάστασις) by the power of God. The fashion (σχῆμα) of this world passes away. In *our* thinking Greek modes of thought, derived from a different spiritual climate, have superimposed themselves unnoticed on the Biblical modes, and traces of them are already discoverable in late Jewish thinking and in certain late parts of the New Testament (e.g. in 2 Pet. iii. 7 and iii. 10–12). Our modern idea of the universe also differs from the ancient, so that acute problems are created at this point for dogmatic theology. But the New Testament evidence is not ambiguous in this matter.

(3) The New Testament Eschatology, as it makes this world the scene and stage of the final redemption of man by God, gathers also within its scope the full course of human history. It is indeed the boundless magnitude of this eschatology that holds open the door to a large hope for history, though by means of the judgement of God and the regeneration of life through the Spirit. If any explicit proof of this is needed, it may be found in two New Testament passages in which, for purposes of warning as well as instruction, a programme of coming events is laid down. The one is the Pauline apocalypse in 2 Thess. ii, the other is the Synoptic apocalypse in St. Mark xiii. Both of these documents warn against the premature excitement of supposing that the day of the Lord has set in (ἐνέστηκεν),[1] that the Parousia has occurred (Ἐγώ εἰμι).[2] Both inculcate patience and quietness, the one saying, in effect, "Go on with your work!", the other saying "First must the gospel be preached to all the nations!"[3] Here is the clearest evidence that *the World-Mission of the Church has stepped into the interval dividing the Incarnation of the Lord from the Age of Glory*. From point to point, apparently, in the history of the apostolic Church there was a temptation to construe contemporary earth-shaking events as the sign of the End of the present order. The apostolic reply is instinctive: "Not yet the End!"[4] Thus the sign of the Last Advent carries us beyond any world-events that can be imagined. The Morning Star stands directly over the path of the Christian mission to the world, but it refuses to be caught up with, until the mission is completed. In this manner the New Testament evangelism leaves the door open to history as the province of the working out of God's purpose of redemption for the world. And it will not do for our theology to close it.

[1] 2 Thess. ii. 2. [2] Mark xiii. 5; 13. 21.
[3] Mark xiii. 10. [4] Mark xiii. 7; cf. 2 Thess. ii. 3.

CHAPTER 4

The Origin of the Christian World-Mission with Special Reference to the Work and Teaching of St. Paul[1]

The inception of the world-mission of Christianity raised questions which were of entrancing interest in themselves and possessed a high degree of importance for the proper understanding, both of the terms of the original kerygma of the Church and of the theological development of that kerygma in the New Testament literature. When, where, and how, we ask, did the Christian world-mission originate? What was the nature of the impulse behind it, and what was its reflex action on the theology, and especially on the Christology, of the Church? What geographical directions did the movement take, and in what relation may we suppose it to have stood to the activity and teaching of St. Paul, its most splendid and most vigorous exponent? These are questions of quite cardinal importance, and perhaps in a short study the best approach will be to observe, stage by stage, and point by point, the course of events which is delineated, or suggested, in the Book of the Acts, our earliest and most indispensable historical record.

(1) In the Acts of the Apostles the beginning of the world-mission is carried back to the numinous period of the Forty Days after the Resurrection of Christ. There, as the climax of the communications received from the Risen Lord, it is intimated to the Apostles that they will be endued with the Holy Spirit and will be the Lord's witnesses to the world's end (Acts i. 8; cf. Matt. xxviii. 19). But it is to be noticed, on the same showing (Acts i. 6), that this intimation to the disciples was not made until an earlier and mistaken conception of theirs, limiting the purpose of the Risen Lord to the glorification of the Chosen People, had been ruled out of their minds. Lord, they had asked, εἰ ἐν τῷ χρόνῳ τούτῳ ἀποκαθιστάνεις τὴν βασιλείαν τῷ Ἰσραήλ;

[1] Reprinted from the Festival Volume of the 1,900th Anniversary of St. Paul's Arrival in Greece, 1953.

(Acts i. 6). The first Christians in Jerusalem were apparently expecting the Lord to return to them. Jerusalem was to be the scene of His manifestation. The restoration of Israel as a nation was to be its object. Even after the dismission of these ideas from their minds, and even after the descent of the Spirit on the Church, the Galilean Apostles and their company still "continued stedfastly" in the temple (προσκαρτεροῦντες ἐν τῷ ἱερῷ, Acts ii. 46; v. 12, etc.). They shelter themselves, so to speak, under the roof of the Jewish institutions. In this they may have been partly influenced by a striking word of prophecy which said: "The Lord whom you seek will suddenly come to His temple" (Mal. iii 1; see also 2–4).

(2) In point of fact the actual beginning of the world-mission came, not through the Galilean Apostles, but through the Hellenist-Jewish Christian Stephen, and as the result of the events set in motion by him, and leading to his martyrdom and the dispersion of his followers. These scattered adherents of St. Stephen were the first carriers of the Christian fire up and down and over the world. We read that that great man, so far from identifying the Divine purpose of redemption with the re-establishment and glorification of Israel as a nation, was definitely critical of the temple and the Jewish institutions. He is accused by his opponents of speaking blasphemous words against Moses and God (Acts vi. 11), of continually decrying the Holy Place and the Law (Acts vi. 13), and even of saying that "Jesus the Nazarene intends to destroy this Place and to alter the traditions which Moses handed down to us" (Acts vi. 14). It is true that these charges come from the lips of suborned witnesses, but there is, as we shall see, other evidence to show that, while the charges may have involved some distortion of Stephen's actual expressions, they were not a pure fabrication. Stephen was in revolt against the attitude which his contemporaries (including the "Hebrew" Christians of Jerusalem) took to the Mosaic law and the cultus.

(3) What then, we ask, explains the fact that Stephen, πλήρης χάριτος καὶ δυνάμεως, and working great signs and miracles among the people (Acts vi. 8), had definitely come into opposition to the ritual ordinances and to the law and tradition of Israel? and that he had done so with an openness not shared, at least as yet, by the Apostles who had been with Jesus? It was not apparently any merely doctrinaire attitude expressing itself in the preference of an inward, as opposed to an external, standpoint in religion. There were Jews of the Diaspora who, in their zeal to win Gentile proselytes to the Jewish

religion, were not averse to turning the cloak of the Law inside out, keeping its prophetic and ethical content to the front, and relegating its exterior and ritual requirement into the background. In lines foisted from some Hellenistic Jewish source on to one or another of the Greek poets, we find sentiments expressed such as the following:

> Do'st think by offerings, thy sin to hide,
> Thou bring'st, O man, the Godhead to thy side?
> Astray thou art, and foolish is thy thought,
> For man to God by goodness must be brought.
> Thy soul must answer to the measuring rod.
> Justice alone is sacrifice to God.[1]

Nothing, however, in the Acts record suggests that the polemic of St. Stephen was of this doctrinaire character. We must look further into that record to discover the real nature of his argument against the Jews, and indirectly of his differences with the "Hebrew" apostles.

(4) We find the explanation, first, in the great apologia which Stephen addressed to his judges at his trial (Acts vii). The whole motive of this impressive retrospect of religious history is to show that from the beginning God had an eschatological purpose for His people Israel, a future End towards which He was directing them, and for the sake of which He did not permit them to settle down in the world or to become fixed in their traditions. Neither past experience nor traditional custom was suffered to stand in the way of the unfolding of that purpose. For example, Abraham, the father of the faithful, was called to "go out" from his country and kindred and father's house and to seek a country which God would show him (Gen. xii. 1 ff.). Moses, again, was called to lead Israel "out of Egypt" (Exod. iii. 1 ff.). The fathers of Israel were Wanderers in the desert. The sign of God's presence with them was the transient "tabernacle" or tent, a thing never confined to one place but moving ever forward with God's purpose for His people, the symbol of their unceasing dependence on the Divine will and grace. The time came when, with the consolidation of the Hebrew kingdom, David desired to build a static, a permanent, shrine for God, which however, it was left to Solomon to rear; yet Solomon's own words at the dedication of the temple confessed that the Most High did not reside in houses built by human hands (Acts vii. 48 f.). The temple was not intended to be a permanent foundation, nor were the Jewish ordinances to last for ever. Here, turning on his

[1] The Greek text in E. Schürer, *Gesch. des Jüd. Volkes* (1909), Bd. III, p. 137, note 4. English translation s. in my *Epistle to the Hebrews* (1951), p. 29 f.

Jewish opponents, St. Stephen accused them roundly of having always resisted the eschatological purpose of God, and this they were still doing through their obdurate refusal to see that with the coming of Jesus the Messiah the temple and the law were superseded. The time had come to leave these things behind, and to go out, as Epistle to the Hebrews was later to express it, "looking to Jesus", who is now "the Pioneer and Consummator of our faith" (Heb. xii, 1 f.). Such at least would seem to be the logic of the apologia.

(5) We find the explanation, secondly, in St. Stephen's dying vision. The martyr, we are told, lifted his eyes to heaven, saw Jesus standing at the right hand of God, and exclaimed: "Behold, I see the heavens opened, and the Son of Man standing at the right hand of God" (Acts vii. 56). The expression "the heavens opened" suggests that here, if anywhere, is to be found the real heart of the revelation to Stephen's soul, and the fact that in this passage alone in the whole New Testament the Son of Man title is found on any lips except those of Jesus shows that the conception of Jesus as the exalted Son of Man was of peculiar interest and significance to this man. We ought not, therefore, to regard St. Luke's putting of the word into Stephen's mouth as an accident. On the contrary, Stephen's eschatological attitude to history gives us every right to consider it as evidence that Stephen first, and Stephen alone in these primitive days, apprehended and understood the full significance of what Jesus meant by the coming of "the Son of Man". Stephen saw that Jesus was more than the Jewish coming of Messiah, and that His reign had a vaster compass than any kingdom restored to Israel. For did not the chapter in Daniel which spoke of the dominion given to "the one who resembled a son of man" say that "all peoples and nations and tongues" would serve Him? (Dan. vii. 14). The Jews doubtless took this to mean that in the kingdom of God the foreign nations would become subservient to the Jews, but to Stephen it may well have signified that these other ethnic peoples would, equally with the believing Jews, be sharers in the grace of the Messiah. At any rate, after the martyr's death (Acts viii. 1–4) we find Stephen's followers going out and preaching Christ, not only to Jews (Acts xi. 19) and Samaritans (Acts viii. 4 ff.), but to Greeks at Antioch (Acts xi. 20), and presently to Gentiles in every quarter.

(6) Putting these things together, then, we may conclude with some confidence that, while the Galilean Apostles at the beginning believed in a Christ for Israel and thought of Israel as the kingdom

of the Christ, Stephen and his followers believed in a Christ for the world, a Son of Man who was raised up for all men, and for whom the empire of the world was destined. This becomes now in fact the message of the Church's mission. Instead of waiting for a Messiah who would return to Jerusalem or Palestine, the Church must go out to all the nations, and proclaim a Son of Man who is Lord of all, the Head of a new humanity.

We may now consider briefly, first, the external course of the mission and, secondly, its gospel and theology.

(7) The Book of Acts describes certain stages in the development of the mission, but for the most part only along one particular line, namely, Jerusalem—Samaria—Antioch—Asia Minor—Macedonia—Greece. One of the remarkable episodes in its early progress was the conversion near Damascus of Saul of Tarsus, the persecutor of Stephen's followers, who, being soon swept into the current of the world-mission, at Antioch, in Asia Minor, and in Europe, rapidly becomes the leader and spearhead of the Church's advance. To this man it was given, rising in spiritual stature above his associates Barnabas and Mark, while counting himself the least of the apostles, to "labour more abundantly" than any of the others, though in making this claim he adds: "Yet it was not I, but the grace of God which was with me" (1 Cor. xv. 9–10). St. Paul felt himself under profound obligation to give the gospel to all men without distinction, to Greeks and to barbarians, to wise and to foolish, and if not to be the first to plant that gospel at Rome, at least to preach it there, at the centre of the world's life. For, he wrote, "I am not ashamed of the gospel. It is God's mighty means of effecting salvation for all men, the Jew first, and the Greek also, since in it is disclosed God's own provision of righteousness" (Rom. i. 14–17). But while the Book of Acts narrates the progress of the mission along this particular route, there were other directions in which it travelled, of which Acts contains no report.

For instance, the gospel must co-evally have been carried to Alexandria, since we hear in Acts of an Alexandrian Jew of the name of Apollos coming to Ephesus about A.D. 51 or 52, who had received some institution in Christian teaching at an earlier period (Acts xviii. 24 ff.), and we know from other evidence that the gospel must have reached Rome before A.D. 49. It is therefore credible that followers of St. Stephen had been active, not only along the line Antioch–Asia Minor–Greece, but along the line Alexandria–Italy–Rome. In fact, when we turn to the New Testament literature in its various phases, we may see evidence for recognizing at least three routes of Christian expansion: (a) the route to Asia and Greece, marked by the Pauline Epistles; (b) the route via Alexandria to Italy and Rome, marked probably by the Epistle to the Hebrews; and (c) another route reaching to Ephesus after St. Paul's time and marked by the Johannine literature.

(8) What now of the gospel and theology of the world-mission? Let us by way of first approach to this question place ourselves at the standpoint of one who, conscious in his soul that Judaism with its law and cultus and all its institutions of grace had passed away, faces towards the future, and sees Christ, the exalted Son of Man, standing at the right hand of power. How now shall the future of divine religion be conceived and presented to the souls of men? What will be the gospel to be preached to the world? Will it not go on to shape itself in the form that the hope of acceptance with God and salvation must now for the Christian depend utterly on the power put forth by God in the resurrection and glorified life of His Son? Because He is on the throne, we must seek and find our life within the sphere of God's saving grace in Him. Judaism with its historic privilege, its covenant with God, its law, its temple, its other means of grace, is over. Faith must henceforth orient itself to God's purpose for us in Christ. We look to Him as the triumphant Lord of life. We believe that, because He lives, we also shall live. Our faith is grounded in Him, bounded by Him, and sustained from Him. In fact, we are led to the conception that Christian life is life "in Christ" (ἐν Χριστῷ), as St. Paul and, later, the Johannine writer were to express it.

And with this recognition of the Son of Man as for all men, and of His dominion as embracing all peoples and nations and tongues, all the barriers hitherto dividing races and classes are now seen to be removed. This thought is to receive special emphasis in the preaching and in the Letters of St. Paul.

But furthermore, if the risen and triumphant Christ is for all the nations, it means that He may be proclaimed as "the light of the Gentiles", as the Wisdom and personal Word of God. It is an interesting fact that, in the literature connected with all three great lines of world-mission expansion we get this thought that Christ is the Wisdom or Logos of God to the world. We get it in St. Paul (e.g. 1 Cor. i. 30, viii. 6; Col. i. 15–20, iii. 3, etc.), we get it in the Epistle to the Hebrews (i. 1–4), and we get it (with the express name, the

Logos) in the Johannine writer (St. John i. 1–18; 1 John. i. 1–2). As this identification of the Christ with the Wisdom or Logos of God had not been effected in Judaism, we must conclude that it first became explicit in early circles within the Church's world mission which were out to offer Christ as God's answer to the whole world's quest of truth, and which transmitted this teaching along all the lines of their evangelism.

(9) Only a few words can be here said, finally about the reflection of the world-mission gospel in the theology of St. Paul.

It is not without interest that Saul of Tarsus in his early days as a righteous Jew, a zealot for the law is reported to have been present at the execution of Stephen: ὅτε ἐξεχύννετο τὸ αἷμα Στεφάνου τοῦ μάρτυρός σου, καὶ αὐτὸς ἤμην ἐφεστὼς καὶ συνευδοκῶν (Acts xxii. 20). Stephen's religious position must have been well known to Saul.

But the apostle had had his own personal experience of grace. It had been given to him, above all others, to make the full test of the law of Moses as an efficacious instrument of salvation, and the experiment had been disappointing. When grace stooped to him in the manifestation of the risen Lord to his soul on the Damascus road, it marked the end of the law so far as the convert was concerned. It was the *reductio ad absurdum* of all his existing ideas of religion. The neophyte, raised to his feet by grace, is left alone with God and Christ. God in Christ was now the only future left to him. Henceforward religion means one thing only, namely, the completest appropriation of the Divine righteousness, love, and power in the Redeemer. All other values have been abandoned.

'Αλλὰ ἅτινα ἦν μοι κέρδη, ταῦτα ἥγημαι διὰ τὸν Χριστὸν ζημίαν· ἀλλὰ μενοῦν γε καὶ ἡγοῦμαι πάντα ζημίαν εἶναι διὰ τὸ ὑπερέχον τῆς γνώσεως Χριστοῦ 'Ιησοῦ τοῦ κυρίου μου, δι' ὃν τὰ πάντα ἐζημιώθην, καὶ ἡγοῦμαι σκύβαλα ἵνα Χριστὸν κερδήσω καὶ εὑρεθῶ ἐν αὐτῷ, μὴ ἔχων ἐμὴν δικαιοσύνην τὴν ἐκ νόμου, ἀλλὰ τὴν διὰ πίστεως Χριστοῦ, τὴν ἐκ Θεοῦ δικαιοσύνην ἐπὶ τῇ πίστει, τοῦ γνῶναι αὐτὸν καὶ τὴν δύναμιν τῆς ἀναστάσεως αὐτοῦ καὶ κοινωνίαν παθημάτων αὐτοῦ, συμμορφιζόμενος τῷ θανάτῳ αὐτοῦ, εἴ πως καταντήσω εἰς τὴν ἐξανάστασιν τὴν ἐκ νεκρῶν (Phil. iii. 7–11).

The central points of connection between the world-mission gospel and St. Paul's doctrine of grace are briefly these:

(a) Christ is "the end of the law" for all who believe. The institutions of Judaism have ceased to possess significance for faith, and are superseded. The Mosaic law has fulfilled its function to bring the world to the consciousness of its sin. It has been the παιδαγωγός to bring us to Christ (Gal. iii. 21–4; Rom. x. 4, etc.). We pass now to Christ.

(b) With the passing of the law and the first covenant, all distinctions between men and races are abolished. Christ is for the world, and all men are offered fullness of life in Him (Gal. iii. 26–8, iv. 6; Col. ii. 9, etc.). He is the Man from Heaven, the Head of the new humanity of God (Rom. v. 12–21; 1 Cor. xv. 44–9; Col. i. 17–18).

(c) On its inner side, the life of religion is constituted by the indwelling of Christ in the Christian through the Spirit of God and the indwelling of Christians in Him (Gal. ii. 20–1, iii. 27; Rom. vi. 1–11). St. Paul's theology is centrally defined from the position that our life as Christians is life ἐν Χριστῷ. This means that we are not any more under law or in solidarity with Adam, or subject to condemnation and death, or only "in flesh". Christ is the ground of the new life, He is also its sphere, He is also its substance, or content, for the new life is drawn from Him. Reconciliation to God, righteousness with God, holiness and victory over sin are aspects of this new existence, inasmuch as the Christ offered to our faith is Himself the righteousness, the holiness, the wisdom and power bestowed by God. Here the substance of the presentation owes very much of its rich elaboration to the unique intensity of St. Paul's personal experience. When the risen Lord stooped down to the convert at his earth-level on the Damascus road and raised him to his feet, it meant that St. Paul had experienced in his own person the atonement wrought by the death of Christ and the power of His resurrection. Christian life is dying in Christ to sin and rising with Him to newness of life.

St. Paul assumes all this to be common ground for all who have responded to the world-gospel.

Ἢ ἀγνοεῖτε, he asks the Roman Christians, ὅτι ὅσοι ἐβαπτίσθημεν εἰς Χριστὸν Ἰησοῦν, εἰς τὸν θάνατον αὐτοῦ ἐβαπτίσθημεν; συνετάφημεν οὖν αὐτῷ διὰ τοῦ βαπτίσματος εἰς τὸν θάνατον ἵνα ὥσπερ ἠγέρθη Χριστὸς ἐκ νεκρῶν διὰ τῆς δόξης τοῦ πατρός, οὕτω καὶ ἡμεῖς ἐν καινότητι ζωῆς περιπατήσωμεν (Rom. vi. 3–4).

(d) Lastly St. Paul took over and developed the Wisdom-Christology of the world-mission. Christ is for him, as we have noted, the Wisdom and Power of God (1 Cor. i. 24, 30), and to Christ in His cosmic significance he assigns all the attributes which Jewish Wisdom-theology had predicated of the figure of the Logos. And for St. Paul this had all the practical significance attached to the conception of the heart of the world-mission—Christ the Light of the Gentiles!

Therefore the Apostle never ceases to pray for his converts that they may be filled with the knowledge of God's will ἐν πάσῃ σοφίᾳ καὶ συνέσει πνευματικῇ, περιπατῆσαι ἀξίως τοῦ κυρίου εἰς πᾶσαν ἀρεσκείαν, ἐν παντὶ ἔργῳ ἀγαθῷ καρποφοροῦντες καὶ αὐξανόμενοι τῇ ἐπιγνώσει τοῦ Θεοῦ, ἐν πάσῃ δυνάμει δυναμούμενοι κατὰ τὸ κράτος τῆς δόξης αὐτοῦ (Col. i. 9–11).

CHAPTER 5

The Biblical Doctrine of Mission[1]

I

The subject appointed for our conference concerns the place which "mission" occupies among the concepts of Holy Scripture, and by "mission" in this connection is meant, of course, mission to the world, the obligation which rests upon the Church to offer the Gospel to every creature.

The point which I shall try to make, and which, I think, it is important for us to consider, is that in the Bible the conception of the Church's universal mission is bound up, first and last, with the thought of the Church being "the Israel of God". Behind the Church and the Christian religion, and behind the consciousness of the universality of the Christian message, stands an older reality, a small exclusive people with a unique historical beginning and a particular and very remarkable sense of divine election and privilege. How is the connection of these two things—Hebrew-Jewish particularism and Christian universalism—to be established? How did it come about?

ISRAEL

To begin with, Israel's emergence as a nation and its particular consciousness of destiny date from the Exodus, the mighty event associated in all later tradition with numinous happenings of an extraordinary kind, through which the soul of a people was born and a new departure made in history. The salient features of the Exodus-event were the deliverance of the Hebrews from Egypt, their safe passage through the Red Sea, the institution at Sinai of a Covenant with their God and the settlement of their families, with kindred tribes, in the land of Canaan. Because of the mass of later accretions which have gathered around the story, we are not able to penetrate back to the

[1] The first part of an address delivered at the S.C.M. Theological College Department Conference, held at Swanwick, 29 December 1952–2 January 1953. Reprinted from *International Review of Missions*, July 1953, pp. 257–65.

original incidents, but nothing prevents our recognizing in the Exodus a mighty wave of religious awakening which swept over the Hebrews in Egypt. The movement was introduced and accompanied by revelations and mighty acts of Yahweh, their God, and it was carried through under the hand of Moses. In Exodus iii, we read of God's mysterious name being communicated to this great man. It was in the form of "*I will be what I will be*", a language implying a purpose of God for His people which was not yet disclosed, which indeed could not be disclosed in its entirety in advance of its fulfilment (cf. Exod. xxxiii), but which was nevertheless at work in their history.

Further, in chapter vi we hear that the name "Yahweh" was a new name not previously made known to the fathers. So at the head of the Law given to Israel, as set down for later generations in the Book of the Covenant (Exod. xx), we get the preamble: "I am Yahweh, your God, who brought you out of the land of Egypt, out of the house of bondage. You shall have no other gods before me," and the Covenant of God with Israel is ratified by sacrifice in terms of His commandments (Exod. xxiv).

The Exodus in Israel's Religion

The Exodus left an indelible mark on Israel's spiritual life and history as these came later to be interpreted by the prophets.[1]

(1) The election and the blessing of Israel were projected back into the past to include the patriarchs of the nation. Old stories were gathered. Abraham repeatedly, and also Jacob, are said to have been given the promise that through (or in) their descendants all the families (or nations) of the world would be blessed.

(2) The Exodus became the foundation-fact of the whole later life and religion of Israel. It is the constant starting-point of the prophets, as far back as the times of the judges and Samuel. By reference to the Exodus, Israel is reminded of the difference between itself and other peoples, and of its peculiar historical position. From the Exodus the supreme events in the nation's life are dated: thus Solomon's building of the Temple is said to have begun "in the four hundred and eightieth year after the people of Israel came out of the land of Egypt" (1 Kings vi. 1). (The Exodus furnished the *Ab Urbe Condita* of the nation's history.)

[1] In this section I acknowledge a debt to Professor John Marsh's book, *The Fulness of Time* (Nisbet, 1952).

(3) The whole cultic or ceremonial life of Israel was given a meaning by reference to the Exodus. The great festivals of the religious calendar—Passover, Pentecost and Tabernacles—were all at first agricultural festivals originating in natural or fertility rites, but in the Old Testament they have all been given an exclusive relation to events in Yahweh's redemption of His people out of Egypt. The old myths have been historicized. The festivals bear witness no longer to recurrent events of the natural order, but to the mighty acts of God at the beginning of His people's life.

(4) The Exodus afforded a permanent criterion of the genuineness of prophecy. The mark of the false prophet (or deceived Israelite) is that he incites by dreams or signs to the worship of "other gods" in rebellion against Yahweh, God of Israel, who had brought His people out of Egypt, and who has set it on its distinctive course of life (Deut. xi). The true prophet is the one who stands in the tradition of Exodus-witness.

(5) Eschatology, when it arises in sinful Israel under the pressure of the prophet's awareness of the holiness and judgement of God shapes itself in large measure round the conception of the Exodus. Amid sin and punishment there arises the announcement of the New Covenant with its interior law of God (Jer. xxxi), and indeed the prediction of a *New Exodus* (Deutero-Isaiah). Because the New Covenant carries with it an inward law, it is said by Jeremiah to be not like the Covenant which Yahweh made with their fathers, but in reality it represents the Old Covenant in its eschatological, at-last-complete accomplishment. The Exodus goes on. It is an eternal Divine event which announces itself afresh at all times of Divine illumination and crisis, and which will have its final realization in a New Age to come.

(6) The redemptive event of the Exodus underlies the Gospel of Jesus and the inauguration of the new era of Christianity. The pattern of the Exodus can be clearly traced behind the events of the Incarnation and the Death of Jesus, as, for example, in His baptism at the Jordan and His temptation in the wilderness, in His teaching on the Mount as presented in St. Matthew's Gospel, in His transfiguration as described in *St. Luke* and in His institution of the Last Supper, with its Passover background and reference to Covenant-blood. With Jesus, however, we have the fulfilment of the redemption of God, not a mere additional chapter in Jewish religious history. Thus, while the Exodus from Egypt is the "salvation-fact" of the older history, the Death-and-Resurrection of Jesus Christ is the salvation-fact of

Christianity. Baptism takes the place of the crossing of the Red Sea. The Old Covenant is replaced by the New. Moses has given place to Christ. The Church of Jesus has become the Israel of God.

So much for the Exodus. It has left an imperishable mark on the religion of the Bible. Israel carries the blessing, the outward and inward possession of the promised presence, virtue, energy, holiness, truth and life-giving power of the Redeeming God. What now is the relation of Israel to the other nations of the world which, it is promised, are to be blessed in her? Has Israel a mission? And if so, what?

Israel and the Nations

Israel's earliest attitude to the other peoples is the naïve one that these nations are to be driven out before the Chosen People and exterminated. But as history develops its complexities, and as Israel comes under judgement for her sin—as the great prophets from Amos onwards tell her—when the Assyrians become a flail in the hand of Yahweh to smite His people, Israel learns that her election and her calling are not so simple a matter as was ordinarily supposed. Sacred history becomes terribly involved with secular history. As Professor John Marsh puts it: "the meaning of history, the interpretation of its facts, is something which belongs to the objective and not to the subjective order". Israel thinks she will get the blessing in one way: she actually gets it in quite another way.

"You only have I known of all the families of the earth. Therefore will I visit your iniquities upon you" (Amos iii. 2).

At the same time Israel is told that God has a historical use for other peoples.

"Have not I brought up Israel out of the land of Egypt, and the Philistines from Caphtor, and the Syrians from Kir? Behold the eyes of Yahweh God are upon the sinful kingdom, and I will destroy it," etc. (Amos ix. 7–8).

Thus Israel's election is not for conquest but for judgement, for sifting, for humiliation, for purification. But while the doom of God upon the sins of this pecular people is driven home to it by the prophets, the fact of Israel's unique election to the knowledge of God remains.

For ask now of the days that are past, which were before you, since the day that God created man upon the earth . . . did ever people hear the voice of God speaking out of the midst of the fire, as you have heard, and live? Or hath God assayed to go and take him a nation from the midst of another nation, by trials, by signs, by wonders, and by war, by a mighty hand and an outstretched arm, and by great terrors, according to all that Yahweh your God did for you in Egypt before your eyes? . . . Out of heaven he made you to hear his voice. . . . (Deut. iv. 32–6).

Two things then—Election and Judgement: Knowledge and Guilt: Blessing and Suffering. Israel passes through the fires. In the Exile, as her most inspired prophet taught, she receives double for all her sins, but the Covenant God in His mercy proposes a New Exodus for her. "Israel came to see", says Professor Marsh, "that God's servant must suffer extinction before the purposes of God could be fulfilled in her." And Israel's function in this matter is representative; at its supreme height her experience reveals itself as vicarious (Isa. liii). God says to His Servant:

It is too light a thing that thou shouldst be my servant, to raise up the tribes of Jacob, and to restore the preserved of Israel; I will also give thee for a light to the Gentiles, that thou mayest be my salvation to the end of the earth (Isa. xlix. 6).

Here, then, at the highest point of the prophetic religious insight of Israel, the mission of the Servant comes into view. The election and the blessing, the spiritual function and the historical destiny of Israel are all seen in one tremendous moment in terms of the suffering—vicarious, as now appears—of her greatest Son. In a flash of divine revelation, Second Isaiah and those who listened to his voice saw what Jesus saw as He entered at His baptism on His ministry and fulfilled that ministry on the Cross (cf. Mark x. 45; Luke xxii. 37; John xii. 23–4; 31–2, etc.).

We are now in a position to understand a little better what it means for the people of Israel to become a blessing to the nations. Israel's mission is to be achieved by her purification under the hand of God and her glorification through His grace. And as a matter of fact, when we read the Old Testament observantly, we find Israel's world-significance and world-responsibility to be constantly stated in the form that, through God's redemptive purpose being wrought out in her, the Gentiles will come to the light and will share the benefits of her salvation. Their salvation will come about by their being drawn to Israel, by their being incorporated in the holy nation. For example:

Isaiah ii. 2 ff. (cf. Mic. iv. 1 ff.):

And it shall come to pass in the latter days that the mountain of the Lord's house shall be established in the top of the mountains . . . and all nations shall flow unto it. And many peoples shall go and say, Come, and let us go up to the mountain of the Lord, to the House of the God of Jacob, and he will teach us of his ways, and we will walk in his paths; for out of Zion shall go forth the law . . . and he shall judge between the nations.

Then follows the promise of international disarmament and world peace.

Isaiah lxii. 1–2. God speaks:

For Jerusalem's sake I will not rest, until her righteousness go forth as brightness, and her salvation as a lamp that burneth. And the nations shall see my righteousness. . . . And thou shalt be called by a new name which the mouth of the Lord will name.

Isaiah lx. 2–3.

For, behold, darkness shall cover the earth, and gross darkness the peoples: But the Lord shall arise upon thee, and his glory shall be seen upon thee. And nations shall come to thy light, and kings to the brightness of thy rising.

Psalm xcviii. 2–3.

The Lord has made known his salvation; his righteousness he has openly showed in the sight of the nations. He has remembered his mercy and his faithfulness towards the house of Israel; all the ends of the earth have seen the salvation of our God.

Israel's evangelism, therefore, is indirect. Her mission to the nations means, first of all, her own redemption. Through the grace of God to her the nations will be attracted. She does not go to them, but they will come streaming to her, and will become beneficiaries of her salvation. This is true even if prophetic voices are sometimes heard declaring that other peoples will be given a standing by the side of Israel in the redeeming purpose of God. The principle holds even when Jonah goes to Nineveh, and Nineveh repents. So far as I can see, there is no hint at all in the Old Testament that God's purpose of grace will be offered to Gentiles on their own ground, so to speak, or that their redemption will be accomplished apart from Israel. There is no hint of it even in what is said of the Servant of the Lord in Deutero-Isaiah. Rather, the salvation of the nations means, first and last, that by God's grace these nations will come to Zion, which means in the end that they will be incorporated in the Holy People.

Jesus Christ and Israel

"He came unto his own, and they that were his own received him not. But as many as received him, to them he gave the right to become children of God, even to them that believe on his name" (John i. 11–12).

We have been speaking of Israel at the height of the great prophetic interpretation of her destiny, according to which Israel had a representative and vicarious function to fulfil on earth. Alas, in the centuries between the prophets and the coming of Jesus, Israel's religion, as embodied in the teaching of the Pharisees, had sunk and hardened into legalism. Israel's religious privilege, her Abrahamic descent, her nationalistic dream of glory, her claim to possess righteousness in herself, had driven out the sense of her sheer dependence on God. She was the self-righteous nation, and when the Servant of the Lord appeared in Jesus, there was no beauty in Him that she should desire Him.

Alternatively, as another religious tendency of the time, we have the rise of the apocalyptic movement of thought in Israel. This despaired altogether of the present world, and rested all hope on the coming of a "new heaven and a new earth".

What, then, is the relation in which Jesus Christ stands to the great line of thought which we have seen running through the Old Testament? On the one hand, we see Fulfilment; on the other hand, Transcendence. Let us look at these two sides of the manifestation of God in the incarnation of Jesus.

(1) He came unto His own. The word was made flesh. The word dwelt among us, full of grace and truth. "Us" in this passage refers to the Jewish people (John i. 14). St. Paul, too, asseverates that Christ was made "a minister of the circumcision for the truth of God, that he might confirm the promises given to the fathers", and if the Apostle adds the words "and that the Gentiles might glorify God for his mercy" (Rom. xv. 8–9), he is still, as his quotations show (Psalm xviii. 49; Deut. xxxii, 43; Psalm cxvii. 1; Isaiah xi. 10), keeping formally within the bounds of the Old Testament blessing, and of the mission and the hope given to Israel.

In the Synoptic Gospels, too, we read that Jesus not only came to Israel, but deliberately confined His mission to that people. To the Syrophoenician woman, when she came with her supplication to Him,

He said "Let the children first be fed" (Mark vii. 27). In a later Gospel His word has the more uncompromising form: "I was not sent except to the lost sheep of the house of Israel" (Matt. xv. 24). It may be that our Lord, at this time a proscribed and homeless wanderer in Israel, already felt the pain of His rejection by His own people, but there it is. In the same Gospel, Jesus says to the Twelve: "Go not into any way of the Gentiles," i.e. take not any road leading to any Gentile centre, "and enter not into any city of the Samaritans, but go rather to the lost sheep of the house of Israel" (Matt. x. 5–6). Though these words come from the M source of *St. Matthew*, there is no real reason for doubting that they are words of Jesus. Even if the same Gospel reports solemn warnings of Jesus about the doom which will fall upon Israel if it remains impenitent, as when He says, "I say to you, that the kingdom of God will be taken away from you, and will be given to a nation bringing forth the fruit of it" (Matt. xxi. 43), it is plain that Jesus conceived His task along the lines of the Old Testament promise, that when Israel's righteousness should go forth as brightness, only then would the nations flow towards it. Thus it was for Israel that He gave Himself, laboured, hungered and died upon the Cross. The salvation of the rest of the world was to be through Israel.

(2) If, however, He came to His own, He came to fulfil. With Jesus the new age is not only announced but inaugurated. This applies to kingdom, blessing, mission, sin-bearing, New Covenant with God, and everything else that had been spoken of by the prophets.

For instance, the kingdom or reign of God: Jesus' first word to His times, according to St. Mark i. 14 f., is "The time is fulfilled and the kingdom of God has drawn near: repent and believe in the tidings of joy". He asked for faith, faith in the immediate power of God to bring the hope of the centuries to pass, and this word "faith" now becomes on the human side the key-word of the soul's response to God. It means the willingness to make way for God in human life and in the world's history. Jesus not only declares the Advent of the reign of God, but He offers to men at once a share in its supernatural power. By His acts He represents the character and the reality of the reign of God. The kingdom is in the midst. He embodies the kingdom of God, and He creates the life of it in men. He is its Fulfiller and its Fulfilment.

Again, blessing: He says to His followers:

Blessed are your eyes, for they see; and your ears, for they hear. For amen, I say to you, many prophets and righteous men desired to see the things which you see, and saw them not; and to hear the things which you hear, and heard them not (Matt. xiii. 16–17).

In other words, the mystery of the reign of God has at last been disclosed to His disciples: what to those outside remains a figure of speech, a metaphor, a myth, has become reality to this little Israel within Israel. So when Jesus says to them, "Blessed are ye poor . . . blessed are you that hunger now . . . blessed are you that weep now . . . blessed are you when men shall hate you . . . for the Son of Man's sake" (Luke vi. 20–2), it means that the blessing of which Israel was to be the bearer, all that virtue, energy, holiness, truth and life of God which was promised of old to Israel, has materialized in Jesus, who is not only the pronouncer of the great benediction but its substance—at once its Fulfiller and its Fulfilment.

Once again, sin-bearing: Jesus does not only allude to the destiny which according to the Old Testament prophet was to be wrought out by the Servant of the Lord; He does not merely cite it as something containing instruction for Himself and His followers, but He makes the Servant's destiny His own. He acts the part of the Servant by taking the sins of the nation upon Himself, as at once Priest and Victim, Revealer and Revelation, Form of the Word and Substance, Fulfiller and Fulfilment. So by His death He not only speaks of, but institutes the New Covenant, not only refers to the Paschal rite of His people, but substitutes Himself as the sacrifice, not only recalls the Exodus from Egypt, but inaugurates a new Exodus. In all ways He incarnates the New Age, the last time which fulfils all time, because He is the substance of the life of that New Age, the promised Day of God.

Henceforth, accordingly, His followers will say: "We are not righteous, but He is righteous; we are not good, but He is good; we are not wise, but He knows all things; we cannot make atonement for our sins, but He has atoned; we cannot raise ourselves, but He is risen and at God's right hand." He is not only the sign but the substance of the new humanity. The New Age has dawned.

(3) What then of the Church's mission to the world? Before we answer that question, let us attend to one other point.

The work of Jesus in history was not only to fulfil but to transcend the Old Testament hope. The reign of God which He proclaimed stood in transcendent relation to all previous history. For example, it is not Moses, the servant of God, who speaks to us in the Sermon on the Mount, but one who is God's Son. The law was given through Moses, but grace and truth came by Jesus Christ. In the proclamation of His message Jesus had to warn His hearers that an impenitent Israel could not hope to retain the blessing which it had come to treat as a property or monopoly of its own. The Kingdom of God, the theocracy of grace, would be taken from it and given to "another nation", producing adequate returns. At the same time, Jesus cut Himself loose from the nationalist conception of Israel's salvation. He made a definite breach with official Judaism. The Old and the New Israel draw apart. Nevertheless, as the exponent and the substance of the redemption promised to Israel, Jesus is Himself Fulfilled Judaism; and those who have received Him, and who will later be described by St. Paul as "the body of Christ", are in Him the Israel of God. This enables us now to answer our question about the mission of the Church to the world.

We have, in fact, to take the idea of fulfilment and the idea of transcendence together if we are to make the right approach to Christian universalism.

Jesus broke with Judaism and was rejected by its official representatives, and between His followers and the rest of the nation there stood now the stark and irreducible fact of the Cross. Yet the Christ who hung and suffered on the Cross fulfilled Judaism, and the Church, which is His body, represents fulfilled Judaism. Over against this now stands "Israel after the flesh", the Israel that hangs on to past historic claim and privilege. The Church, on the other hand, as the Israel of the New Covenant, has been set free from the past, for it has for its principle of life the inward law of the Spirit, which it has received from Jesus, and its future history is to be determined, not by tradition, but by this Spirit. For example, the ground on which the Church was very soon to discontinue the requirement of circumcision for converts entering the new Israel of God was that both at Caesarea, when St. Peter preached, and on other occasions, the Spirit descended on uncircumcized persons (Acts xi. 15–18). Thus the New Covenant was in operation, and the requirements of the Old Covenant fall into the past. In Christ, neither circumcision nor uncircumcision matter, but "the new creation" (Gal. vi. 15). But as in the same breath St. Paul makes reference to the Church as "the Israel of God" (Gal. vi. 16), we are given the solution of our problem. The Church of the new creation, which offers the Gospel to every creature irrespective of race or ritual distinction, is the true inheritor of the Divine election and blessing, so that all who respond to its message enter by that act into the Israel of God.

II[1]

In the second part of our study we return to the realities and hopes in the strength of which the world mission of the Church started on its way and developed.

(1) We begin from the fact that the new age, or new creation, of which the prophets in the past had spoken, and for which the saints of Israel had longed—compare Simeon and his *Nunc Dimittis* in Luke ii. 28–32—was no longer a purely future thing which had to be prepared for, but a reality of the present which was to be received and entered into. The definitive signs of the new creation were the Resurrection of Jesus and the descent of the Holy Spirit on the Church (Acts ii. 32–3; iii. 18–20). However difficult it may be for us to represent to ourselves the nature of the numinous experiences belonging to the tremendous days after the Crucifixion, in which the Resurrection-faith of the Church was born, we have to recognize in these events the rending of a veil which had lain upon the minds of the disciples of Jesus, and which till now had prevented that understanding of His destiny which He had striven by word and parable to effect (cf. Luke xxiv. 16, 31–2). In the same experiences we see the translation of their souls into a new spiritual world. The age of the Resurrection had begun.

It follows from this that the gifts and blessings and powers which the Church was now to offer to men in the name of Jesus were the gifts and blessings and powers of the *eschatological time*. For example, justification, the gift to sinful men of a rectified relation with God—the prophets of the past had denied to the existing age the possession of "righteousness" in the theological sense of the clear manifestation of God's justice in human affairs, in other words, of God's salvation, and they had projected the hope of righteousness into the age to come. But now, particularly by St. Paul, justification by act of the divine grace is put into the forefront of the Christian message. Again, sonship to God. Sonship to God was the pattern of life which Israel had been called to realize (Exod. iv. 22; Hos. xi. 1) but which it had failed to achieve. This sonship—the "adoption"—is now offered to men through Jesus (John i. 12; Rom. viii. 15; Gal. iv. 5). Once more, the

[1] Reprinted from *International Review of Missions*, Oct. 1953, pp. 389–96.

Spirit. This gift that in the prophets had been reserved for the New Covenant or the Last Days (Ezek. xxxvi. 24–7; Joel ii. 28–32) has been poured out on the Christian community. Two orders of life, therefore, *two ages* have come to coexist in Christianity. The New Age has begun, the Old has not ended. The New dates from the Resurrection, the Old will last until the final manifestation of Jesus Christ in glory.

(2) The Christian Church and the world mission therefore fulfil themselves under conditions of *tension*. The new life in the Spirit or, as St. Paul also expresses it, the new humanity, has come into existence in Christ, but it is in conflict with the old life in the flesh. How acute that tension is St. Paul shows movingly in the eighth chapter of *Romans*. While there is "no condemnation" resting now on those who are united to Christ, there is, he says, conflict between the Spirit and the flesh in Christian life, there is the constant sense of coming short of Christian duty, there is suffering and incompleteness, there is the struggle and felt incompetence of the soul in prayer. And though in all this tension, inseparable from life in this intermediate aeon, we have the help of the Spirit, yet our sense of incompleteness throws us on hope as a necessity, and this gives rise in Christianity to a new eschatology of the things-which-are-not-yet-seen, an eschatology of glory which looks to the final victory, or *Parousia*, of Christ. While the new Christian age represents the fulfilment of the old prophetic eschatology, nevertheless Christianity by the very nature of its experience is impelled to a further end. There can be no thought of the Church in the present world-age, even though it is the age of grace, attaining a sufficient or self-contained existence. There is no perfection here. The Church remains at every point dependent on the grace and energy of God, it is subject to His judgement and correction, it is complete only in Christ.

The aspect of this situation which most concerns us now is that the Church is in the world; and it is within *secular history* and with reference to it that the Church's mission is to be wrought out. Here we can see a parallel between the old Israel and the new. Ancient Israel thought that the divine blessing was something which guaranteed that the nations would be simply subdued before itself, but in the working out of things Israel found itself terribly involved in the complexities of secular history. It is heavily punished for its sins, and it learns that only through suffering can its mission to be a blessing to the nations be accomplished. So perhaps the Church in the first apostolic days thought that it would avoid the complexities of world history by sheltering under the eaves of the Temple on Zion, and even thinking of the Kingdom of God as a preserve of Israel (Acts i. 6). If so, it was soon forced out of that position by facts and forces which it could only explain as the work of the Spirit of God, and which from the start indicated suffering and dispersal as the condition of its mission being fulfilled. The Church was to learn, as the old Israel had learnt, that fulfilment of its mission could not come about apart from its own purification by grace, and the manifestation within it of the life of the crucified and risen Lord. No complacency about itself was here possible for the Church. St. Paul is witness to this fact. He had had many advantages as a Jew but he had gladly, as he says, renounced them, and treated them as worthless:

> that I may gain Christ, [he says] and be found in Him, possessing no righteousness of my own by the law, but that which comes by faith in Christ, that righteousness which faith receives from God: that I may know Him [he resumes], and the power of His resurrection, and share with Him in His sufferings, and be thereby conformed to His death in the hope that, if possible, I may attain to the Resurrection from the dead. (Phil. iii. 9–10).

(3) The mission of the Church, however, is a phenomenon of the new creation, and therefore, like the rest of the new creation, it is sustained by supernatural grace and truth. It looks to the final coming of Christ in His power and glory, and its notes are hope and a sense of urgency. God has His elect, the predestined members of the true Israel, in every nation, and if they are to be reached it must be by a proclamation of the Gospel among all peoples. But the time is short, for the coming of the Lord is at hand. This sense of the nearness of the *Parousia* belongs very definitely to the world mission. But does this concern of the Church signify only a hope of plucking a supposed elect remnant on earth from the doom awaiting the rest of humanity? Does it mean that secular history is meaningless, and that the world as a whole is marked for perdition? These questions can only be settled by watching the progress of the Christian mission. Does it reach a point at which it appears satisfied that it has completed the task of reaching the elect? If not, can it be said ever to reach the point at which general history is disposed of, or to be written off as an absolute loss? These are questions of great interest for us at the present day, in a time of crisis in the history of Christian missions, and we shall devote the remainder of this statement largely to a discussion of these issues.

(4) It must not be forgotten that the Christian Church in its world mission was inspired by something which Israel had never known in its experience, the love of Christ to men. The revelation of God's love to the world in Christ (John iii. 16) imparted passion and urgency to the prosecution of the task, for was not the time short and were not the issues of infinite importance? The love inspired by Christ was an absolutely new thing in the religious history of man. Therefore no conceptions based on past religious teaching and no analogies drawn from Jewish apocalyptic expectation were to the point in the new situation in which Christians found themselves, a situation in which "the powers of the world to come" were already operative through the Spirit. And here something further has to be considered.

I have elsewhere tried to explore the origins of the world mission of the Church in the first century, and do not think it is necessary to go over the ground again. Rather would I approach the problem which is before us by enquiring a little more particularly into the character of the message which the Church proclaims.

In my book on *The Epistle to the Hebrews*, where I have sought to explain the secular range of the mission by reference to St. Stephen's vision of the Son of Man in *Acts* vii, I have said something about the doctrine of Christ in the mission. I pointed out that in the Letters of St. Paul, in the *Epistle to the Hebrews* and in the Johannine writings—three sections of the New Testament literature which we may well regard as marking so many independent channels in the stream of the world mission as it poured out into the world of the first century—it is possible to detect a common element of great interest, viz. the identification of Jesus Christ with the Wisdom or Logos of God. This equation of the Messiah with the principle of Divine Wisdom is not to be found in Judaism, though the potentiality of the synthesis was present there. On the other hand, it is found in New Testament Christianity, and its occurrence along three separate lines of world mission thought suggests that it dates from a point before the divergence of these lines took place, i.e. from a point very near the beginning of the mission. Probably we may connect its presence in the mission literature of Christianity with the thought of Christ being "the light of the Gentiles", a function ascribed in Second Isaiah to the "servant of the Lord" (Isa. xlii. 6; xlix. 6), and later ascribed to the elect "Son of Man" in 1 *Enoch.* This function is explicitly assigned to the Christ in Simeon's Song in *Luke* ii. 32. It would be natural in the world mission to present the Christian Redeemer as *Lux Mundi,* as the answer given by God to the religious quests and yearnings of men. Christ is the refutation of their false wisdom (cf. 1 Cor. i. 21–5; ii. 16), and the only source of a right understanding of the divine mysteries. As such, He may be called "the Wisdom of God" (1 Cor. i. 24; i. 30). St. Paul's words are worth quoting:

> For seeing that in the Wisdom of God the world through its wisdom failed to know God, it was God's good pleasure through the foolishness of the (Christian) kerygma to save those who believe. Seeing that Jews ask for signs and Greeks seek after wisdom: but we preach a crucified Messiah, who is to Jews a stumbling block, and to Gentiles foolishness, but to those who are called, a Christ who is God's power and God's wisdom (1 Cor. i. 22–4). To God you owe your being in Christ Jesus, who was made to us wisdom from God, righteousness and sanctification and redemption (1 Cor. i. 30).

The Gospel as source of divine illumination stands in completely paradoxical relation to secular philosophy, but that only proves its transcendent origin. For if Jesus is the real wisdom of God, who is the refutation of false philosophy and the source of the true, He stands necessarily in positive relation to the cosmos and to humanity, even if these are sunk in sin and in ignorance of God. The sign of Christianity is, indeed, the Cross and the Cross inexorably proclaims that life can only come to the world through death, Christ's death for us and our death in Him. Yet if this Cross is the manifestation of God's love to the world, who can put limits to the range of its effect? But there is a further aspect of this Wisdom-Christology which has to be considered.

As we pursue the Wisdom-teaching of St. Paul, and take with it the teaching of *Hebrews*, and the Fourth Gospel, we find that the doctrine of Christ as the Wisdom of God goes deeper than the idea that heavenly light has come through Jesus. The doctrine strikes down to an ontological or metaphysical level of reality. Jesus is the Wisdom or Word of God, not only because He illumines the soul, but because He expresses the very substance of the real, represents in fact the underlying cause and ground and sustaining principle of creation itself. Compare these passages:

> Col. i. 14–17. In Him we have redemption, the forgiveness of sins. He is the image of the invisible God, the first-born of all creation; for in Him were all things created, in the heavens and upon the earth, things visible and things invisible . . . all things have been created through Him, and for Him; and He is before all things, and in Him all things consist.

Heb. i. 1–3. God spoke in old time to our fathers through the prophets. It was in manifold and very varied ways. He has now at the close of these days spoken to us through a Son—one whom He has appointed to be the universal Heir. Through Him also He made the world. He, the radiance of God's glory and the very expression of His essence, the sustainer also of the universe by his word of power, has now, after effecting the purification of our sins, taken His seat at the right hand of the Majesty on high.

St. John i. 1 ff. In the beginning was the Word, and the Word was with God, and the Word was God. This Word was in the beginning with God. All things came into being through Him, and apart from Him nothing came into being of what has come to be. In Him was Life, and the Life was the Light of men. . . . And the Word became flesh and dwelt among us, and we looked upon His glory . . . full of grace and truth.

In all these passages Jesus Christ appears not only as the agent of redemption, but as the underlying principle of creation and history. The predicates applied to wisdom or the Logos in Jewish-Alexandrian theology have been appropriated to Him and absorbed in Him. In other words, redemption in Christ stands in relation to the structure of the cosmos and to the fulfilment of history. Despite the ruin and defacement wrought by man's estrangement from God through the Fall, there is something in the natural and in the historical order which corresponds with the manifestation of God in Christ. Even if the return of the world to God can only come about through its death and resurrection in Christ, the correspondence remains. The return of the soul to God, though it can only come about through Christ, is in accordance with the original purpose for which creation was designed. In other words, redemption is also the restoration of all things, the *apokatastasis* to which reference is made in Acts iii. 21, the consummation for which all creation yearns (Rom. viii. 20–3). Having now such a doctrine, is it likely that the leaders of the world mission would be pessimistically disposed or even neutral towards the result of the preaching of the Cross, or that they would ultimately acquiesce easily in the prospect of an early termination of the course of history?

It is interesting in this connection that the formation of a sombre judgement on the future of human history is most characteristic of those theological circles which are most opposed to the Logos element in the Church's doctrine of Christ. A case is the direction taken by theology on the continent of Europe at the present time. The emphasis of this theology is *away* from the Logos theology, which it regards as a "Greek" importation into Christianity, and which it accepts only subject to the putting of a strictly Hebraic interpretation on it. This school of theologians therefore tends to an apocalyptic judgement on human affairs which places it in marked contrast with the tendency of thought in Britain and in America.

Of course, the whole Church looks, and must ever look, for "new heavens and a new earth, wherein dwelleth righteousness" (2 Pet. iii. 12). But the recognition that a transformation of the existing order through Christ must take place, a transformation of which there is no adequate symbol except the death and resurrection of all things in Christ, is compatible with different degrees of hope as to the salvability of mankind, and with different estimates of the time-interval to be allowed between the Incarnation and the end of the present age. What the Gospel may do for the reclaiming of the world and of history can be put to no test except that of the Gospel itself. On the other hand, it belongs to the nature of the Gospel that the issue which is placed before us is urgent in the extreme, and it may be that to slacken in the work of the world mission and to count confidently on time, saying "My Lord delayeth His return", may be to precipitate a doom upon history which only the mercy of God at present restrains.

I have recently read Bishop Leslie Newbigin's book, *The People of God: Lectures on the Nature of the Church*, and I take the opportunity to commend it as a very valuable study, not only of the nature of the Church but of the urgency of the Christian message at the present hour in the history of humanity. In this matter it bears out with moving powers of expression the kind of argument I have just been advancing.

I will only add two considerations. The first of these applies to St. Paul and concerns his philosophy of history, something that he describes in Romans xi. 25 as "this mystery". In general, St. Paul was faithful to the principle that God's salvation was first sent to Israel, and in every centre he first addressed himself to the Jewish synagogue and to the fringe of spiritually-minded Gentiles who had gathered round the synagogue. But in centres like Corinth (Acts xviii. 5–6), where Jewish opposition to the Gospel interposed a practically insurmountable barrier, he turned to the Gentiles. His justification was the fact that in the Christian world mission from its first beginnings at Antioch (Acts xii. 20–1) and at Caesarea (Acts x. 44–7; xi. 15–18) the Holy Spirit had come on the uncircumcised when the Gospel was believed by them, and they were baptized. But while Gentiles thus came into the Church, and it was recognized that there was no longer any distinction between Jew and Gentile before God, the apostle warns the Gentile enclave in the Church at Rome against presuming upon the grace they had received (Rom. xi. 13–24). He reminds them that they are a wild slip which has been grafted into the olive tree of the Israel of God, and that it is not they who carry the root, but the root that carries them. And then very strikingly he develops the thought of a divine ordering of affairs which is also an unfathomable mystery (Rom. xi. 33–6), according to which God has cleared a space in time for His elect among the Gentiles to be received into grace. So far from this, however, meaning a final rejection of Israel, St. Paul says it has been revealed to him that the ultimate purpose of this temporary passing of the Gospel to the Gentiles is to hasten the conversion of the Jews, and "what will their reassumption into favour be but life from the dead"? (Rom. xi. 15).

Despite St. Paul's expectation, therefore, of a very early date for the *Parousia,* we are witnesses of a process by which history opens up to him new vistas of divine possibility. He speaks of "the reconciliation of the world" as being promoted by the temporary withdrawal of grace from the Jews, and of the winning of the Gentiles as preceding the recovery of the Jews. Does not this suggest that already for the apostolic generation the *Parousia* lay right over the path of the world mission, and that its coming would be conditioned by the fulfilment of the missionary task?

Secondly, I would refer to the concurrent evidence of such teaching about the *Parousia* as we find in 2 Thess. ii and in the "Little Apocalypse", as it is called, in Mark xiii, with the parallels in *Matthew and Luke.* Here in the clearest way we see the Christians of the middle decades of the first century (A.D. 50–70) being warned of the dangers of coming to precipitate conclusions regarding the End of the Age, and being counselled to patience and steadfastness. Three things are made clear in the teaching of the passages:

(1) The danger of apocalypticism in the Church threatening not only the peace of the Christian community but the continuance of its missionary effort in the world.

(2) The recognition by apostles and others in the Church that no contemporary secular events are to be identified with the coming of the Lord.

(3) The consequent postponement of the coming of the Lord and of the End of history to a future date which, though near and certain, leaves room for results yet to be attained by the progress of the Christian mission. This, in effect, leaves the door open to history. It

is a refusal to foreclose the issue of history, now that the Gospel has gone out into the world and its powers are at work. The stage for the final dénouement is set, but "the End is not yet". In any event, the road to the End is the path of the world mission. It is above that path that the Morning-Star of the *Parousia* of Christ coruscates and shines.

I. Index of Scripture References

II. Index of Names